GURU GOBIND SINGH JI'S
ZAFURNAMAH

About the Author

Dr. Harjeet Singh Gandhi was born in Jalandhar, Punjab. After graduating from medical college in Amritsar, he spent much of his early adulthood in the United Kingdom. He is an orthopaedic surgeon, currently living and working in Canada. He is married to Amrit Laure and they have two grown daughters, Dante' and India.

Dr. Gandhi enjoys reading ancient Indian literature and Sikh history to connect with the world's variegated humanity. The present translation of Guru Gobind Singh Ji's *Zafurnamah* is his second book. The strength of his work lies in his ability to relate events in order to create a better understanding of human nature and the intellectual behaviour of "Man," a social yet cruel animal. At present, he is working on the instructive philosophy of the *Bhagavad Geetaa* and trying to comprehend the instinctive mind of Guru Nanak Dev.

A Challenge and a Sermon

GURU GOBIND SINGH JI'S
ZAFURNAMAH

Set in Historical Perspective
Its Consequences and Outcomes

English Translation by
Dr. Harjeet Singh Gandhi

Rock's Mills Press
Oakville, Ontario
2021

The original artwork "Pure @ Heart" preceding each chapter of this book is the creation of Dr. Harjeet Singh Gandhi, and was sketched to specifically symbolize the philosophy of Guru Gobind Singh.

The cover design was created by Amrit Laure.

The contents of this book have been thoroughly researched and verified to the extent practically possible, given that many historical facts may be impossible to validate because of the loss of information over the centuries and the fact that historians may interpret those facts in various ways so as to suit their feelings, interests and moral differences. As well as setting out historical facts, the author has on occasion expressed his opinions of those facts, in the full realization that different people may hold different opinions on the same facts.

Copyright © 2021 by Harjeet Singh Gandhi. All rights reserved.

Acknowledgement and Appreciation

Dr. Daljitam Singh Ajrawat introduced me to the *Zafurnamah* written by Guru Gobind Singh, and encouraged me to translate it into English. Uttering the verses in Persian passionately to me, he was instrumental in transmitting all the emotions of the events, which many of you will experience as you read them. The historical background of this excellent literary work is important, but becomes insignificant once you feel its power and emotions by reading it time and again, with interest.

I thoroughly appreciate the modernistic attitudes of my parents, the late Sardar Mohinder Singh and Sardarnee Harjinder Kaur, and I am thankful for their total support during my formative years in school and higher education abroad. With their realistic optimism they made wholehearted efforts to achieve a better future for the whole family, living during the vicissitudes of the post-independence era of the nation.

Contents

Preface ... 9

1. Introduction ... 17

2. The Tractable Hindu Society in Mughal Hindostaan ... 25

3. A Recapitulation of the Life and Times of Guru Gobind Singh ... 37

4. *Fatehnamah* ... 67

5. *Zafurnamah* ... 71

6. *Fatehnamah* in Prose ... 87

7. *Zafurnamah* in Prose ... 89

8. Aftermath: The Rise and Fall of Banda Singh Bahaadur ... 97

9. Conclusion: A Critical Review ... 103

A SELECTION OF PHOTOGRAPHS ... 115

10. Descriptive Glossary ... 125

Appendices ... 169

References ... 179

Index ... 181

Preface

Since the golden age of Bhaaratvarsh (India), its northwestern frontier, the Khyber Pass, had always been a gateway for invaders, until it was blocked by the regional forces of the one-eyed champion of the Punjab, Maharajah Runjeet Singh. Many centuries later, after the retreat of the terrorizing Macedonian and Greek forces, and the rise of Chandergupt Mauraya, the Afghaans and Turks (of Turkestaan, Central Asia) invaded to loot and desecrate the "sacred land" of plenty, establishing themselves as rulers for more than half a millennium. At the same time, high-caste Brahmans deluded the superstitious and illiterate lower classes, while the upper classes lived in luxury. The Islamic rulers, oblivious to Manu's philosophy, exploited the socially divided Hindu society to convert the lower Hindu classes to Islam to strengthen their grip on power. This undermined the dignity and confidence of the Hindus, leading to further disintegration. These actions intensified and reached new heights during the reign of the last Mughal emperor, Aurangzeb. It was to protect the social and religious rights of the citizens that Guru Gobind Singh raised his sword (verse 22 of *Zafurnamah*) against the emperor and his agenda to convert all inhabitants of the subcontinent to Islam.

22. When all (peaceful) acts and strategies are exhausted,
Then it is legitimate to brandish the sword in hand.

Like his predecessors, the Guru challenged Manu's doctrine of birthright, which he believed perpetuated a divided society. He encouraged the enfeebled lower classes to enlist in his military force to defend the democratic principle of equality for all. To put these innovative ideas in practice, he strengthened his authority at Anandpur soon after his ascendency as the new Sikh guru, to deter the tyranny of Mughal imperialism.

Guru Gobind Singh originally wrote *Zafurnamah* in Persian, after he evacuated Anandpur. The emperor guaranteed his safe passage, swearing by an oath written on a copy of the Qur'an. Writing *Zafurnamah*, an official letter to Aurangzeb, was the most meaningful way for him to express his feelings and declare a moral victory over the bigoted and cruel Mughal emperor. In the letter, Guru Gobind Singh explicitly described the action-packed battle of Chumkor and subtle challenges. He rebuked Aurangzeb and his officials for breaking their oath and killing close members of the Guru's family. For the Guru, leaving the fort of Anandpur and the town was an honourable act, intended to prevent the unnecessary loss of his entrapped soldiers because of a blockade cutting off food and drinkable water supplies. He did not want to injure the esteem of his famished and physically weakened Khalsaa men by making them an easy prey to the Mughal forces. The moral victory of Guru Gobind Singh lay in his firm belief in the Almighty, and the strength of his people.

The complete version of *Zafurnamah*, as originally written by Guru Gobind Singh, is not available. It has been put together from available remnants over time in verse. A brief history of its discovery and further editions is given on page 67. Whether the letter was originally in prose or verse is a subject of controversy. It has been printed many times in various newspapers and magazines. It is possible that many words and even the order of the verses have been altered during its numerous reproductions.

An effort has been made in this book to present the couplets in the most suitable order to follow the flow of the events. Despite minor variations in the present-day editions available for reference, the main corpus of the work remains a meaningful expression of the feelings of Guru Gobind Singh, and seems authentic to the author.

It is impossible for another soul to imagine what feelings and thoughts might have inspired Guru Gobind Singh to write the letter to the emperor. Each word chosen by the Guru has a very specific meaning, which neither the present author nor anyone else may be able to understand completely. We can only speculate and seek diverse meanings to make the words and phrases meaningful to our own minds.

For ease of reading, I also present a prose version of the epistle, something which has not been done before to my knowledge. Every effort was made to maintain authenticity of the original work and at the same time to make it meaningful to a questioning mind.

Persian is a rich poetic language. For effect, Guru Gobind Singh frequently employed proverbs. A literal translation of *Zafurnamah* might seem ungrammatical in places. Unfortunately, the English alphabet has fewer letters (26), and is less phonetic in its construction than Persian, Arabic, Devnaagri, Hindostaani as written in Urdu, and Gurumukhi, which has 35 letters. The English language does not lend itself well to a system of short and long vowels (a, aa, i, ee), s, sh, t, ta, d, dh, r, a*r*d, etc., or to accentuating symbols for nouns and adjectives of Sanskrit and Hindi languages. For this reason, the English transliterations of some of the names of the people and places are presented here with unconventional spellings, including appropriate consonants and extra vowels, so that they sound closer to the pronunciation of the indigenous language. Still, for the sake of authenticity and understanding, it would be preferable to make hybrid words using the alphabets of the local language. For example, the place name is "Ropa*r*d," said softly without much emphasis on the italicized *r*. It is not "Ropar" or "Ropad." The author hopes that the readers will accept this approach. Readers would also note that "Amrit," the sanctified sweetened solution made in an iron bowl stirred with the iron "Khandah," a double-edged sword, during the Sikh Khalsaa initiation, has been spelt as "Umrit," the *u* to be pronounced as in "umbrella." In the past the name of the city of Amritsar had been spelt "Umritsur."

The "Khalsaa" is an orthodox initiated and conscientiously purified Sikh male and female member, who is supposed to live a lifestyle based on precepts as defined by Guru Gobind Singh. The root word "Khalas" entered the Gurumukhi vocabulary via Urdu, Persian, and ultimately from the Arabic word "Kalis," which means pure (*The Penguin English Dictionary*, third edition, 2007).

A translation of *Fatehnamah*, also originally written in Persian by Guru Gobind Singh, has been included. It is believed to be the prelude to *Zafurnamah*. Following the translations, there is an account of the period under the leadership of Banda Singh Bahaadur, after the assassination of Guru Gobind Singh. The last chapter presents a brief analysis of the outcome of the Guru's actions and the long-term influence on the culture of the nation as a result of numerous alien rulers in the last one thousand years.

Many translations of *Zafurnamah* are presented in English and Punjabi transliterations alongside the Persian script. I believe such accompaniments are unnecessary as Persian has neither been taught nor spoken in daily life for more than fifty years. Although the present work has been written to interest a wide variety of readers, it is mainly intended to acquaint the youth of the nation with an important chapter of Sikh history.

The present work has been written to bring *Zafurnamah* to the people of Bhaaratvarsh who are now touring Sikh historical places with much greater frequency. The present-day highway from Anandpur to Sabo-dee-Talwandee, Guru Gobind Singh Marg, follows the historic route which Guru Gobind Singh and his men journeyed after their expulsion from Anandpur. It celebrates the Guru's moral victory over Aurangzeb. Almost all the significant places visited and inhabited by Guru Gobind Singh are regarded as sacred by the Sikhs and over time their historical importance was marked by erecting numerous Gurudwaras along and near this historic route. I had the opportunity to visit some of these places. Some photographs of these monuments have been included in the book.

A comprehensive glossary at the end of the book explains the meaning and purpose of some of the terms, places and persons mentioned in the main text. The entries in the glossary are marked with an asterisk in the text. Most of the Vedic literature is enigmatic, without specific authorship, likely elaborated on multiple occasions over more than 2,500 years with an accompanying mutation of original concepts and philosophy, particularly in the transition from oral invocative versions to written texts. Since ancient times, the fertile landscape of the Greater Punjab has attracted numerous nomadic tribes and well-organized invasive forces across the Hindu Kush mountain range. Up till now, the trickle of immigrants to the region has continuously brought changes in its demography, culture and language. The author here has tried to critically review some of the controversial subjects, maintaining an indifference to the mundane mythological meshwork of the Indian subcontinent. The appendix highlights one of the major factors that have changed the history of the world since 1493 CE, through religious bias and racial discrimination in the name of God, by aggressive explorers-cum-invaders, contrary to the philosophy of the Sikh Gurus. During the same period they were canvassing and fighting against socio-religious inequality, to bring victory to the same Supreme entity.

Here I would like to acknowledge the assistance of my wife Amrit Laure for going carefully through the text and my friend, the late Sardar Kanwaljit Singh Bakshi, for reviewing it. I appreciate the patience and sincere effort of Mr. David Stover, the editor, to enhance the quality of the text for greater understanding of *Zafurnamah*.

Dr. Harjeet Singh Gandhi
Lindsay, Ontario, Canada

Map 1

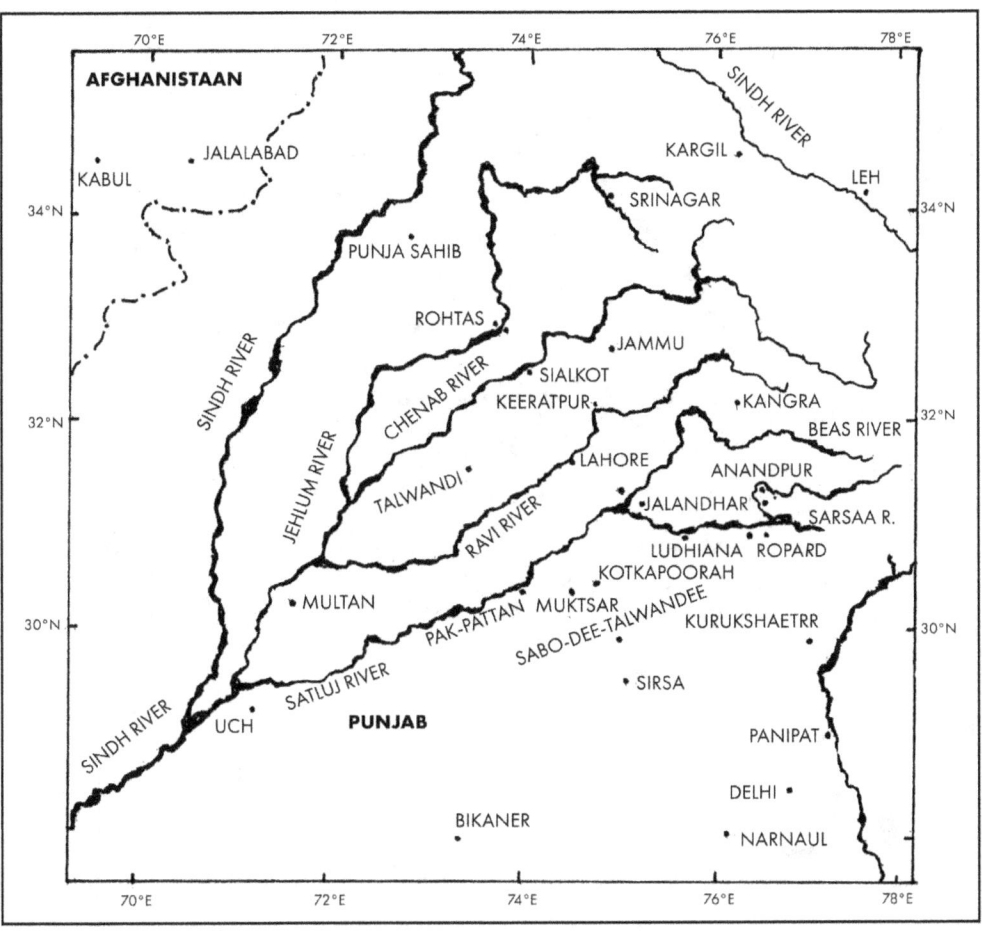

A map (not to scale) of Greater Punjab, showing five rivers joining the river Sindhu/Sindu, and names of key places.

Map 2

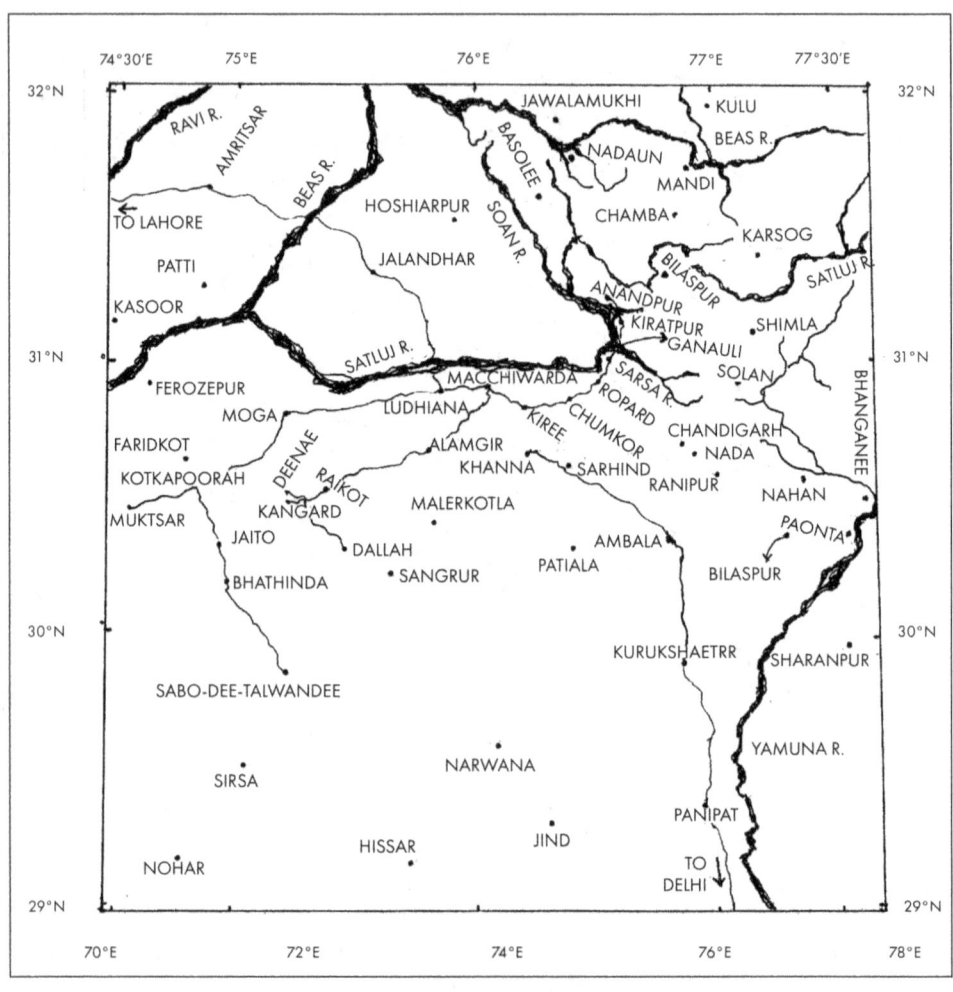

A map (not to scale) showing names of places en route
from Anandpur to Sabo-dee-Talwandee.

1. Introduction

Of all the creatures living upon this earth, man is considered the most mobile, cruel, and adventurous, always looking for greener and greater pastures. Looting and destroying the peace of others, man subordinates the weak for self-interest. One such young, spirited, aggressive and terrorizing warrior was Alexander* from Macedon, who, wandering through Asia Minor and north-east Africa came to the threshold of Bhaaratvarsh and then turned back. He terrorized the human race on a large scale across multiple international boundaries to extend the extremities of his "empire." He became an archetype of international terrorism. Like him, many attempted to invade Bhaaratvarsh, but failed to establish themselves for long in the fertile plateaus sloping down from the Himalaya mountain range.

The Khyber Pass, on the northwestern frontier, had always been a gateway to enter Bhaarat. At the beginning of the last millennium, it was the turn of the Afghans and Turks of Turkestaan, Central Asia, to follow in Alexander's footsteps, initially as traders, and later as rulers.

These were the times when the Lodee rulers were squandering local resources, living in luxury, and caring for no one else in society. Their weakness brought Babr (meaning "lion"), the first Mughal ruler, to the northwestern frontier, setting the scene for the Mughal rule in Bhaaratvarsh. It was after multiple attempts during the early 1520s across the Northwest Territories that Babr (1483–1530 CE) found his roots in Bhaaratvarsh. The foreign domination brought with it untold atrocities upon the local people. The first Sikh prophetic teacher, Guru Nanak Dev (1469–1539 CE), was born at this critical period in the history of the country. The challenge taken up by the Guru Nanak, with his conscience awakening words of wisdom, finally reached its climax with the sharp edge of the sword, the Bhagawtee, the god/goddess of strength and righteousness.

The event that brought invaders to the golden land was when the great king Ashoak* of Patliputrr (now Patna in the state of Bihar) buried his mighty sword deep in the battlefield of Kalingaa, realizing a loss of human life numbered in hundreds and thousands, caused by him and his forces. He was shamed to see the Buddhist monks roaming the battlefield taking care not only of his injured soldiers but also those of the defending state. This made him to convert to Buddhism, and it became the state religion of Mauraya Empire. Although at the time he acted righteously, but made the nation defenseless against future invasions. By doing so, he had put the race of kShatriya into a long peaceful slumber with deafening chants of Buddhism, initiating the ideology of non-violence, weakening the defence of the Northwest Territories. Over time the nation was divided into smaller provincial governments, and its borders were left to weak border kingdoms. It took nearly two thousand years to reach the day when a new warrior was conceived on the soil of Patliputrr, but with a difference; when Gobind Rai, the son of the ninth Sikh Guru Taeg Bahaadur, was born. At the time the thriving Mughal state occupied almost two-third of Bhaaratvarsh, and Aurangzeb was furiously fighting against the Marathaa*, in the southwestern state of Maharashtra.

As the wheel of time rolls through history, it tends to gather grievous historical events like wound-scabs on its circumference, picked up from one place and shed elsewhere. It so happened that the scab of the peace-inducing chants of Buddhism not only provided comfort to society, they also unarmed the ruling kShatriya after the battle of Kalingaa, leaving the vast borders of the Maurayan Empire defenceless and numbing their response to constant invasions. The scab concealing the desire for retaliation began to lift off nowhere else but in Patliputrr itself with the birth of the Gobind Rai. Thereafter, the oppressive regime of the Mughals seemed to accelerate the peeling-off of the scab, which was finally shed in the Shivaalik hills of Anandpur in the province of Punjab, the seat of the ninth Sikh Guru. It was here that Gobind Rai grew up to be an astute soldier and raised his mighty sword against the Mughals. The minds of the large majority of peace-loving, innocent and humbled Hindu of Bhaaratvarsh over the centuries had buckled under the biased and misconstrued Vedic philosophy, which was inflicted upon them by their own people, and were easily taken advantage of by the Mughal. The so-called high priests and high-caste Brahmans were undermining the will of the already weakened and the illiterate, while the kShatriya remained no better than a scarecrow.

The unenlightened and militarized "Mughals" (Mongols and Turks), originating in Fergana and Samarkand (Turkestaan), could not understand the Sanaatan (Hindu) principles enshrined by the ancestral scholars of the Bhaaratvarsh, which revealed hundreds and thousands of gods and goddesses for their countrymen to pick and choose a model to follow, leading them to the same goal of righteousness. With the introduction of Islam, and ever-increasing religious degradation, the differences in the practice of the Sanaatan idolaters and Islam brought loss of dignity, lack of national integrity, and a famine of self-esteem. Just in time, self-made warriors like Guru Hargobind Rai and his grandson Gobind Rai, later to be revered as Guru Gobind Singh, appeared on the scene. Guru Arjan Dev and Guru Taeg Bahaadur had already sacrificed their lives for the cause of the same socio-religious rights for all citizens.

Guru Gobind Singh (1666–1708 CE) acceded to the title of tenth Sikh Guru at the tender age of nine. He had just lost his father, Guru Taeg Bahaadur, who had been protecting the religious rights of the Hindus, the Brahmans of Kashmir, at the command of the Mughal Emperor Aurangzeb. Guru Taeg Bahaadur had been a visionary, who recognized difficult times ahead and began preparations to defend his people. To achieve this objective he made sure that his son Gobind Rai was trained in contemporary warfare and horsemanship. At the same time, Gobind Rai was educated in Sanskrit, Persian, and Gurumukhi by the local scholars. On becoming the tenth Guru he established his "rule of state" at Anandpur, to oppose the brutalities and fanaticism of the Mughal officers.

To achieve his objectives it became essential for the tenth Guru, Guru Gobind Rai, to raise an army of fearless loyal soldiers who were ready to die for the rightful cause of others. The existing members of the present-day families of the disbanded army of Guru Hargobind Rai enlisted unhesitatingly, and also encouraged many others to do the same. To increase the potential of his defensive program, Guru Gobind Rai set about to ignite and infuse courage among the downtrodden and emasculated lower classes. He did so in a very dramatic way, on a Baisaakhi day, a day in the month of Baisaakh, in the year 1699, by creating a new turbaned and bearded dedicated class among the existing disciples of the Nanak and men of other clans, "castes" and classes, giving them the title of "Khalsaa."*

The creation of the "Khalsaa" changed the face of northern India forever, giving birth to a force ready to guard against the perennial invasions of its northwestern borders. Guru Gobind Singh's vision for his new creation was aimed at an amalgamation of all of the four classes under the Manu's social system of social segregation, which had divided a society filled with prejudices to promote the prerogatives of so-called Aarya* over the indigenous tribal population. The doctrines of Manu* were intended to prevent fraternization with the natives, while using their skills and services to the rulers' own advantage. Manu classified the Aarya (currently the origin of the Aarya is a controversial subject, explained in the glossary) as kShatriya (ruling warriors), while dividing the remainder of the citizenry into Brahman (priest), Vaishya (trader), kShuderr (insignificant semi-skilled and unskilled, providing manual and menial labour). Guru Nanak Dev recognized the centuries-long corrupt traditional establishment of the ruling and other higher classes. He refused to accept the intentional segregation of the citizens into quarters, and found it restrictive and threatening, particularly to the potential of lower classes. Guru Nanak Dev succeeded in awakening his followers to the concept of monotheism, the *"Naam"* (an impersonal, undefined, unnamed entity—neither Hindu nor Muslim nor of any other religious denomination), the one creative "Being" of the whole universe. To further the ideology of his predecessors and strengthen the oppressed society, Guru Gobind Singh planned to reignite the militarization process left dormant after the passing away of his grandfather, to empower all classes against Mughal imperialism. He enunciated the slogan, "Become literate like a Brahman, brave and upright like a kShatriya, hardworking and productive like a Vaish, and be humble to offer service for the needy, like a kShuderr."

Guru Gobind Singh was faced with opposition from the Hill Chiefs, who had befriended the Mughals to seek protection through mischievous diplomacy. Hill Chiefs and regional Mughal rulers (Vazeer) felt threatened by the rising strength of Guru Gobind Singh in and around Anandpur. The unpredictability of the Guru's activities created in them fears for their security. On the request of the Hill Chiefs, Emperor Aurangzeb appointed General Sharazey Khan to lead an offensive against the Guru. On hearing this, the Guru stationed his Khalsaa military on the banks of river Satluj (Sutlej) to defend his territory. On the battlefield, Sharazey Khan and his special officers lost their lives. Mughal forces, despite being large in number, fled the battleground afraid for their lives, thus bringing a decisive victory to the Khalsaa. This caused immense psychological trauma to the supposedly invincible power of Aurangzeb.

Knowing the immense faith of the Guru in religion, and his God-fearing nature, the defeat led the Mughal to hatch an underhanded plan to surprise him. It was decided to send an invitation to the Guru to leave Anandpur, with a friendly handshake. Written on the cover of a copy of the Qur'an, the presentation was taken by the Guru as a sworn oath. The following verses quoted from the Qur'an, known to any religious person, would make him or her believe that a written promise with the seal of the Emperor could be nothing other than a sworn oath:

Chapter 2 Verse 2.25 *"And make not Allah a target for your oaths that you may thereby **abstain** from doing good and acting righteously and making peace between men. And Allah is all Hearing and All Knowing."*

Verse 2.26 "*Allah will not call you to account for such of your oaths as are vain, but He will call you to account for what your hearts have earned. And Allah is most forgiving and forbearing.*"

"It is indeed an act of blasphemy that one should use the name of Allah, to abstain from doing good deeds. Again, it is a gross violation of the sanctity of Allah's name that it should be used as a butt, or target for profane or purposeless oaths. Taking an oath is a serious matter, but some men are in the habit of swearing without meaning anything. Such oaths as are taken thoughtlessly or as a matter of habit or those taken in a sudden fit of anger do not call for expiation." —*The Holy Qur'an*, edited by Malik Ghulam Farid, published by the London Mosque, 1981)

Guru Gobind Singh accepted the invitation partly because of his own ethics and the way the oath was presented and partly under duress from his mother and men. The Guru, his family and loyal men evacuated Anandpur and proceeded towards the town of Kangard. Hereafter, the personal life of the Guru and his family changed forever.

At the same time, Aurangzeb ordered Subedaar Zabardast Khan to proceed to Anandpur, along with some of the Hill Chiefs, to ambush the oncoming party of Guru Gobind Singh. Near Ropard, on the banks of rivulet Sarsaa, a bloody battle took place. It was here that the Guru was separated from his immediate family, taking with him his two eldest sons, Ajit Singh, and Jujhaar Singh. His wives, Sundaree and Sahib Kaur, left for Dilli* (Delhi) in the company of Bhai Manee Singh. The two younger sons, Zoravaar Singh, and Fateh Singh, accompanying their grandmother, Gujree, went to a village near Sarhind with the family cook by the name of Gangoo. However, Gangoo betrayed and delivered the family to the Subedaar of Sarhind, Vazeer Khan, who walled off both the boys alive on their refusal to embrace Islam.

Meanwhile the malicious intentions of Mughal forces became very clear to Guru Gobind Singh. He advanced to the village of Chumkor, along with his two older sons and forty chosen soldiers, to take refuge. But to ensnare the Guru and his Khalsaa, a huge Mughal army lay in wait for a final assault on them. They were attacked under the administration of Naaher Khan and Khawaza Khizer. The Guru portrayed the battle of Chumkor vividly in his letter, *Zafurnamah*, to Aurangzeb. The Khalsaa soldiers fought courageously, causing massive losses to the Mughal army. Here, the Guru lost both his older sons along with the majority of Khalsaa men. The tiny remaining contingent of Khalsaa could not withstand the huge Mughal force. Realizing the possible danger to the life of the Guru, an escape was planned for him, leaving behind the few remaining soldiers.

Disguised as "Uch da peer," dressed like a Sufi-saint, he escaped via Maccheewarda and, with the help of two Pathaan brothers, Ganny Khan and Nabbhy Khan; he reached the village of Deenae-Kangard. Here he wrote the *Zafurnamah*, while taking refuge at the residence of Deysaa Singh in the village Dinae. He gave the *Zafurnamah*, a letter of moral victory in principle, to Bhai Diyaa Singh to deliver to Aurangzeb. In the letter the Guru deplored the callous behaviour and unjust practices of Aurangzeb's officers, and denounced the dirty trick of falsely swearing an oath upon the holy Qur'an. In addition, he denounced the betrayal of Aurangzeb, and proclaimed the supremacy of a pervasive, all-knowing, just and gracious God. Thereafter, he continued his journey towards Kotkapoorah, where in time, he raised a new army. The Khalsaa finally defeated the royal forces at Khidraaney-dee-Daab, the place now known by the name of Muktsar.

Guru Gobind Singh believed himself to be a mortal being, born with a mission to protect and render peace to all. To prove his worth he raised himself above all, like a fountainhead. He was an extraordinary character. The Guru was confident of his actions and carried them through with dignity, like a true warrior. He had total faith in "Bhagawtee," the goddess of Strength, and in the power of his own people behind him, who believed in his philosophy of equal rights for all. The weapons of Guru Gobind Singh were neither sacred nor ecclesiastical destructive instruments of divine origin as described in mythological epics. Instead, he had grown within his human corpus a divine soul, industriously practiced his instruments, and transmitted the same to his "Khalas" men. His sword, the Kripaan, was an instrument of kindness to bring peace and equality among all races and creeds. His objective, like those of his predecessors, was to institute freedom of social and religious democracy for all humanity. The Khandah, a heavy double concave-edged pointed sword used to stir sugared water, and a sacrament—Umrit—were employed to recruit ordinary village folk of his time living in fear of the Mughals to become "Khalas" warriors. Guru Gobind Singh wanted his "Khalas" men to resist the insatiable greed for wealth and worldly pleasures like the ruling Mughals, Hindu royals and other higher classes. It was the belief of the Guru in the inexhaustible blessings of the Supreme Being that fuelled his courage to thrive during the most hurtful personal events in his life.

Guru Gobind Singh strongly denied his superiority over others, and also denied any direct kinship with God. He hailed the mighty sword of righteousness, believed in his strength, and had complete faith in the Supreme Saviour to protect him and his rightful followers. The scriptures and personal experience taught him patience, perseverance, courage and strength. He raised himself above all the chiefs and governors of the time as an extraordinary leader and a soldier, striving to protect the common people from the wrath of the Mughal regime. His mission was to recruit soldiers from within and outside the fellowship of the holy order of Khalsaa to include people of all classes. Thus, he created a new breed of soldiers.

The recurring loss of immediate family is very personal and private. The Guru not only lost his father during his juvenile years, but also his four children and mother within a short period of time. Although he felt deceived and defeated by his cunning enemy, he was not angered. Despite this intense trauma Guru Gobind Singh was steadfast and unyielding to the challenges that confronted him.

In *Zafurnamah*, he successfully expressed his losses, exposed the lies of the Mughal officers and the despotism of Mughal rule, and challenged the ultimate authority of Aurangzeb.

Extraordinary as he may have been, he was, after all, only a human being with human feelings. His Bhakti and Shakti (prayers and physical strength) were compelling enough to encourage him to fight for the rights and freedom of his people against the atrocities committed upon them by the Mughals. Putting his pen to paper to write this poetic epistle must have been a great relief. What better means could a scholar employ to ease his dammed-up emotions; filled with anguish at having lost his near and dear ones. It must have meant sleepless nights and ruthless days to be at peace, while strengthening his own confidence and that of his men, maintaining his strong composure to lead an army and planning to strike strategically at his enemies.

To fully appreciate the depth of the Guru's feelings one has to try to experience within oneself the strong sense of retribution the Guru felt after having been deceived outright by a callous opponent and the lying Mughal officials. Unlike a true king, Aurangzeb acted like a fallen creature never to be trusted again. He was a man without principles and integrity. What to say of his dishonest diplomats and their baseless randomly contrived diplomacies. On the other hand, Guru Gobind Singh, the man with a steadfast nature despite defeat, raised himself out of the ashes of Chumkor like a forceful spirit. Steeped in courage, he led an army of faithful soldiers ready to sacrifice for the cause.

The state of mind of Aurangzeb after reading the *Zafurnamah* is inconsequential, as his deeds were irreversible, and he could not be acquitted in any court of justice, including that of Allah. The self-awakening of his guilty conscience and the desire to suffer could have been no more than a self-induced penance to escape the fires of hell.

As the translator I must confess that I have no significant working knowledge of the Persian language. During my discourses on multiple occasions with Brigadier Dr. Daljitam Singh, the *Zafurnamah* was read in Persian and translated into Punjabi with great enthusiasm. The other references were Punjabi and English transliterations and translations as the original document is not available. I note variations in the order and number of the verses, in certain words, and in their spellings in the references. In the present translation, there are 119 verses following a commonly accepted order. A list of references is given at the end. Enough historical background has been given above to allow any reader to enjoy this work without going into the nitty-gritty of the Guru's personal life.

The objective here is to highlight the successful leadership and management skills of Guru Gobind Singh in representing people of all "castes" and classes in society. His first objective was to lift them up to a common level and then lead them to a common goal; secondly, to empower all to actively engage and achieve socio-religious freedom by throwing off the centuries-old social burden of "caste" discrimination; and finally to arise to oppose the oppressive Mughal regime. He was not only a social reformer and a perceptive politician, but also a scholar and possessor of an innovative mind.

Preceding the translation of *Fatehnamah* and the legendary epistle *Zafurnamah* is a historical exposition that sets out reasons for the poor state of and response by the easily tractable Hindu society of the time to the Mughal occupation of Bhaaratvarsh, followed by a biographical sketch that describes major events in the life of Guru Gobind Singh. The work has been thoroughly researched, but it is not written for academic consumption. However, any interested student would benefit from reading it. Every effort has been made to maintain the originality and correctness of the work.

2. The Tractable Hindu Society in Mughal Hindostaan

After the golden age of the Mauraya Empire, Bhaaratvarsh once again gradually divided into small kingdoms. This weakened the territorial defenses on the northwest frontier. Through the crevices of the Hindu Kush mountain range and the valleys of Afghanistaan multiple small and large invasive forces started to make their way into the land of the Hindus. It was in the battle of Narain that Qutab Uddin Aibak, an Afghaan, successfully decimated the dwindling might of the Hindu dynasties in 1193 CE. Following his victory, from the moment he established his rule, he turned his attention to the goal of annihilating the Hindus and Hinduism.

The Hindu rulers of border provinces did mount resistance, but failed utterly to collaborate with each other to repel the forces seeking to occupy their lands. Hundreds and thousands of Hindus were slaughtered. At each step of the conquest of the northwestern provinces, the Afghaan army destroyed Hindu temples, razing them to the ground. The process of insulting Hinduism started by the Afghaans was continued by the Turk Zahir Uddin Babr* who desecrated places of worship upon his arrival from Kabul, undermining the strength and self-esteem of the Hindus. Although there was greater tolerance of Hinduism by Jalal Uddin Akbar, the pace picked up once again during the brutal reign of Muhyi Uddin Aurangzeb.

It had been one of the strategies of the rulers and practitioners of Islam to either destroy the sacred places of other faiths or convert them for use as mosques. Doing so proved a successful tactic to sway the emotions of conquered peoples and undermine their resistance. Very early on Mohammad and many other preachers and missionaries realized the importance of religion in bringing people together to fight off a common enemy. Almost every Moghul ruler razed the superstructures of existing Hindu temples and erected mosques on their foundations, and the forced conversion of Hindus to Islam began in earnest. After the initial struggles the Hindu rulers and the people did not resist further, as they sought to avoid physical cruelties, prevent unnecessary loss of life and escape high taxes, including social and religious levies.

The self-esteem and courage of the kShatriya were badly injured and the integrity of the Brahmans was at its lowest point. There are no significant historical chronicles of the events written by Hindu scholars that describe the plight of the people. However, there are several accounts written by Muslim scholars and historians of Islam that describe the cruelties inflicted by the domineering regime to isolate Hindus who resisted conversion to Islam. The royal Hindu families faced a similar predicament first at the hands of the Afghaans and later the descendants of Temoor. This continued for more than three centuries.

Of the Lodee dynasty, Behlol, Sikander and Ibrahim ruled over Hindus between 1451 CE and 1526 CE. It was the Vazeer of Punjab, Daulat Khan Lodee, who invited the first Temoori Turk, Babr, to invade Hindostaan and take over the throne of Dilli. Babr defeated Ibrahim Lodee in the battle of Panipat to establish Mughal (Temoori) rule over Hindostaan. Finally, by the end of the Mughal period, the Mughal Empire covered almost two-thirds of Bhaaratvarsh.

During the late Lodee period and early Mughal rule, the first Sikh Guru Nanak Dev (1469–1539 CE) described the heartbreaking state of the Hindus. He was born of upper "caste" Hindu parentage and had a reasonably good upbringing and education. His questioning mind and desire to experience the world led him to undertake exploratory travels, not only across the length and breadth of Bhaaratvarsh but to Arabia, Persia, Afghanistan, Tibet and Sri Lanka. All of his well-known work is recorded in the Sikh scripture *Sri Guru Granth Sahib*. Although Guru Nanak Dev was a Punjabi, his affections extended beyond the borders of Bhaaratvarsh. He was a complex, liberal nonconformist, who sharply defined his opinions and outgrew the traditional wisdom of the Vedic and Puraanic mythological literature that invoked illusive metaphysical concepts. He was well-read and well-informed about current examples of social, political and religious discrimination that led to struggles in the daily life of the ordinary Hindus. He deplored discrimination between upper and lower social classes and openly socialized with people of lower social status in his daily activities.

Before the beginning of the Christian era, with the gradual decay of the complex Vedic literature, many Hindu scholars developed popular mythological epic tales and a network of stories relaying high moral principles. These novel and delightful interconnected stories portrayed numerous man-made gods and royal dynasties set in a hierarchy that has clouded the intelligence of Hindus to this day. These intensely true-to-life fictional works have impaired the social, sacred and spiritual development of ordinary Hindus, who have believed these tales to be true and based their daily lives on them. It seems these stories were intentionally created by the elite Brahmans and social scientists of the time to drive the masses away from the ideal Sanaatan principles of a disciplined life as it was lived during the ancient Vedic period.

Unfortunately, these tales turned out to be so realistic that the god-like images of the characters intensely engaged innocent and illiterate minds. These characters overshadowed the Vedic spiritualism by becoming the centre of their own ritualism. It transformed the concept of spiritualism into the impractical Hinduism of rituals and false asceticism filled with superstitions through the medium of these exciting bedtime stories. No doubt, these god-like mythological characters are great models to follow but they have always had a limited application in real-life matters since they were made sacred, no more than lifeless dolls sitting on Morning Prayer shelves and in temples, rather than true sources of inspiration and innovation. Still, to this day, politically motivated and power-hungry intellectuals cite the condemnable immoralities included in these epic tales as essential truths about daily activities that are destined to occur if one wants to lead a worldly lifestyle. This kind of attitude underlies dishonest and discriminatory behaviour based on the idea of destiny. Failure to successfully emulate these godly characters and achieve divine success can lead to huge dejection. It can become a cause of self-denial and loss of self-esteem that introduces an idle state of detachment from society and results in prevalent good-for-nothing asceticism. Most of the messages projected in these stories are conflicting and politically motivated, not progressive, leading to human injustice and prejudice. Even though the two monumental epics, *Raamayan* and *Mahabhaarat*, are not considered parables by some scholars, they have resulted in intense subliminal mental conditioning and effects on the life of Hindus and the rest of the population of Bhaaratvarsh.

In the epic of *Raamayan*, the lead characters are Shree Raam: (these dots in Sanskrit are called "visarg"; to pronounce it, start softly and end firmly, with a sound close to "visargaH"; it represents a noun, and because of this symbol the name has been inappropriately pronounced and written in English transliterations as Rama, when it should be RamaH) and his wife Seetaa (this name has a long vowel). They belong to a utopian kingdom, Ayodhayaa, a land without active warriors, as there are no political and territorial conflicts. The couple is an example of an ideal master and mistress. Shree Raam: is the reincarnation (identified as a metaphor) of the god Vishnu (he is the organizer of humanity and deals with dualities of life; he is mirror image of Shiv: and is a mirror to the human beings). Another key character, Hanumaan,* demonstrates total servility and affection towards them. To serve them well, Hanumaan has a narrow focus for his actions. He possesses divine powers and strength without any display of deliberate selfless acts or sacrifice for a larger cause. Hanumaan is a chimerical human-like primate and in appearance is portrayed as a less evolved human being, unlike the ruling masters. The creation of such a character subliminally encourages racial discrimination, servility, and subjugation in the less endowed natives of a land. The abduction of Seetaa during exile and her release from the clutches of the demon king Raavan of Lanka (at present Sri Lanka) is a very well-crafted plot.

The father of Shree Raam:, Dashrath:, was an accomplished charioteer and a benevolent king. The king, instead of standing firmly up to his youngest wife, who demanded exile for Raam: and the throne for her son, instead dropped dead on knowing that his firstborn was to be banished to the forest for 14 years. It was only a temporary event and such self-destructive and selfish behaviour signifies weak mental strength in a king! The focus of the epic is on theoretically high morals and the successes and failures of personal conflicts. At the end, Raam: sacrifices his wife, the queen, based on the judgment passed by the citizens of his utopian state and submerges himself in a river. There are no pragmatic events in the tale that can be put into practice for the development and progress of Bhaaratvarsh.

The second epic, *Mahabhaarat*, generally misunderstood and ill-applied, is the longest poem ever written. It is an unconventional, well-engineered congeries of long and short interwoven stories. The famous scripture *The Bhagavad Geetaa* is one of the sections of this great epic. The plot portrays the conflict of the Kuru (from the Sanskrit root word kRi, meaning "to do"; an extended meaning of the word Kuru is to act, perform and have the ability to execute, enact and negotiate intense political game play by whatever means to accomplish one's final goal within accepted rules, and at other times by deception as well) royal families, comprising third-generation cousins, five Paandav and one hundred Kaurav brothers, over the kingdom of their fathers. It is seemingly filled with sworn promises, familiar upheavals and the immoralities of human relationships. The lead characters have the fortune to acquire divine weapons of destruction, and many of them break rules to deceive each other. The nucleus of this epic tale is Shree Krishan (a performer, who acts to the point, possessing strength of a dark metal, such as iron), sometimes referred to as Ironman, who has numerous titles to describe his personality and character. He possesses a metamorphic metallic personality.

Metaphorically, Shree Krishan identifies himself to God, the "*Me*", in Geetaa, which is a dialectic discourse, a point of view to theoretically find the "*Truth*", argued through rhetorical reasoning about how to reach an optimal resolution. Most of it is truly an inspirational monologue to encourage Arjun: to shed his defeatist attitude and compromised mental state, let go human relations and pick up his divine weapons with a purpose in self-interest. It is not to kill the opposing force because he tells Arjun: that nothing dies, as the "*Aatamaa*," the individual "*Self*" entity is immortal being the seed of rebirth, the concept of reincarnation. To act with reason and purpose is the true meaning of the concept "*Kerm*". To convince Arjun:, Shree Krishan elevates himself above all the humanity and, like a father to child-like Arjun:, he seems to be dilated and colossal in appearance as an influential personality. Hypothetically, despite the fact both sides have large forces, it is a clash between two families. Statistically speaking, Shree Krishan is confident that the odds are that he will pull the Paandav brothers through as winners; however, the probability is that either can be winner or loser. The whole ideology is rooted in principles of courage, inspiration and motivation through conditioning of the mind to defend self-interests, to act with reason and fruitful purpose without the knowledge of its final outcome, the reward. Shree Krishan tells Arjun: that the outcome is unknown before the act is executed, hence it is waste of energy to miss the opportunity while dreaming and thinking about the reward even before acting. The idea is not a sacred doctrine. It is obligatory to *concentrate* on the "*Kerm*" to complete it successfully. It has been largely misunderstood or intentionally misconstrued to mislead ordinary people.

Shree Krishan very clearly expresses his concern over "caste," class and gender discrimination: "come and take refuge in '*Me*.' Whether of low birth, women, skilled workers, or slaves [you] shall achieve higher goals … how much virtuous a Brahman may be and worthy royal seer, all must transgress this unpleasant humanly planet, hence must devote to each of their action, the *Kerm*, with reason and purpose" (*The Bhagavad Geetaa*, Chapter 9, verses 32 and 33). Shree Krishan never said that he is "God." He acted well at the right time and right place to bring victory to Arjun: and his brothers. The scripture has nothing to do with the entity "God"; the Sanaatan principles dictate a way of life and do not constitute religious philosophy. Geetaa is about human relationships, the act of righteousness, the definition of true "Dharam", to perform ones duty conscientiously, for all of humanity. It is for these ideological characteristics that Shree Krishan too was identified as reincarnation of the god Vishnu. He realizes and develops an insight into how the drama is going to unfold—that there is no other way than to lead both the families to a battlefield to resolve their conflict.

The way the character of Shree Krishan has been developed as a divine being in human form makes him distinctively different from other characters. He possesses an unmatchable divine power of intellectual vision, and is a great master of politics and diplomatic manipulations. He provides timely deceitful advice to undermine and even terminate an opponent without spilling a drop of blood of the enemy himself. He skillfully decimates an army of hundreds and thousands of Kaurav by driving the five Paandav brothers onto the battlefield of Kurukshaetrr (the field of Kuru), bringing them home victorious unscathed. With the ideology of *Kerm* (misconstrued as the actions and deeds of past births) and "reincarnation," he provokes Arjun: (a person who can procure anything divine) to invoke intrinsic strength to use weapons to kill kinsmen (his equals in every respect) with purpose, rather than cause genocide blindly for ill-defined reasons. Shree Krishan passively assists, not in vain to sacrifice innocent humanity but based on the very simple yet fathomless concept of "Aatamaa," which refers to one's individuality. It does not mean the same thing as the word soul, the spirit of a dead person, unless the soul is considered equivalent to Aatamaa as the spiritual individuality of a person. What is left at the end after death and cremation is "ashes," the final residue, which can neither be cut, dried further nor burnt again, and is free of all ego and desires.

At the end, on the eighteenth day of the battle, the day of "Victory," to finish the conflict, Shree Krishan: directs Bheem, one of the Pandav brothers, against the rules of duel, to strike the thigh of Duryodhan: (a person who is an evil warrior), the eldest brother of the Kaurav, to break his femur with the mace. Shree Krishan was very well aware of the fact that once the longest and strongest bone of the body is broken, Duryodhan: will never rise again after he falls to the ground, making him an easy target for a final blow, and that he will ultimately bleed to death. One can say that Shree Krishan incited violence between two families of renowned warriors, and fooled gurus and other intellectuals of the land in order to lead the clan of Kuru and their armies, families and friends onto the battlefield. As he led the Paandav to the battlefield he had clear objectives, strategies and a vision, to act with purpose and reason, and to bring home the Paandav brothers victorious.

Shree Krishan did not sacrifice even one hair of his head for the sake of humanity. In summary, Shree Krishan made use of vicious strategies to sacrifice hundreds and thousands of innocents and warriors equipped with divine weapons to demonstrate his deceitful intellect and divinity. At the end, the older brother of Shree Krishan, Balraam: disagreed with his underhanded approach to favour the Paandav brothers. Despite his divine wisdom, he failed to come up with a real world humanitarian strategy!

Once truth, righteousness and human reality are taken out of the equation, the deceitful attitude of the intellectuals fails humanity terribly. Well-intended and morally sound epics followed religiously can cause immense harm to an entire society. A peaceful, religious society following impractical philosophies is weak and defenseless against a well-equipped army under a power-hungry, religiously and racially motivated leader. To fulfill his lifelong dream, the vicious Babr, approached Hindostaan at a fast and furious pace accompanied by his army of soldiers from Turkestaan, Khoraasan, Mongolia, Persia and Afghanistan, who followed him to get their share of the loot. Each soldier acted of his own will without the thought of reward in advance until the "*Kerm*" was done. What Shree Krishan: narrated in 700 verses of the Geetaa, Babr stated in seven lines before he launched his attack against Rana Sangha on 27 March 1527:

Baegs and warriors!
Whoever comes into the world will die, a beggar or Shah;
What lasts and lives will be Allah.

He who has taken his first breath,
Will at last drink the cup of death.
Better than life with a bad name
Is death with a good one.

Unfortunately, Babr never read the *Bhagavad Geetaa* to learn what more is required of a leader beyond success in battle. History is witness to what came thereafter: three centuries of rule by the descendents of Temoor.

The battle was concluded in less than a day and Rana Sangha escaped. Babr's strategy was very simple, always the same and reproducible, like a play in a football (soccer) game intended to get to the goal. He advanced behind the centre in an array; the forces on the right and left would move around the enemy, squeeze and crush. On 29 January 1528, Babr conquered the fort of Chandiri in mere hours. The Raajpoot failed to hold firmly despite the advantage of being on a hill. Instead of setting swords in the hands of the women to defend the fort to the death, the cowards first set them alight and then beheaded all the men, to the surprise of Babr. He ordered a pillar to be erected from the heads as per tradition.

The laudable concepts of the *Bhagavad Geetaa* have been manipulated by its expounders, who could read and understand Sanskrit, without offering its advantages to the ordinary people of Bhaaratvarsh. The British rendered it into English and popularized its philosophy in such a way that the ultimate meaning of the scripture was lost in translation. This provided a new opportunity for the Anglicized Hindu intellectuals to disadvantageously apply the concepts of *Geetaa* piecemeal, using them to pacify the population, instead of inspiring citizens of the nation to take control of their destiny. To this day it is etched in people's minds in such a way that it is difficult to shift the status quo. Otherwise, the philosophy is simple, inventive and inspiring, encouraging self-interest free of greed and profit over others. The *Geetaa* is not a religious scripture, as generally presumed. It is certainly an instrument to motivate and intrigue the human mind.

During the period of Guru Nanak Dev the Hindu society had become heterogeneous, divided into numerous sects and groups. Most destructive of all to the unity of Hindu society was the intensification of ritualism, with deepening of the wedge between castes and sub-castes, alienating each other in every aspect of life. The respect and esteem the women had enjoyed during the Vedic period was lost. Under Islamic rule, the nation was made an easy prey to outsiders. Invaders like Temoor came, who not only plundered and stole natural resources but killed Hindus and abducted their womenfolk. The Muslim governments of the era were extremely theocratic and offered Hindus two options. They could either face death or convert to Islam. Already-suffering lower "castes" could be easily motivated to accept Islam with little incentive. This induced degradation and demoralization among the Hindus. They had to abandon their ancient signs and symbols; scriptures, culture and language; religion, rites and rituals in order to survive the onslaught of Mughal fanaticism. The Brahmans who embraced Islam were given the title of "Sayyid" (the hereditary title given to a descendant of Prophet Mohammad) to help convert other Hindus to Islam. Hindu women were frequently molested and then auctioned off in bazaars for few coins and traded across Afghanistan into Arabia and Persia.

To curb any kind of political uprising, Hindus were forbidden to keep thoroughbred horses and the upper classes could not wear white turbans as symbols of respect and authority. The Raajpoot, known for their valour, were suppressed and their daughters forced to marry Mughal princes as part of this political subjugation. By the time Aurangzeb came to power, Hinduism was almost on the verge of disappearing. The change in national identity from Bhaaratvarsh to Hindostaan meant the firm rooting of Islamic culture and the replacement of Sanskrit, Hindi and other indigenous languages by Persian and Arabic, diminishing the ancient literature of Bhaaratvarsh.

All the great Hindu kingdoms, the ancient Solar and Lunar dynasties, were made to feel impotent and forced to live a life restrained within their palaces and small holdings. The disgraced Brahmans started to debate among themselves over the metaphysical and philosophical complexities of Vedic literature in order to prey upon the illiterate middle and lower classes who were unable to read or even understand spoken Sanskrit. This caused further division in Hindu society, spreading communal hatred and jealousies among the new converts to Islam due to altered social and religious values. The trust among citizens was lost. There was no mechanism that could provide support and solidarity among the remainder of Hindus.

Despite his birth and childhood in an orthodox Hindu family, Guru Nanak Dev very early on realized the superficiality of Hindu practices. As he grew older, he became critical of the biased and poorly understood theological objectives of highly revered Vedic literature and developed a strong resistance to the fictional Puraanic tales of Hindu mythology. In his poetic hymns, he boldly expressed his dislike for the transgression of Hindu society, "caste" distinctions and the tyranny of the Mughal officers. He painted a miserable picture of moral and cultural degradation. He lived during the final decades of the Lodee dynasty and had firsthand experience of invasion by the Mughal forces under the command of Babr.*

The reaction of Guru Nanak Dev to the barbarous killing of the Hindus is impressively revealed in some of his hymns, recorded in *Shree Guru Granth Sahib*. The following are some exemplary excerpts from the *Guru Granth Sahib*:

> Justice is rare, devotion towards family is changing into selfishness, faith in religion is more formal than sincere ... the degradation of the country is due to the failure of the leadership ... the saints are after power and money, the warriors have adopted foreign language, and self-respect is no longer sustainable ... the Hindu kings had lost sense immersed in merriment and pleasures ... the Brahmans bathe in holy waters, and kill living beings ... the yogis are blind to mindfulness and do not know how to unite with the higher self ... the Muslims in higher administration tell lies and accept bribes ... the subjects are oblivious to true knowledge and are like corpses ablaze in worldly fire ... the wise (convert Brahmans) dance and play musical instruments for entertainment and decorate their bodies ... the foolish Brahmans have the wisdom for arguments and greed of materialism ... the virtuous practice virtues but get no reward.

Describing the invasion of Babr, Guru Nanak Dev wrote:

> He [Babr] rushed on from Kabul with his army like a dancing marriage procession full of sinners to gather all the wealth by force ... with the help of Khoraasan [Turks and Mughals from the region west of Afghanistan], Hindostaan was frightened. The blame lies with us and not the Creator, who has sent the Mughal as the angel of death. [Describing the plight of the womenfolk:] The heads on which the hair-plaits were beautifully arranged, with vermillion on the parting, the scalp hair were sheared by scissors and dust of molestation rose to the necks ... the dwellers of palaces now do not find the company of their husbands ... the messengers who carried them in palanquins were ordered to rape them ... without the sacred floor how the Hindu women could bathe, dress and put the bright red bridal mark on their forehead. Before they never remembered the Lord Raam:, now they are prohibited to utter the Lord's name.

Even before the Mughal Emperor Aurangzeb ascended the throne of Dilli, socio-religious inequality was already well established. It was out of the unremitting harassment of Brahmans from Kashmir and the cold-blooded sacrifice of his father, Guru Taeg Bahaadur, that Guru Gobind Rai, the tenth Sikh guru, initiated the Khalsaa breed of self-motivated followers of the Sikh faith, to defend the socio-religious rights of all citizens. Neither Guru Gobind Singh himself nor the Sikh disciples ever identified the Guru with any existing godly figures or reincarnation of a higher divinity. He was a soldier and a saint; a perceptive politician, without guile and free of deceit. He and his heroic soldiers did not possess any divine weapons of destruction except that they had the spirit of a fearless lion, true to the given suffix "Singh" and "Khalas," (pure) at heart; belonging to the non-lineage dynasty of the "Gurus" as one family. It would be difficult to suggest that the Guru raised his sword against the Mughal emperor directly due to a personal conflict or as a matter of revenge. After the events of Chumkor, despite the loss of his family at the hands of the Mughal, he lent his Khalsaa force to assist Muazzam Shah during the struggle of ascension to the throne of Dilli, when the Guru could have turned down the request.

The reason to establish the uniformed Khalsaa force was to fight against socio-religious inequalities, the repressive regime of the Mughals and finally to dismantle their rule. In the battle of Chumkor, which lasted less than 24 hours, 40 Khalsaa soldiers fought against a well-equipped Mughal army numbering in the hundreds and thousands. In this unbalanced battle the Guru sacrificed two older sons in action while the two younger sons were entombed alive behind his back upon refusal to accept Islam. To keep alive the drive against the Mughal to defend the interests of his countrymen, he temporarily deserted the battlefield of Chumkor, leaving it in the hands of the last few Khalsaa soldiers. His focus was never on personal gain. Rather, he raised a military force consisting of self-motivated ordinary members of the society to fight for a much larger cause.

The Temoori (Mughal) Empire lasted for almost 350 years, after which the British gradually encroached as the Islamic imperial regime lost hold over Hindostaan. The nation acquired a new identity as India under the British Raj. As before, centuries-old divisions borne of religion, language, social structure, and political weakness within the country due to foreign domination, together with the largely unprotected northwestern frontier and a vast undefended coastline, made the nation easy prey to invaders who said they came as traders. The divisive British administrative policies and the underlying agenda of plundering the country's natural resources and making use of its manpower meant that the self-serving new imperial power prevented the development of the country's people through common interests. The already debilitated Hindus and now the shattered Muslim society too suffered enormous setbacks and a loss of dignity at the hands of a common enemy. The divided feelings of nationalism created understandable confusion in the minds of citizens, contriving against each other in self-interest. This provided extremely fertile grounds for the British to practice their own divide-and-rule philosophy.

Unfortunately, even now after 75 years of independence, there is very little genuine inclination on the part of the masses towards true nationalism in terms of one nation, one language and the practice of meaningful religiosity. The injured trust and self-esteem of the lower strata are far from healed and to do so would require a genuinely equal distribution of wealth at its source, rather than trying to redress inequities through charities and handouts that are seen as favours granted by the rich, further hurting the dignity of the poor. One possible way to address the epidemic of poverty is to institute much higher wages right across all social ranks to narrow the gap, and to put a check on the draining away of national wealth to developed countries to pay for higher education for youth and the transfer of personal funds for permanent immigration.

A nation cannot progress as long as its people are corrupt, do not love each other and do not develop a feeling of belonging to the whole land without racial, linguistic, religious and provincial boundaries. This ancient nation can never recover its former glories under the imposed identities of India and Hindostaan. The diverse nation can never remain united under one flag and effectively defend its borders until the nation once again identifies itself as and takes pride in becoming Bhaaratvarsh.

3. A Recapitulation of the Life and Times of Guru Gobind Singh

The philosophy of Sikhism originated in the thoughts and ideas of the prophetic first Sikh guru, Guru Nanak Dev, towards the end of the fifteenth century. He was a contemporary of Zahir Uddin Babr, the first Temoor sovereign to establish Temoori (Mughal) rule in Dilli (Delhi), followed by a line of his successors. In the preceding centuries, the invasion of Persian culture and Islamic values into the land of Bhaaratvarsh through traders had influenced the indigenous people. The underprivileged section of society was denied religious equality, and its social segregation from the upper "caste" became an easy target for foreign religious cults. The society, already weakened by inherent division into the "caste" system, suffered rapidly further degradation and disintegration under Islamic rule.

In addition, the Brahmans, so-called higher men of religion, began to change the values of the Vedic religion, either through ignorance or by deliberately misinterpreting the philosophy in order to gain the favour of the ruling Chiefs, which resulted in further injury to the underprivileged people. With the change of the Vedic Sanaatanic way of life to the more prevalent name of Hinduism by the Mughal rulers, and the arrival of Islam, the people of the upper "caste" too felt troubled in their own motherland. To protect their centuries-old traditions they buried themselves deeper in formalism and ritualism. This completely segregated the people of lower "caste." To make things worse, the social matrix of Hinduism, studded with many power-hungry, frightened royals and greedy Hindu officials, became pawns of the Mughal rulers. The decaying status of the Hindu social life and the many cultural intrusions dishonoured the purity of Vedic culture. This affected not only ordinary illiterate people, but also the educated and wise, as well as the existing provincial rulers of Bhaaratvarsh.

The inquiring mind of the Sikh Gurus caused them to develop a clear understanding of the existing state of society. To them, self-realization was more to be found within the material world than in an abstract philosophy of mysticism. In their minds, the relevance of any religion lay in fulfilling the needs and wants of present times successfully, to embrace the whole humanity as a unified society, so that all can enjoy the beneficence of earthly life. Through this objective they attempted to perpetuate the idea of realization of self being the realization of the Divine, to understand the design and work of God's creation.

During the time when the Sikh Gurus were disseminating their message of spiritual liberty, the Mughal emperor Nour Uddin Jahangir ordered the execution of the fifth Guru, Guru Arjan Dev, to smother attempts at gaining religious freedom by the Sikhs. Following the peaceful reign of Jalal Uddin Akbar, Muhyi Uddin Aurangzeb imprisoned his father Shihab Uddin Shah Jahan, and killed all his brothers in order to occupy the throne. Mughals were staunch Sunni Muslims and wanted Bhaaratvarsh to become an Islamic nation. The Afghaans before the Temoori rule had already changed its name to Hindostaan. Aurangzeb wanted to erase Hinduism completely. Like the Afghaans, Aurangzeb and his officials engaged themselves aggressively in building mosques on the foundations of razed Hindu temples. Being an iconoclast and intolerant of the Hindu way of worshipping idols of gods and goddesses, he had the idols removed from the temples and placed in the foundations of the stairways approaching the mosques to offend and further belittle Hindus.

The offensive behavior of Aurangzeb did not stop there. He felt threatened by the growing sect of Sikhism within the stronghold of the Islamic northern zones of Greater Punjab. Even the Raajpoot* Hindu Hill Chiefs, pawns to the Mughal ruler in northeastern reaches of Punjab, showed their revulsion toward Sikh principles of equality among all "castes," and teachings against idol worship.

Worse still, there was a government policy of forced conversion to Islam, thus denying individuals the right to practice the religion of their choice. This frequently led to persecution of ordinary people as well as leading figures in society. During this process all the Sikh Gurus suffered severely, but the execution of the fifth and the ninth Gurus was followed by the adoption of military force. Thereafter, the Sikh philosophy of Guru Nanak Dev changed completely. The phenomenon of militancy took birth out of the peace-loving saintly roots of Sikhism. First, it was Guru Hargobind Rai who recruited an army and commanded from Akaal Takht (timeless throne), within the premises of Har-Mandir (Golden Temple), in Amritsar. Later his grandson, Guru Gobind Singh, the last Sikh Guru, once again gathered forces to strike back at the Mughal emperor with his original and unique democratic philosophy, giving external features and symbols to future followers of Sikhism.

It was the year when Shah Jahan died, and his son Aurangzeb had already been on the throne for nearly eight years, that Guru Gobind Singh, the warrior and the saviour of the people's faith, was born on 13 Poh 1723 Bikrami (22 December 1666 CE) at Patna (Patliputrr) in Bihar. At the time his father, the ninth Guru Taeg Bahaadur, was on a religious mission in the far eastern quarter of the country. He was the only child born to Guru Taeg Bahaadur and his mother Gujree. As the news of the child's birth reached him through Mehar Chand and Kishan Chand, he announced the birth, naming the child Gobind Daas. Guru Taeg Bahaadur was so engaged in his missionary work that he only stopped briefly in Patna to see the newborn. From there he continued his journey to Punjab, to settle in the region of Anandpur, in the foot hills of Shivaalik.

The child Gobind Daas (also sometimes called Gobind Rai), surrounded by the immediate family of his mother and grandmother, spent the first few years of his life in Patna. He began his primary education there and left for Anandpur sometime during the year 1672 CE to join his father. He was admitted to a madrasa headed by Peer Mohammad Qaazi, Munshee Sahib Chand, and Pandit Kirpa Chand to learn Arabic, Persian, and Sanskrit. Punjabi Gurumukhi script was taught by Harjas Rai, and at the same time he was introduced to the *Adi Granth* (the Sikh scripture). By the age of nine the child Gobind Daas also became conversant with Vedic literature and Puraanic epic tales. Under the tutorship of Bajar Shahadara Pargana Vazirabad, he was trained in horse riding as well as the basic skills of a soldier.

The missionary work and grace of Guru Taeg Bahaadur brought followers from all over to Anandpur. Apart from faithful religious activities, it became a haven for scholars, and artists under the aegis of the ninth Guru. He was regarded as an uncrowned royal of the region, holding court to deliver sermons and to bless his visitors. He believed in righteousness and the right to religious freedom. The event that brought a definite change to the externals of Sikhism began when Pundits from Kashmir approached Guru Taeg Bahaadur for his support to repel the forces of Aurangzeb, who was converting the Hindus of Kashmir to Islam. This event sparked the remark by the young Gobind Daas to his father that none could be more worthy than him to make a sacrifice for the cause, which led to the martyrdom of Guru Taeg Bahaadur.

Along with an envoy of six followers Guru Taeg Bahaadur arranged a missionary tour to Agra, where he was arrested and sent to Dilli* (Delhi). On the orders of Aurangzeb, he was beheaded on the 11th day of December, 1675 CE along with his immediate companions. He inflicted this sacrifice upon himself for the right of freedom for all human beings, rather than any specific religious sect. However, the immediate cause of this incident was Brahmans from Kashmir seeking his protection. Historically, it became a significant event of sacrifice by the Guru to voice the rights of socio-religious freedom of all the Hindus nationwide, despite condemnation of the Hindu religious practices by the antecedent Sikh Gurus.

The self-sought sacrifice of Guru Taeg Bahaadur cemented the desire of the people of the northern region of the Mughal Empire to stand up for the right to practice the religion of their choice. The young Gobind Rai seeded new ideas and philosophies in the minds of the people to create a new social order, which was exclusive and unparalleled, leading to the creation of a powerful self-sacrificing male gender that would be the best in every respect. This not only discouraged further strengthening of the alliance between the Hill Chiefs and the forces of Aurangzeb but later the British also, to block them for years through the strength of Khalsaa Sikh and strategic reality of Punjab geographically, until the reign of Maharaja Runjeet Singh.*

Gobind Rai acceded as the next Sikh Guru at the age of approximately nine, as previously ordained by his father. He grew into a tall, strong, and energetic handsome youth. He is always portrayed as immaculately and richly dressed like a prince, with a plumed crest on his peaked turban, armed with a sword, shield, spear, and bow with a quiver of arrows. One would never miss his "logo", a white hawk, perched on his left wrist while he rode his favourite steel-blue white horse. Apart from his royal style, he was a natural genius, acquiring literary skills at a young age. He composed a large volume of his own poems, mostly in Persian, on various subjects to infuse martial spirit in his followers, and devotional material expounding religious philosophy, later to be collected under the title *Dasam Granth* (compilation of the tenth). He became a phenomenon in himself. His goals were very distinct and different from those of his predecessors. Hence, he kept his literary works separate from the main Sikh scripture *Adi Granth*, containing the works of other Gurus. In his court at Anandpur, due to a more congenial environment, many scholars and poets settled permanently. They contributed to the education and enhancement of religious knowledge of the local people, by translating Vedic literature from Sanskrit to the more prevalent indigenous saral bhaasha in Punjabi Gurumukhi script. He also wrote his own interpretation of Puraanic (ancient) legends, included in *the Dasam Granth.*

There is confusion over the circumstances and number of his marriages. Such controversies are beyond the scope of this present work. Even before turning twenty, he was married to Sundaree (Sundar Saroop; its diminutive Sundaree is an adjective meaning beautiful maiden), on the 13th day of July, 1685 CE. His alleged second marriage was solemnized with Jeeto, on the 28th day of January, 1686. It is believed that Sundar Saroop and Jeeto may be the names of the same person as he affectionately addressed Sundar Saroop as Sundaree. Secondly, in accordance with the usual practice of giving a brand-new name to a newlywed girl, Jeeto could have been the name given by her parents, and Sundar Saroop was her post-nuptial mutational name, when she joined him in January of 1686 CE. By the beginning of November, 1688 his eldest child Ajit Singh was born. Three other sons, Jujhaar Singh in 1690, Zoraavar Singh in 1696, and Fateh Singh in 1699, were also born. His other partner in marriage was Sahib Dewan. He married her against his will on the insistence of her parents and his own mother in 1699. It is believed that the marriage was never consummated. Sahib lived as a virgin moral wife to him all her life, accepting a role as a spiritual companion in his day to day activities.

With the assistance and support of the followers of Sikhism, Gobind Rai raised a well-trained private army and constructed the fort known as Anandga*r*d. He organized a military force. Weapons, fire arms, ammunition, horses and other warfare accessories were received as part of offerings from devoted admirers and supporters who believed in his cause to militarize the willing Sikhs. Such preparations were undertaken to defend the interests and freedom of ordinary people based on past experience, the assassination of Guru Arjan Dev and his own father. However, during his early peaceful years, he mainly kept himself busy in literary and religious activities. To establish his role as leader of a huge following at Anandpur, a kettle drum, Runjeet Nagaa*r*da,* was played to announce his daily spiritual activities and exercises of his armed forces. Indirectly, the kettle drum symbolized freedom, righteousness, and recent victories over skirmishes with Hill Chiefs. He aroused strong feelings of patriotism and nationalism among his followers. Such a display and the progressively increasing popularity of the Guru irritated and offended the Hill Chiefs in the surrounding provinces. They felt threatened by his growing strength and force. Although the estate of Makhowal (Anandpur) and surrounding forested zone was a freehold property acquired by his family on return of his father from the east, it supposedly fell within the territory of Chief Bheem Chand of Kehloor (now Bilaspur). Bheem Chand considered himself as the leader of Member Hill States and felt threatened by the assertion and military display of Gobind Rai on his territory. The beating of the drum made him increasingly intolerant and the perceived presence of the Guru seemed a potential danger to his independence.

The Raajpoot* Rajas of hill principalities did not have the courage to face the Mughal rulers. They had no sense of patriotism anymore, and were constantly attempting to preserve their self-interests. They found it difficult to believe the revolutionary change that had occurred in the members of the underprivileged Hindu classes enlisting as soldiers in Sikh forces, under the leadership of the tenth Guru. These Hindu Chiefs and Rajas were political slaves, forced to pay tribute in the form of taxes, ensuring loyalty to the crown in Dilli, and expecting protection in return. This mechanism had been in existence since the days of Akbar, by keeping a prince from every state as a hostage to seal the fate of the native royal families. By nature Hill Rajas were always competing with one another to win the favour of the ruler. They never hesitated to foolishly engage in territorial battles and skirmishes amongst themselves. This suited the Mughals, as it prevented any aggression by the Hindu royals against the capital, Dilli. Adolescent Guru Gobind Rai, antagonistic to the Mughal court, openly condemned the servile attitude of the Hill Chiefs. Realizing the Guru's military strength they all vied to have an alliance with him to fight each other.

Although Guru Gobind Rai was a neutral figure in the region, Raja Bheem Chand of Kehloor (Bilaspur) did not like his cordial relations with the Raja of Handoor. Such personal agendas and envy became the cause of skirmishes and battles between the Guru and the alliances of the Hill Chiefs. Guru Gobind Rai had neither territorial interests nor personal reasons to fight them. He only wanted to establish the concept of equality for all, and inculcate the idea of religious tolerance among the rulers of the country. Once threatened and invaded by the alliance in collaboration of the Mughal forces by the orders of Aurangzeb, his defensive war finally became a critical campaign to protect interests of his family and the newly established creed of "Khalas" men, women, and their families. The maltreatment received by his predecessors was sufficient evidence to make him engage in battles against Mughal alliances to protect his own interests and the socio-religious rights of indigenous people, even at the cost of his whole family. When left with no choice he armed himself as a crusader, to retaliate with total trust and believing that it was the will of the Supreme Being.

The battles started when Raja Medni Parkaash of Sirmur, Nahan, in April 1684 CE, invited Guru Gobind Rai to spend time at the palace along with his five hundred chosen men. In return, Medni Parkaash expected military favours from the Guru. Medni Parkaash had a longstanding territorial dispute with Raja Fateh Shah of Ghardwal. Instead, Guru Gobind Rai tried to convince them to create a united front against the domination of Aurangzeb. In the process, Medni Parkaash offered the Guru an estate on the banks of river Jamuna (Yamuna,* sister river of Ganga*). After a short stay with the host, the Guru decided to move out and lay down his convoy on the accepted peaceful romantic spot by the banks of Jamuna, naming the site Paonta.* Shortly thereafter at the site he constructed a fort to settle down, expecting a peaceful time. During this period at Paonta he created some of his literary works. From here he sent some of his favourite Sikh scholars to Kaashee* to learn Sanskrit and to help with translations of Sanskrit literature. His time in Paonta was relaxing and productive. He had significant time to spare following his spiritual duties to socialize and to enjoy an adventurous lifestyle. Once on a hunting expedition, singlehandedly, he killed a tiger with his sword, defending himself with the shield.

A Muslim by the name of Saiyyad Budhu Shah, an admirer of the Guru, visited Paonta to engage in a spiritual discourse. He was impressed by the philosophy of Guru Gobind Rai, his cause and his reaction to the socio-religious oppression by Aurangzeb. Budhu Shah suggested that the Guru should offer employment to nearly five hundred Pathaans dismissed from the Royal army. The Guru accepted the abandoned Pathaans in the hope of strengthening his own forces in anticipation of troubles ahead from the Hill Chiefs and Aurangzeb.

Guru Gobind Rai kept up his efforts as a mediator to improve the relationship among Raja Fateh Shah of Ghardwaal, Raja Medni Parkaash and the other Hill

Chiefs. Unfortunately, the situation ignited when the Guru sent a wedding present to the daughter of Fateh Shah, due to marry Ajmer Chand, son of Bheem Chand. Guru Gobind Rai had already accepted the invitation of Fateh Shah to attend the wedding. However, as expected, Bheem Chand objected, feeling that this was a kind of discriminatory attitude displayed by Guru Gobind Rai by not sending gifts to his son as well. To remain neutral in dealing with his friends and not cause any displeasure on an occasion such as a marriage, the Guru decided to send Nand Chand with a company of one hundred Sikh soldiers as his representatives to deliver wedding presents to Fateh Shah. Whether the wedding party of the bridegroom on its way to Ghardwal took the route through Paonta intentionally or just to lessen the travelling time is unclear. Despite the careful gestures on the part of the Guru to avoid any conflict when Nand Chand and his men were returning after delivering the precious gifts, the soldiers of Bheem Chand, escorting the wedding party led by the men of Fateh Shah, attacked them. Surprised Sikhs faced them bravely, killing most of the offending men in self-defense. The winning party of the brave men reached Paonta mostly unhurt, and reported their victory. This was the first victory of the Guru against an organized attack by Hill Rajas, demonstrating the strength and faithfulness of his men, thus building new confidence in him. It was no surprise to the Guru, as he had trained his Sikhs very well for such eventualities. Hearing this news many more Sikhs as well as Pathaans left Mughal forces to join his army. He established a base in Paonta before returning to Anandpur.

As expected, the relationship between the House of the Guru and the surrounding Hill Chiefs deteriorated. An alliance of the Hill Chiefs under the formal protection of the royal army led to development of a full-blown battle from September 1688 CE onward, in Bhanganee,* a village ten kilometres from the banks of Jamuna. Hearing the news of an impending battle, nearly one thousand soldiers including the Pathaans betrayed the Guru at the eleventh hour. Undisturbed by the situation and with the timely support of the distressed Pir Budhu Shah along with seven hundred of his men, four grandsons, and his nephews, the Guru encouraged new men to join, accumulating an army of two thousand on his side. Bhai Rama of Banaras (Varanasi/Kaashee*) supplied wooden cannon. The enemy lines were made up of ten thousand soldiers under the command of Hill Chiefs Bheem Chand, Kirpal Chand of Kotar, Kesari Chand Jaiswal, Hari Chand, Prithi Chand and other Hill Chiefs. In the battle, there were heavy losses on both sides. With the death of Hari Chand, the frightened Hill forces scattered, leaving the field and bringing a decisive victory to Guru Gobind Rai. Defeating the alliance was no less than a miracle. On his return from Paonta, the Guru received the news of his first son's birth in Anandpur. The theme of the moment was victory, so he named him "Ajit."

Soon, Bheem Chand extended a friendly hand, but the Guru mistrusted such friendly attitudes on the part of the Hill Chiefs. He continued to strengthen his army, and built more fortresses, namely Lohgard, Fatehgard, and Keshgard, around the estate of Anandpur. Encouraged and motivated by the rebellious spirit of the Guru, some of the Hill Chiefs also tried to flex their muscles, refusing to pay the usual taxes to the emperor. Soon the tax collector, Dilavar Khan from Dilli, landed on the banks of the river Yamuna. He sent Alif Khan to Nadaun, a place on the banks of the river Beas, near Kangarda to collect taxes from Kirpal Chand. In turn, Kirpal

Chand asked Alif Khan to first seek taxes from Bheem Chand, the leader in refusing to pay taxes. Bheem Chand again refused point blank and, expecting trouble, asked Guru Gobind Rai for assistance. Reluctantly the Guru participated in the skirmish between the allied forces of Alif Khan and Kirpal Chand against the rest of the Hill Chiefs on the bank of Beas in Nadaun. In the very first engagement, following a grievous injury to Kirpal Chand, frightened Mughal soldiers declared the invincible strength of the Guru, leading them to retreat from the region overnight. This was the second effortless victory, without much loss of life for the Guru, in the spring of 1691 CE.

In order to have a trouble-free relationship with Aurangzeb, Ajmer Chand, the newly enthroned son of Bheem Chand, called a regional summit in 1692 CE. He invited Vazeer Khan of Sarhind,* Hussain Khan of Kangarda, Dilavar Khan of Lahore, and Abraham of Jammu to build an alliance with him. The alliance warned Aurangzeb of the Guru's increasing strength in the foothills of Shivaalik, claiming that the Guru was a major obstruction in collection of taxes. In reply, Aurangzeb sent orders to the Guru to give up his royal status by disarming, and to either choose the life of a saint like his predecessors or face exile. This encouraged the alliance to take a hostile attitude towards the Guru, who took appropriate steps to strengthen his army and fortification around Anandpur further. In 1694 CE, Dilavar Khan of Lahore sent his son Rustam Khan to attack Anandpur. But a shower of arrows on reaching Anandpur sent him back to Lahore.

This made Dilavar Khan very upset, and he decided to lead the alliance against Guru Gobind Rai himself. After extensive preparation, the following year in the company of Hussain Khan he advanced toward Anandpur. To prevent devastation of the region Gopal Chand Gularia and Ram Singh went to see Hussain Khan. After being turned down and attacked by Hussain Khan's men, Gopal Chand requested Guru Gobind Rai to come forward for assistance. Guru Gobind Rai sent a small contingent led by Lal Chand and Ranga Ram. They fought bravely against the alliance, killing Kirpal Chand and Hussain Khan. When news of these events reached Aurangzeb, he appointed his son Muazzam as viceroy of the northwest regions, including Punjab. As soon as Muazzam acquired office at Lahore, Aurangzeb sent a large army under the command of Mirza Jaffer Baeg, to attack dithering Hill Chiefs and Anandpur, during the summer months of 1696 CE. Mirza plundered and troubled the Hill Chiefs, and returned without proceeding to Anandpur. On hearing about the military strength, saintly attitude and neutral interests of Guru Gobind Rai, Muazzam was so impressed that he decided to take a softer line on diplomatic relations with the Guru's household instead of following the hard line of his father.

While Muazzam was the viceroy, the Guru enjoyed a trouble-free period to once again engage in his literary activities. This gave him ample opportunity to further his role as a religious leader and to expand Sikhism. He wanted to revitalize the decayed Sikh missionary organization, called the Masands,* that had been set up during the era of Guru Arjan Dev. Many of them had become corrupt, engaging in immoral practices and embezzling offerings of the Sikhs. In February 1698 CE, he formally announced the dismissal of all the Masands, and advised his followers to send all their contributions directly to Anandpur. He sought contributions of arms and horses, to strengthen his existing military force. To reform further and bring in an entirely new philosophy of "people power," he began his efforts towards the creation of the "Khalas" men and women, who would be loyal and pure at heart. He sent out messages of equality for all "castes," advising them to give up unnecessary religious rituals and to socially break away from the Turks.

Finally, with a complete blueprint in his mind to create a new righteous and socially equal society without the barriers of "caste," he sent out messages to all his followers to gather in Anandpur on the 30th day of March, a day in Baisaakh of the Hindu calendar, in 1699 CE. Following the morning prayers he addressed the crowd of Sikhs in front of a tent with a flashing sword in his hand. He called out for someone loyal and brave who would be ready to sacrifice for social equality and righteousness. Eventually five men, Daya Ram from Lahore, Dharam Chand from Dilli, Himmat Rai from Jaganath Puri, Mohkam Chand from Dwarka, and Sahib Chand from Bidar, came forward, one after the other. The Guru took them, one at a time, behind the tent and reappeared with his sword dripping with blood. Bravely each followed him thinking that the man prior to him had been killed. But at the end, the Guru brought all of them unharmed back to the front to honour their fearlessness and willingness to die for socio-religious freedom for all.

These beloved five men, who were called "Khalsaa,"* were nominated as founding members of the new community called "Khalas Panth," a wing of empowered Sikh society pure at heart, loyal and sincere in their deeds and lifestyle, ever ready to sacrifice for the cause of righteousness. The Guru offered them a drink called "Umrit,*" made of water and sugar stirred with a Khandah (a double-edged sword) and served in a common iron bowl. Then he asked the five men to initiate him by offering the "Umrit" from the same bowl. This unique and simple act was intentional, to break down the "caste" barriers among the emerging Sikh community, to establish a brotherhood of fearless men, and finally to erase the distinction between the Guru and his disciples. They were asked to change their surnames to "Singh," as if belonging to the same family. He applied the suffix "Singh" to his own name as well, becoming Guru Gobind Singh, shedding the "caste"-distinguishing surname of Rai. Traditionally he is known as the father of the Khalsaa, and his moral wife, Sahib Dewan, is called the mother of the Khalsaa, as she assisted him through this celebration. He denounced the idea of social apartheid and religious exclusiveness, and upheld the concept of social mobility, in which people were to work out their destiny according to their own potential through self-effort. Thus, he laid the foundation stone of equality and democracy, a distinctive event in the history of the nation.

Each member belonging to the community was advised to wear five external symbols, commonly referred to as the five K's.* They were asked to keep long hair and unshorn beards (**Kaesh**); to carry a miniature comb (**Kanghaa**); to wear modest knee-length shorts (**Kacchaa**) and an iron bracelet on the right wrist (**Ka**r**daa**); and carry a short sword (**Kripaan**). In the literature, except for the sword which is self-explanatory, there are varied explanations discussing the practical value of these symbols. At the time of creation of the Khalsaa order, the immediate need was to gather an army of fearless and fierce self-motivated brave men in uniform symbolizing the Khalsaa force, to set them apart from both the Hindus and the Mughals, with high self-esteem and human integrity. His true intentions in introducing such symbols were to promote personal hygiene, high moral values and spiritual development among his followers rather than create a brutal military force. To him these symbols were not intended to portray the power or superiority of the Khalsaa over others during peacetime or to strike fear among ordinary people of other religious denominations. He always maintained supremacy of one and the only one God, the Supreme Being. In "Bachittrr Naatak" (enigmatic drama) he very clearly expounded his philosophy on external appearances of the people. He said, *"God does not take notice of those who acquire disguises to standout. Everyone must understand for once and all, the Supreme Being does not live among the disguised. The men who disguise to show off and influence others, at the end are butchered to pieces and thrown in hell. Do not search afar as God does not reside in the costume."*

Symbols should promote inner self-worth and adherence to the universal moral values of that symbol. The wearer must show and earn genuine respect for it. Those who put on symbols, false garbs as disguise, as fashion to form a special group of people joined together in the name of God under the pretext of religion to hurt humanity—for them such physical markers do not have a true value of what they represent. To the Guru, such external changes were temporary and did not have inherent value. There should be a well-defined objective to become uniformed, to represent unity of purpose for the well-being of humanity. To maintain a high level of self-discipline he forbade his uniformed men to consume any kind of intoxicants and Halal meat, that is, meat of an animal slaughtered by being bled to death while Islamic prayers are said. Following this historic event thousands of men and women descended upon Anandpur to be initiated as Sikh Khalsaa. Formally, a council of five initiated members was given the right to perform the ceremony to initiate the interested members of the community. This helped many more loyal men voluntarily enlist in the Khalsaa force, ready to sacrifice themselves for the cause of equal socio-religious rights.

The aim of the Guru was to create a nation of "pure" (the Khalas), loyal, and fearless people to be warriors, full of martial spirit to fight against the forces of injustice. The new sect of Khalsaa aggravated Brahmans, elite Hindus, and strongly irritated the Raajpoot Hindu Hill Chiefs all over northern territories of Bhaaratvarsh. The Khalsaa initiation ceremony infused martial spirit among all the lower "castes," diminishing the prerogative of the kShatriya. Armed men on horses visiting and living in Anandpur virtually converted the town into a cantonment. However, the Guru did not have any intention to offend anyone but only sought to defend the interests of the citizens living under the tyranny of Mughal rulers. This became a major cause of concern for Hill Rajas and the emperor presently fighting the Maraathas* in the south of the country.

The peaceful days of Guru Gobind Singh were interrupted by the perturbed Hill Chiefs, who began to conspire to somehow evict him from the region. They sought the military assistance of the Mughals to uproot the House of Sikhism once and for all. When democratic thinkers, anti-Mughal Hindus and Sikh followers sympathizing with the Guru, gathered at Anandpur in support, this fuelled the situation further. The coalition of Hindu Rajas sent messages about the military activities of Guru Gobind Singh to Dilli, inflaming the authorities against him. This was to voice their concern to the emperor that the Khalsaa sect, if left in existence, would cause a rift and preclude any kind of possible association between Hindus and Muslims. They worried that the newly amalgamated socio-religious group of upper and lower classes under the banner of "Khalas Panth" would act like a wedge between them. This fear led to many skirmishes and ambushes between the Guru and the Hill Chiefs in alliance with Mughal forces. It caused unnecessary loss of human life, beginning at the doorstep of Anandpur, ripping apart Guru Gobind Singh's immediate family, and ended in Khidrana, the present-day town of Muktsar.

In 1701 CE, the Nawaab of Sarhind* received orders from the south to check upon supposedly threatening activities in the region of Anandpur. The Mughal forces moved to surround Anandpur under the command of Dina Baeg and Paendey Khan. They blocked supplies of daily consumption to the fortress, Anandgard. But fearless and enduring Sikhs within were unmoved. Realizing the strong will of the Guru's men, Mughal generals adopted deceitful means by falsely promising safe passage to the occupants of the fortress in return for abandoning the town of Anandpur. Agreeing to the deal for the safety of his men, the Guru left the fort and headed towards the village of Nirmoh, near Keeratpur. The Mughal army chased them there, attacking his encampment. At the site, in the ensuing skirmish, Hill Chiefs and Sarhind forces could not withstand the swift response of brave Sikh soldiers still sitting stern and steadfast in their saddles. The allied enemy forces retreated, and the Guru returned home victorious once again. Soon afterward, on the invitation of Raja of Basolee, Guru Gobind Singh went to Basolee. During the visit, daring Bheem Chand did not hesitate to show his muscle by intruding into the territory. However, he had to compromise his aggressive stance towards the Guru, flanked by the host and Raja Jaiswal. Thereafter, the Guru spent the next couple of years in peace, consolidating his domain.

Regional Vazeers and nervous Hill Royals surrounding Anandpur continued to see even the peaceful attitude of the Guru as a potential threat to the Mughal Empire. As always, the self-proclaimed leader of the Hill Chiefs, Raja Bheem Chand, felt the irritation of the Guru's continued presence and sent an envoy led by his son Ajmer Chand to the capital. Distressed Aurangzeb, already troubled by the rebellious Maraathas* in the south, wrote to Guru Gobind Singh, inviting him to visit his court in peace, as a holy man. In reply, the Guru told him, *"Sovereign who has made you emperor has sent me in to the world to do justice. He has commanded you also to do justice, but you have forgotten His mandate."* The angered emperor ordered Nawaabs of Sarhind and Lahore to march to raze Anandpur.

At mid-year in 1704 CE, a large Mughal force numbering in thousands reached Ropard. From there they converged upon Anandpur, joined by soldiers from Bilaspur, Kullu, Mandi, Gulaer, Chamba, Jammu, and Gardwaal, led by their ruling heads.

Allied forces coming from all directions converted the town into a war zone. The resistance of the Sikhs from within the Fortress of Anandgard prevented the alliance from storming in to engage in face-to-face combat. Failing so, the offenders decided to lay siege to the town, blocking all the portals of entry and exit. The fortress was completely isolated. Stopping all the food and water left the occupants high and dry. Mughals tried to break open the gate of the fortress with an intoxicated mad elephant that was bravely killed by Bachittrr Singh.

With the prolonged siege the allied forces started to feel the scarcity of provisions. The state of the Khalsaa soldiers trapped inside the fortress, with limited stores, can well be imagined. No doubt, some of the soldiers stuck inside felt frightened being faced with the impending shortage of food and water. The Guru realized the complexity of the situation. Knowing the stamina of the Guru's followers, the exhausted Mughal generals decided to deceive the starving Sikhs on the suggestion of Hill Chiefs. When ordinary communications and false oaths failed to stir the Guru, to make an oath convincing enough, they decided to write one on the cover page of a copy of the Qur'an. It promised safe passage to all the Khalsaa, including the Guru and his family, on evacuation of Anandpur, and that they would not be harmed in any way. Past experience had taught the Guru not to believe or have any faith in the oaths of Mughal officers. However, on the strong insistence of the suffering Khalsa he permitted the desirous to go free, providing they subscribed to the Bey-dawa (indisputable memorandum).

Realizing his depleted manpower, judging difficult times were ahead, and being unsure of the promised oath, the forsaken Guru decided to evacuate the fortress. During the cold and wet night between the 4th and 5th of December 1704 CE, in the company of his most loyal men and family, he abandoned his home to escape towards the region of Malwa, Punjab. As expected, soon after the band of Sikhs neared the stream Sarsa, the allied forces engulfed them from all directions. Even before approaching Keeratpur, skirmishes between the rearguard of the Khalsaa army and the Mughals had begun. The ratio of soldiers between the two, as always, was discouraging. Once again the Guru was cheated by the broken promises of Mughal officers. That night even cruel nature was not in his favour. He faced heavy winter showers, and the swollen Sarsa was waiting to swallow most of his soldiers and destroy the precious literary works in their possession.

The loyal soldiers in command of Uday Singh fought bravely, and perished, holding the enemy back so as to give full cover to the Guru and his immediate companions. Before the first sign of dawn the Guru and his family reached the bank of the uninviting Sarsa. The hot chase by the large number of Mughal soldiers left no viable choice for him but to leap into the rising waves of the stream. Jeevan Singh Rangrheta was given the command on the proximal bank, with a detachment of five scores, to offer resistance. During the crossing a large number of soldiers met their end, and the whole family of the Guru got scattered in the flooding waters midstream before reaching the opposite bank. As fortune would have it, his mother along with the two younger sons got separated from the rest of the party, later to be led away by the family cook Gangoo. His wives Sundaree, and Sahib Dewan, were safely escorted away by Bhai Mani Singh, to Dilli, disguised in male attire.

Once on the other side of the stream, Guru Gobind Singh, his two older sons and the surviving soldiers entered the village Ghanaula. The intelligence reported the fresh reinforcement of Mughal forces from Ropard heading towards them, leaving no time for deliberation. The Guru decided to reach Kotla as soon as possible to pass the rest of the day in the haveli (mansion) of Kotla Nihung Khan. As a defensive measure he split his men into two groups, giving command of one to Bachittrr Singh, whom he advised to take the shorter route to Kotla. He himself, leading the other group, followed the longer route along the bank of the river Satluj (Sutlej). On the way he did not meet any resistance and reached the haveli of Kotla Nihung Khan safely. Unfortunately Bachitrr Singh and his group had fierce encounters with the Pathaans of Ropard and the Ranghars of Malakpur. Most met their end and the badly wounded Bachittar Singh was later rescued by the Guru's eldest son Ajit Singh.

In the meantime, the Guru's mother Gujree and his two younger sons, expecting no trouble, chose to accompany Gangoo to his village Saheyerdee. On the night of arrival the deceitful cook tried to steal their possessions and also informed the local guards about his companions. This led to the capture of the children and their grandmother, and the next day they were sent to Sarhind. They were put into prison—Thanda Burj*—in the precinct of the present-day Gurudwara at Fatehgard, Punjab. The following morning they appeared in the presence of Nawaab of Sarhind, Vazeer Khan. The children refused to bow to any kind of threat. Vazeer Khan decided to punish the children severely, despite the intervention of the Nawaab of Maleyrkotla, who petitioned to free the children and their grandmother. Ultimately, under the direct supervision of Vazeer Khan, the children were walled off alive in the last week of December 1704. Whether they died of suffocation with time or were beheaded is unclear. Hearing the tragic news killed their grandmother that very night while still in captivity.

A landlord by the name of Buddhi Chand escorted Guru Gobind Singh, along with his accompanying sons and forty Khalsaa soldiers, to the village Chumkor. The Guru decided to station himself in the mansion house of Buddhi Chand, built of unbaked bricks. He strategically placed all his Khalsaa inside the construction, converting the modest double-storey shelter into a fortress. The fatigued and famished men, exhausted by the December chill and finding solace in the newly found cover, left their fate in the hands of the Almighty. By the following dawn, the dark clouds of the allied forces were hovering expectantly all over the village, surrounding the mud fortress. Unfortunately, the shelter became a death trap for the Khalsaa. The family of three men, plus forty Khalsaa was now faced with hundreds and thousands—metaphorically speaking, a "million"—Mughal soldiers. There was no obvious mechanism that would help them to escape out of this trap. With total faith in the Supreme Being, the miniscule brigade of forty Khalsaa could only think to sacrifice themselves, fighting bravely rather than surrender to the tyrants.

In the pandemonium of the crowded village, the Mughal soldiers began a fierce battle raging at the mud fortress. Initially, the strategically stationed Sikhs within the mansion frustrated the storming enemy. Once the Sikh soldiers' hand-missiles were nearly depleted they were forced out of their protection into the open. Guru Gobind Singh planned to send out batches of five men, each to engage in one to one combat. He and his sons positioned themselves in the observation attic to monitor and give cover to the advancing band of the Khalsaa. The brave Khalsaa proved their worth, forcibly piercing the throng of hundreds of Mughals, flashing their swords, cutting up enemies in all directions. Once in the thick of the raging crowd they came to the end of their lives. The Khalsaa were involved in the making of history, matchless history among the battles of the world. By midday it was Ajit Singh's turn to lead the next five, followed by his enthusiastic younger brother, Jujhar Singh, who also wanted to display his skills in the battlefield. Both lost their lives fighting bravely, killing many soldiers. In the *Zafurnamah* to the emperor, the Guru very clearly portrayed a real-time picture of the actions and events in the battlefield of Chumkor.

The battle of Chumkor was a total mismatch in men and weaponry on the two sides. There were forty-three exhausted and starving men against a well-provided and refreshed enemy, numbering in hundreds and thousands. The Sikhs were fighting with self-will, courage, and enthusiasm, without seeking any treasures in return. By late evening, apart from the Guru, seven other Khalsaa soldiers were left. It was enormously clear that winning and escaping alive was impossible for all of them. The falling darkness of the evening brought calm on either side, giving them a much-needed respite. The remaining seven Khalsaa counseled the Guru to escape the region so as to keep the crusade alive. Five chosen Sikhs, according to the tradition of the Khalsaa council, unanimously advised Guru Gobind Singh to escape in the company of any three of the remaining men during the quiet hours of the night. Abiding by his own set of principles and the rules of the Khalsaa council, he could not refuse and accepted their request. He undid his crest and plume, and respectfully placed it upon the turban of Sant Singh.

At the decided hour, accompanied by Daya Singh, Dharam Singh, and Maan Singh, he greeted the remaining men, leaving them under the protection of the Almighty. They planned to head out of the fortress, and then follow the route to the Malwa region. The Guru instructed them to move in different directions, hoping to meet up at a suitable place. Soon after midnight, using loud clapping as a diversion, each of the men leaving the mud fortress headed in four different directions, announcing that the Peer-e-Hind* was going. This caused confusion among the enemy camp. The Khalsaa within started a torrential shower of the remaining arrows in stock. Many of the Mughal soldiers leapt towards the fortress beating drums, adding to the chaos. In the dark of the night the confused allied forces started to kill each other. By dawn hundreds of Mughal men were dead. In this scuffle, Ajmer Chand of Kehloor, and other important figures of the Hill forces were also badly injured. Realizing their deadly mistake, the commanders of the Mughal forces made a final forceful assault on the mud fortress, penetrating its portals and killing the remaining Khalsaa.

Seeing Sant Singh, lying dead with the recognizable plume on his turban, Mughal officers presumed him to be the Guru, and made the announcement of their victory over the Khalsaa. One of them severed the head of the dead man, to be certain of the presumed Guru's death. It became a moment of jubilation and celebration for the allied forces. It was noon before they realized that the real Guru was alive and had escaped towards Malwa district. Later that day, after sunset, a woman by the name of Gursharan Kaur gathered the dead Khalsaa corpses and cremated them. The smoke rising from the burning pyre in the sky brought Mughal soldiers back to the scene. She herself was beheaded and thrown into the fire.

In the meantime, leaving Chumkor, the Guru took the route to the village Kiree, and reached there by the next dawn. From there he made his way to Bahiloll. By that evening, travelling with bare feet, thirsty and hungry, his body began to fail him. Somehow he managed to escape into the woods of Macchiwarda. His blistered and lacerated feet were bleeding. His body was aching from fatigue, and the damp winter chill made his joints stiff. Finding a boulder to rest his head upon, he lay down on a bed of hay and spent the night in the woods. The following couplets ascribed to escape of the Guru into the woods of Macchiwarda reveal the state of his mind.

> *Do tell (my) dear friend, the Lord, about the state of the meek,*
> *Despite Thee, (we) are shrouded under the blanket of troubles, living like reptiles.*
> *The parched body, akin to a dried up pitcher, feels like being pierced by pins and needles (spikes);*
> *Dried-up tongue is like a dagger in mouth (tumbler), left to tolerate the butchers.*
> *The warmth of winter hay is manifold better than living in the coziness of a blazing kiln heat.*

He was tired, cold, parched and dejected. He was on the run to escape, chased by the enemy and hurt by the loss of his family. He was faced with cruel and barbaric Mughal soldiers. At that time, the comforts of life meant nothing to him and he preferred a simple existence sandwiched between the sky and the earth.

As the next day dawned, concerned over being noticed by passing people, he decided to move away from the regular path. His chosen path happened to carry him towards the residence of Gulaab, once a Masand to the Sikh mission. The other three men, who had left Chumkor with him, also met up with him there in the nearby orchard of Gulaab.

When Vazeer Khan heard of the folly of the allied forces, he ordered the entire force to find the Guru. Mughal soldiers scattered over all the villages in the vicinity, searching through the fields and wooded lands of the region. It was not safe for the Guru or his party to spend too much time near the woods of Macchiwarda. Instead of staying in the area, the Guru preferred to move on to the safer place of the Pathaan brothers Ganny Khan and Nabbhy Khan, who had supplied him horses and weapons in Anandpur. The legendary account of his disguised escape from the orchard of Gulaab to the place of the Pathaan brothers as an Uch-da-Peer (Peer of Uch village), in blue robes and an uncovered head with his loose hair, is controversial. It is quite possible that his escape was well planned to trick the soldiers chasing him, but the story is intended more to interest and thrill a casual reader. It tells of his shrewdness and courage under such circumstances to escape from the clutches of the enemy unscathed. It was during his stay with the Pathaan brothers that he wrote his first letter to Aurangzeb, "Namah Guru Gobind Singh Ba Aurangzeb," later to be titled *Fatehnamah*. He wanted to put all the events of the ordeal that his family had undergone at the cruel hands of the deceitful allied forces in proper perspective before the reality was masked by the lies of the Mughal officials.

As a disguised Peer, the Guru and his three men continued their journey through Alamgir and Reyherdee in Ludhiana district. Once again the Mughal soldiers, still unaware of his identity as an Uch-da-Peer travelling through the area, only knew that Guru Gobind Singh was still at large. Thus, the party reached Jatpura untroubled. On the way they managed to get a horse, which speeded and eased their journey to Raikot. There he had a Muslim acquaintance by the name of Rai Kalan, who welcomed them at his residence. The Guru accepted his hospitality. Already there were rumours about the death of his mother and two younger sons. From Raikot he sent a messenger to Sarhind to confirm the rumours about the unfortunate event. When the messenger returned with the news, the Guru was calm, and took it as the will of the Almighty. With two elder sons already lost in Chumkor and the other two sacrificed in Sarhind, he had no reason to look back any longer. He had clear objectives and a firm determination to achieve what was already set out by his exemplary ancestors. His vision was to bring socio-religious freedom to his people. He moved on into the territory of Malwa, where his grandfather Guru Hargobind Rai had a strong following in his day. He was confident and determined enough to bring together an army of dedicated Sikh soldiers to continue his just advocacy against the Mughals.

Now the Guru was totally possessed by his chosen mission, and nothing would discourage him from reaching his target as he had nothing else to lose personally. He gathered all the men of his Khalsaa force at the twin village of Deenae-Kangard. There he received a warm welcome from Choudhary Lakhmee and Choudhary Shameer, of Deenae. He settled there for some time, and it was here that he decided to write the famous *Zafurnamah* to Aurangzeb, to elucidate further upon what he had already written. It is believed to be in response to a conciliatory letter from Aurangzeb, inviting the Guru to visit him in the Deccan. In principle, the Guru wanted to pronounce his moral victory over the deceitful Mughal forces and their commanders. For the Guru, the true valour was when opponents are equipped with equal resources in the battlefield, and they stand by their oaths. As the faith had been already broken due to the follies of the Mughal officers, he refused to accept Aurangzeb's invitation. Instead, he was determined to continue with his defensive crusade against the beastly Mughal soldiers still chasing his men all over the region.

The hunt for the Guru by the Nawaab of Sarhind into Malwa had become a very private and personal agenda. Despite having evicted the Guru from his residence in Anandpur and making him heirless, the Nawaab was determined to eliminate him and his Khalsaa army entirely. The new social philosophy of Guru Gobind Singh had made his presence in the region threatening to Hindus as well as Mughal Chiefs. The Guru was determined to once again raise an army of loyal Sikhs to fight on, to his last breath. Mughals on the offence were not retreating either, keeping up with their chase and seeking to force him out of the region.

After dispatching *Zafurnamah*, it was already the spring of 1705 CE. He set about in search of a suitable place in Malwa, where he could raise an adequate number of loyal soldiers to confront the Mughals from the direction of Sarhind. He needed sufficient time to plan and secure his defensive resources, to be able to achieve success in his mission. After leaving the twin village of Deenae-Kangard, he encamped at many places before reaching Kotkapoorah. The Guru was confident he could bring together many loyal Sikhs of the region to fight with fortitude to prove threatening to the enemy. Under the circumstances, geographically he thought that the area was ideal for preparations to launch his offence.

Unfortunately, the local zamindaar (landlord) by the name of Kapura, who owned the local fort, declined any military involvement from his territory. Initially, Kapura was scared of being hurt by the Mughal forces and losing royal favours. However, on the suggestion of Choudhary Kapura himself, the Guru decided that Khidraney-dee-Dhaab, a hillock on the outskirts of the town, would be the next-best place to respond to any imminent attack on the Khalsa force from Mughal quarters.

Once the Guru established his men strategically on the hillock, a contingent of Sikhs from Majha region led by Mai Bhago* arrived looking for the Guru. This included all those men who had abandoned the Guru during the second battle of Anandpur. Fortunately they returned after having been taunted by their women, who had also joined the mounted Khalsaa force, fully armed. Realizing the strength of the Guru's spirit, regardless of his personal losses, shamed them to tears. As there was no time for discussions or exchange of sympathies, the volunteered Sikhs were aligned strategically around the mound in defense against the fast approaching enemy forces. As expected, the Mughals from Sarhind arrived shortly and there was a furious exchange of arrows. The enthusiastic men and women of Majha acted as equalizers to oppose the Mughal forces and thus the Guru and his Khalsaa army held their ground.

By midday, the ferociousness of the Sikhs and the scorching sun of the desert parched the already weakened Mughal soldiers. Many dispersed and retreated to seek water and to escape with their lives. By sunset the fighting-fit Sikhs had turned away the attacking Mughals. In the process, most of the men from Majha, who had signed the Bey-dawa (indisputable memorandum) in Anandpur, and the women, lost their lives. As the Guru had accepted them back, he personally took care of the dead, dying and injured, praising their sacrifice. These men were given the title of "Muktey," the liberated, and are still remembered in daily prayers everywhere in Gurudwaras during final supplication, the Ardaas* of the day. The present day township at Khidraney-dee-Dhaab is known by the name of Muktsar.

After achieving another victory over the Mughals, staying no longer in Khidraney-dee-Dhaab than necessary, the Guru was ready to move out of the area. Before leaving he paid the complaining Birards, who had participated in fighting the Mughals, their worth in money. He proceeded to Sabo-dee-Talwandee. Each movement of the Guru was well-thought-out and planned to yoke the strength of the masses into a new class in society for the betterment of all socio-religious levels. Nothing he did was to promote self-interest. On the special request of Dallah, he decided to stay in Sabo-dee-Talwandee. It was a place of repose for him, and without the constant Mughal presence there was a period of calm for the people without unwanted skirmishes. Once settled there peacefully, the Guru started to attract large numbers of people of all classes, from all over the northwest and further afar from Talwandee. The process of initiating the desiring became a regular event, thus growing the number of the Khalsaa discipline. It brought a fresh opportunity to further establish the Sikh philosophy of equality and self-defence, and to strengthen the teachings of his predecessors.

He also planned to update the *Adi Granth*. He attempted to procure the original copy in possession of a person by the name of Dheermal. Failing to do so, he decided to prepare a new copy with the assistance of Mani Singh, from recollections of his memorized daily prayers of the *Granth*. He managed to successfully complete the works in the company of Mani Singh, who acted as the registrar to him for the compilation of the *Granth*. To the pre-existing text he added the collection of hymns from the works of his father, Guru Taeg Bahaadur. He did not add any of his own hymns, probably to avoid molestation of the work done by his predecessors or simply because his own philosophy had a different scope in the life of the newly created Khalsaa and their contemporary needs. In addition, realizing the pacifying philosophy of the Adi Granth and the continued misinterpretations of influential Vedic literature negatively affecting the new converts to Sikhism, he chose not to include his writings. To eliminate the Vedic influence, as well as to achieve the socio-religious objectives needed so much by the new followers, he also began to reproduce his own works lost during the crossing of Sarsa.

It was in Sabo-dee-Talwandee that he was joined by his wives, Sundaree and Sahib Dewan Kaur, on their return from Dilli escorted by Mani Singh. On enquiry by the mothers of their sons, he replied that he had sacrificed all the four sons in the service of humanity so as many more would live forever. He was always full of praise for the Sikhs who had sacrificed their lives fighting without complaint against all odds, whether in number, resources, or provisions. He resided in Sabo-dee-Talwandee (now known by the name of Damdama Sahib, a place of respite) for nearly a year, and celebrated the seventh anniversary of Khalsaa establishment there. He also received the information that his last letter, *Zafurnamah*, had been delivered to Aurangzeb.

It is believed that the *Zafurnamah* made a deep impact on the mind of the emperor because the letter proclaimed the moral victory of the Guru and the humiliating defeat of the emperor's well-resourced forces. At the time, Aurangzeb was in Ahmednagar, with his forces still engaged in conflict with the Maraathas. Once again, to resolve the differences, Aurangzeb, in reply sent an invitation to the Guru to visit him in the south. In addition, Daya Singh and Dharam Singh also requested the Guru to consider the visit to see for himself the poor state of the Maraatha people, and the devastation that had been caused by the battles in the southern region of the country to establish Mughal sovereignty. To convince the Guru and to assure honest intentions, Aurangzeb, even instructed the deputy governor of Lahore, Munim Khan, to make arrangements for his safe journey.

Sometime in October 1706 CE, Guru Gobind Singh took leave of his followers during a gathering, and in the company of some of his chosen men, set upon the journey to the south. Still on his way through Rajasthan, in February 1707 he received the message that Aurangzeb had passed away. Thus, Aurangzeb never had the fortune to meet the Guru in person. As expected, soon after the death of the Emperor the war for succession began between his sons. Muazzam, being the eldest of all, was the rightful heir to the throne of Dilli. On his return journey to his newly established seat in Talwandee, on the banks of Satluj, the Guru met Muazzam, who was returning to Dilli from Afghanistan to acquire the newly vacated throne. Muazzam, the crown prince, requested the Guru's assistance with the process of succession. It is not clear whether the Guru had any social or political expectations from Muazzam if he acceded to the throne with the Guru's assistance. In any case, the prince did receive full assistance from the Sikh leader to acquire the throne of Dilli, and the nearest rival Azam Khan was killed in Agra. For his support, Muazzam honoured the Guru with a *Khillat*, a jeweled scarf, an aigrette and other gifts.

Muazzam acceded to the throne with the title of Bahaadur Shah and sent his gratitude to the Guru, inviting him for a meeting in Dilli to strengthen ties between them. The scene in Punjab was rather volatile because of the socio-religious philosophy resulting in the merger of a single caste of Sikhs by Guru Gobind Singh and high-class Hindus' strong objections. During the early winter of 1707 CE,

Guru Gobind Singh was still in Agra, when the news of a coup by Bahaadur Shah's younger brother Kaam Baksh, stationed in the south, arrived. The new emperor once again requested the assistance of the Guru and his men to help to quash the desires of his brother. Instead of returning to Sabo-dee-Talwandee, the Guru decided to continue his journey to the south, which he had abandoned earlier on. During his journey the Guru did join the caravan of Bahaadur Shah but as destiny would have it, he decided to drop out of the emperor's armed procession near the banks of river Godavari. Whether this was the result of a diplomatic rift between the two men or caused by other misunderstandings within the ranks of the emperor's own men is not very clear. It is likely that they were unsure of the relationship between the Guru and the newly enthroned emperor, having different religious affiliations. It may be that the Guru felt his efforts to convince Bahaadur Shah to implement the idea of secularism and equal rights to practice religion of choice were futile, and therefore the Guru decided to return to his chosen goal in the company of his loyal Khalsaa who were true to his ideals.

The paths of the two leaders divaricated when Guru Gobind Singh noticed the uncompromising attitude of Bahaadur Shah, who did not show any inclination to lay the foundation for a more congenial social system giving equal rights. He was well aware of the corrupt hierarchy of Mughal rulers. These were enough reasons for the Guru to turn down the request to lend assistance in crushing the coup by Kaam Baksh, and inhibit the smouldering efforts of the Mughals to subjugate Maraathas in the southwest and Raajpoot in the west.

It was almost September of 1708 CE when the Guru decided to settle down in the vicinity of the river Godavari, at a place called Nanderd. At the time his younger wife, Sahib Kaur, accompanied him. During his stay in Nanderd, the Guru came in contact with Madho Das (previously named Lachhman Das, son of a Raajpoot) Bairagi. He was a Vaishnav ascetic (a follower of Vishnu) and practitioner of occultism. He belonged to Pajouri in Jammu, and had settled in Nanderd, building his own hermitage with a huge following of his own. Following an audience and counsel with Guru Gobind Singh, Madho Das decided to be initiated into the Khalsaa sect. He was given a new name, Banda Singh. Within a short period the Guru realized his potential as a strong-minded soldier, and decided to nominate him as a commander of the Khalsaa force. Later, while the Guru was ill with his injuries, Banda Singh was knighted as Banda Singh Bahaadur, to assume leadership of the Khalsaa force. Banda Singh Bahaadur sought permission to head for Punjab to carry on the "war" against the socio-religious divides, while the Guru was still in the south. He received the necessary written credentials addressed to the Khalsaa in Punjab, and left in the company of the very best chosen men. Before leaving, the Guru gave him five of his arrows, wishing him success in his mission and warning him not to proclaim himself to be a Guru. He was also advised to remain celibate to have the freedom from family ties. This merely reflects the Guru's own heartache at the loss of his near and dear ones. When he reached Punjab the Sikhs of the Malwa were ready to join him with open arms, and destroy the Mughal establishment for good. Uncertain of his own activities and the dangers of the volatile war-torn region of Maharashtra, the Guru decided to send Sahib Kaur to join Sundaree back in Dilli, escorted by Mani Singh.

Nawaab of Sarhind, Vazeer Khan, was restless after his embarrassing defeat at

Khidrana. The absence of Guru Gobind Singh from Punjab meant an uninterrupted opportunity for Khan to hatch some new conspiracy against the Guru. The Nawaab sent Jamshaed and Gul Khan to Nanderd to keep track of the Guru and ordered them to kill him at the first opportunity. At the same time, noticing the good relationship between the Guru and Bahaadur Shah, he was frightened of being rebuffed by the new emperor. However, it is also believed that Bahaadur Shah may have been an accomplice in the plot to eliminate the Guru, to stamp out the increasing courage of the Khalsaa order, and the Sikh establishment as a whole. It has been recorded with certainty that these two Pathaans from Sarhind visited Dilli on their way to the south meeting with his first wife, Sundar Saroop Kaur, to find out the whereabouts of the Guru.

At the time, Guru Gobind Singh was actively holding congregations, attracting more devotees and initiating men and women to Sikhism. He believed in the power of the people, and that a greater force could be generated through a united front of the ostracized "castes" against the hardened attitudes of the Islamic rulers. To prove his concept of democratic rule, he had already removed the seats of missionaries and established the institution of Khalsaa. He had set up the idea of instantaneous decision-making by a body of the "beloved Khalsaa quintet" (an initial congress of *Punj Piyarey*, the five revered members, which constituted a council of original five enrolled Khalsaa Sikhs, a democratic institution, "pure in mind and at heart" to make appropriate political and social decisions for the Sikh community) from among the ordinary Sikh citizens, to carry out the process of new enrolments and the running of the daily workings of the Sikh community in his absence. With the rapid expansion of the Khalsaa discipline he was unaware that among the loyal daily audience, there could also be the presence of assassins. He did not suspect that there were two such false disciples in the crowd, waiting to attack him.

On the evening of the 14th of September 1708 CE, while he was resting in his tent, the pair of malevolent Pathaans seeing the opportune moment entered his safe haven. Jamshaed Khan lunged forward to savagely strike the Guru with a dagger, penetrating the left side of his torso. Before the second strike, Guru Gobind Singh reached out briskly to spill the blood of his assassin, with a single deadly thrust of his sword. The escaping Gul Khan was caught by the nearby guards and killed immediately.

From the available narratives it is amply clear that the Guru was very seriously injured, possibly sustaining internal injuries to his abdomen and chest. He ordered Banda Singh Bahaadur to set off towards Punjab and to announce the state of his health to the followers, as well as take up the cause to bring social and religious liberty to society, with the power of the "Kripaan"—the sword—as the final instrument of kindness to establish socio-religious equality, after having failed by all diplomatic means to end the intolerable oppression of non-Muslim communities. In addition, before his impending death, he also abolished the title of "Guru" as one that could be held by any single human being in the future, announcing the *Adi Granth*, the Holy Sikh scripture, would be the future "Guru." The *Adi Granth* was ceremoniously raised to the seat of "the Guru," by saying the essential prayers and performing suitable rituals. It was thereafter to be called "The Guru Granth Sahib."

There is no substantial evidence that Bahaadur Shah sent any medical help to treat the injuries of Guru Gobind Singh as a good-will gesture. The stabbing injury was obviously fatal and inadequate treatment only meant a poor outcome. It can be easily presumed that the Guru developed a serious infection of the inflicted wound, as antibiotics were unknown in that era. As the tale goes, after a few days of rest he gained strength, and when he tried to pull on a stiff bow, the force caused a sudden rupture of his still-healing wound. As would be expected, he must have experienced rapid bleeding from the ruptured and infected wound, leading to his last breath on the 7th day of October 1708 CE. Nevertheless, the assassination of such an important leader, with a huge following, could not have easily occurred without the active connivance of the emperor of the day. The most painful part of the whole event was that the Guru was far away from his wives, own people and homeland at the time of his death.

Guru Gobind Singh had firm faith in the democratic and collective wisdom of the people. For this very reason, he never appointed a hierarchical leader of the newly shaped sect from among his favourite followers. Then again, well before his assassination he had already lost all the male members of his immediate family. His last injunctions to the Sikhs were to search the Holy *Granth* as the mind of the immortal Guru, secondly to accept the words of the assembled beloved quintet of Khalsaa Sikhs as the final authority. Thus, he epitomized the *Adi Granth* as the true Guru, and the Khalsaa quintet as the most judicious unit among the Sikh society. He himself became the fountainhead of the identity of Sikhism, and Guru Nanak Dev as the foundation of the Sikh philosophy. All through his life, the acts of Guru Gobind Singh to raise the sword were not meant to fulfill any offensive objectives. He did not play the game of violence, and only acted in self-defense and defense of his fellow citizens. Like his predecessors, he had no interest in acquiring earthly treasures, but wanted to lift up the downtrodden people of the nation, held down by the Mughals for nearly three centuries. He wanted to clear the idea of meaningless rituals from the minds of the people and make them aware of their hidden physical and mental strength. He wanted to create opportunity for all citizens of the nation, unlike the Maraatha and Raajpoot who fought for territorial and personal interests only. He wanted all citizens to rise for secular freedom, but at the same time not to exercise their birthright irresponsibly, whether belonging to a higher or a lower "caste."

Guru Gobind Singh utilized all his peaceful periods for creative and literary activities. His literary works were meant not only to encourage armed men but also to make them kind-hearted spiritual beings. He was a keen observer possessing cinematographic vision and had superb linguistic skills to put his observations in writing. His broad education in multiple languages helped him to appreciate and critique ancient literature, to clarify its role in the evolution and establishment of Sikhism. The Guru wanted the Sikh community to learn as many languages as possible to enrich their minds, re-orient their own culture, and travel widely to all parts of the nation without fear and prejudice towards fellow citizens. He felt that literacy and self-discipline would help prevent social digressions. The very source of his own chivalrous nature and power to instill fearlessness was strengthened by extensive study and thorough understanding of classic tales and epics, and he possessed an innovative mind to inspire the newly created Khalsaa force.

The fact he housed scholars in his court, and the existence of his own literary writings, demonstrate that the pen of the scribe is no less able than the edge of a sword to bring about freedom of expression in a society torn apart by factions of religions and outmoded religious beliefs. He and his companion scholars expressed themselves fearlessly and without hesitation in condemning and criticizing ancient writings covering a wide range of themes, in order to characterize their own views. Among his scholarly finds was the most meritorious Bhai Nand Lal, who possessed intense feelings and an understanding of human nature. He served the objectives of the Guru better with his pen in the literary field than he might have done so with a sword in the battlefield. To quench and satisfy his mental quests, the Guru successfully established a centre of learning at Sabo-dee-Talwandee, often referred to as *"Guru-Kee- Kaashee."* To him enlightenment meant harmonious synthesis of knowledge and devotion, which combined with ability to reason, he believed, would create a sublime human personality.

Guru Gobind Singh never claimed to be a direct descendant or reincarnation of any dead god, nor did he advertise himself as the son of God nor want anybody to bear any such beliefs about him in their minds. Within him dwelled the faith in the one almighty God. He condemned all kinds of mortal demigods of mythological proportions; however, through his writings he did expound their ideal personalities to follow in daily life, and praised them for their superhuman qualities and deeds. His focus was to battle for truth and righteousness. If he raised his sword, it was only to fulfill God's justice, based on his inner beliefs and lessons learnt from his predecessors. He could not stand by and see the ideal concept of non-violence be mocked by scoundrels and rascals of Islam or any other faith. He justified the raising of his sword in self-defense.

To Guru Gobind Singh, the sword was not a sacred or a divine weapon. He did not believe in intense self-mortification, sitting in meditation for years in idleness in a forest like an ascetic to receive divine weapons of destruction from demi-gods and being able to materialize them during dire straits as described in ancient epics. His sword was neither a "talvaar" (a sword in Hindi is called talvaar, which means to make leveled strike as an equalizer out of revenge) nor a device of violence to let flow the blood of humanity without reason. In fact, it was a "kripaan," (from the Sanskrit word kripaa, meaning compassion), an instrument of kindness and a mechanism to protect the meek against cruel and corrupt power-hungry Mughal imperialists.

Ultimately, it was to stop the incessant conversion of Hindus to Islam and protect the tenets of the newly formed Sikh faith to meet the goals of socio-religious equality. Like Guru Nanak Dev, he had a firm faith in the unity of all humanity, created by one single Supreme Creator—the true king of all kings. The kripaan of the Khalsaa forces was an instrument of kindness meant to bring peace and equality among human beings, even if they had distinctive physical features and cultural variances as a result of genetic and geographical diversity. His acts of violence were guided by reason; when all diplomatic means ran dry, the intent of using the instrument was to protect self-interest and to awaken smothered spirits, while the Khandah, the double-edged instrument to stir the "Umrit" during the ceremonial act of initiation, symbolized spiritualism and gallantry, and was meant to unify his men without "caste" differences into a single formation to defend their socio-religious rights, rather than serve as a political weapon to offend followers of Sanaatan Dharam (the Hindu way of life) or Islam (the followers of the Qur'an) in Mughal Hindostaan.

Bringing together the emasculated lower "caste" and making them responsible citizens proved to them that they were by no means lesser human beings than the self-segregated higher "caste," instituted nearly 2,500 years earlier. The formation of the "caste" system based on birth-right rather than individual skills was intended to impose the domination of the higher "caste" upon the rest of the people under the guise of religion. It was supported by the most ambiguous philosophy of "*Kerm*"(in Hindi, the word is pronounced "term," and is generally written as Karma, and is considered as rationale of human destiny premised on one's actions), in conjunction with the fear-inducing philosophy of past reincarnations (the cycle of birth and rebirths, in Hindi called *Puner-Janam*) linking past actions to one's destiny in the present life. Guru Gobind Singh believed in and submitted to the philosophy of reincarnation in his writings, particularly in the controversial *Bachittrr Naatak* (the enigmatic play), but his faith was firmly rooted in the ideology that one should act to make best of one's life now or never. Hence, he directed his energy to motivate and encourage people of lower "caste" to take on the challenge to expunge antecedent negative or bad "Kerm" and elevate themselves to a higher rank in society as equals.

He ignited the power of the people against the excruciating and spiteful Mughal regime, which was based on an intentional misinterpretation of the Qur'an, rather than opposing the righteousness of the Qur'an itself. Despite a number of defeats in the battlefield, he never let himself be trapped by Aurangzeb. His life could not be extinguished by the storming Mughal forces even when they were millions in number. The defining elements of his moral victory over Aurangzeb and allied forces were his persistent efforts against the Mughal regime, his unconquered spirit, and his total belief in the Almighty as the ultimate victor.

Guru Gobind Singh did not himself become ordinary to join the masses, but instead made the masses extraordinary to follow in his footsteps, to find reasons to move ahead so as to live life with a purpose. Although his leadership provided collective encouragement to create a team effort, at the same time it generated individual strength as well, to demonstrate bravery and a self-sacrificing capacity. He wanted to give birth to kindhearted lions who would rise in defense rather than becoming fearsome and vengeful killing machines. His Kripaan was an instrument similar to "Sudarshan Chakker,"* or "Charkho Taeg,"* referred to in *Zafurnamah* (verse 69) as a merciless wheel of time, that takes care of degenerate human behaviour.

The leadership of Guru Gobind Singh did not demand heads in sacrifice for his own personal cause or to cloak the Sikh people in a distinctive costume so as to threaten Hindus and Muslims. He encouraged people to rise up for their own reasons, to earn what they deserved rather than beg in vain like wandering ascetics, and to become "Khalas," that is, pure and honest, honouring themselves by being victorious in their goals in the name of the Almighty, irrespective of "caste" and costume. His long-term goal was to leave behind a recognizable society of "Khalas citizens," a society which did not accumulate power for the few but cared for all its members, and to teach all to work for their social, religious, economic, and political liberation. For him, only those pure in heart and having a universal outlook could be considered the true Khalsaa. He became a leading role model of his time, fighting evil like the well-known mortal heroes of ancient epics and Puraanic tales.

The struggle of the Guru and his Khalsaa force was not against any one individual or community, it was against the oppression and tyranny of the Mughal rulers. To the very last day of his life, at the age of forty-two, he led a fast-moving life on the battlefield, pursuing socio-religious and political activities for the sake of human equality, striving to be inclusive of both Hindu and Muslim communities. To bring justice to the common people, he preferred violence against villainy, to restore righteousness as the appointed soldier of the almighty God. It was not about demonstrating the supremacy and superiority of his swordsmanship or to try to impress common folks. Rather, it was his assertive and sublime nature filled with human sensitivity towards helpless and submissive people hurt too long by the dogmatic Islamic regime.

Guru Gobind Singh, like his predecessors, was not a miracle man. He was, however, certainly a miraculous human being, a soldier with the strength of steel and a saintly spirit who had a mind of his own. He refused to believe in miracles and did not have blind faith in Vedic philosophies and thrilling semi-religious tales. In instances where he had doubts and felt they were only mind-bending superstitions, he condemned them and ridiculed the proponents of such foolish beliefs. However, if he thought something was of practical value that offered encouragement, he would consider applying it for the benefit of his followers. He strongly denied the magical appearance (by teletransfer, as in *Star Trek*) of gods and goddesses during Vedic austerities, the "Havans," bringing the boon of heavenly weapons. For him such rituals, ceremonies, and idol worship were a complete waste of valuable time and misdirected emotional energy. His immense faculty of imagination and innovative mind were his prime leadership qualities, with the goal of an enhanced religious perspective, improved quality of life, and progressive social values with positive morals.

Despite the opposition of the higher "caste," what began in the days of the Mughal emperor Babr during the lifetime of Guru Nanak, reached its climax with the versatile actions and progressive new approach of Guru Gobind Singh. It weakened the roots of the Mughal Empire in the northwest of the country. He consolidated the foundation of the Sikh community firmly in the northwest reaches of Bhaaratvarsh by establishing the "Khalsaa Panth," based on democratic principles. He managed his leadership boldly, basing it on the opinions of the people, saying that decision-making was not the work of one leader but of a collective body. At the same time, he objected to the fanaticism of the few and discouraged false and aimless kinds of martyrdom leading to unnecessary collateral human losses. To his mind, such meaningless self-mortification was outside the realm of democracy.

Zafurnamah was not an application for mercy, but the most passionate and reasoned document composed by Guru Gobind Singh, demonstrating his acute need to make Aurangzeb realize his religious and political bigotry. It was a warning in the form of a sermon and a subtle challenge to Aurangzeb that unless he changed his attitudes towards the social and political needs of his subjects, he would suffer at the hands of the Almighty. The genesis of a martial race of "Non-kShatriya castes," rationalizing the sacrifice of his immediate family and thousands of self-motivated "Khalsaa," his successful efforts to unify society through the elimination of the "caste" system and the formation of the Sikh community, all ultimately announced the victory of the Guru against Hindu royals and the Mughal Empire. The institutional establishment of the "Khalsaa Panth" was visible statement of success for the tenth Guru, advancing the most challenging socio-political task of amalgamating the centuries-old heritable division of society.

Whether a meeting of the Guru with Aurangzeb would have changed the fate of the nation on the socio-religious front is a subject full of ifs and buts. To say *Zafurnamah* had any influence on Aurangzeb during his morbid state at the end is speculation, based on the letter written by the emperor to his own son Azam. The letter does not clearly make any direct reference to *Zafurnamah*, and is no more than the representative thoughts of a dying person, advice offered by a desperate father to his son. Despite the close relationship of Bahaadur Shah with the Guru there was no indication of change in his attitude towards secular policy. Therefore, after realizing the new emperor's unwillingness to bring about any positive change to heal the ailing community, Guru Gobind Singh decided to leave the caravan of Bahaadur Shah and continue on his chosen course travelling south.

Guru Gobind Singh's defensive expedition was an ongoing war of righteousness, a struggle against injustices perpetrated by Mughal rulers and their provincial chiefs, rather than against Islam. The arms taken up by Guru Hargobind Rai and the Khalsaa force created by Guru Gobind Singh, made up of saintly soldiers, had as their goal the liberation of simple folk from the religious fanaticism advanced under the corrupted philosophy of both Hinduism and Islam. The Guru succeeded in many of his objectives but could not fully achieve all of them because of the cutting-short of his lifespan by the same God in whose name he had fought evil-spirited human beings.

Whether the preceding Gurus and Guru Gobind Singh truly wanted the Sikh community to become another religious sect that would create further divisions in society is debatable, in the light of modern day inter-religious conflicts. This is an extremely difficult matter for modern readers of Bhaaratvarsh to grasp easily. The actions of Guru Gobind Singh and earlier Gurus were such that they have to be understood in the context of their times, as an essential historical fact, intended to protect the interests of Hindu (Sanaatan) society. Islamic customs and foreign values were imposed by Mughals to prop up their rule by converting the lower "caste," encouraging them to turn against their own people. The opposition of the Gurus was not to the Sanaatan Vedic way of Hindu life, but to their blind faith, selective religious practices and divisive social tiers that were a result of Manu's doctrines discriminating amongst human beings who were created equal by the same Almighty God. Whether Manu's doctrines were at the time politically motivated to subjugate natives to menial occupations or intended to set up a well-designed social machinery run by educated Brahmans to isolate higher "castes" and prevent lower "castes" from entering their residences and places of worship, considering them lesser human beings, has been largely left unexplored.

The nature of discrimination was such that lower "castes" and other natives were classified based on their physiognomy. They were forced to remain as semi-skilled and unskilled by birth, to always live in poverty. They were further categorized into sub-castes based on the occupation of their ancestors, denied the basic skill of reading and writing in Sanskrit, which was considered unnecessary for their line of work. Learning a skill outside one's category was emphatically discouraged. One such outstanding example is of a character in the epic *Mahabhaarat*, Ek Lavaya,* a boy of lower caste, who visited guru Drona-Aachaaraya to learn archery, but was refused on the basis of his tribal origin. The people of the land were struck with fear of gods and goddesses, forced to venerate Brahmans and royals as reincarnation of imaginary higher creatures controlling the elements of the universe. The author of the epic *Raamayan* portrayed the tribes of Southern Bhaaratvarsh as "Vaaners," literally meaning monkeys, supposedly lesser human beings, and making up the army of Shree Raam:, a Suryavanshi (direct descendent of Sun) Aarya-born, who attacked Sri Lanka to get his wife Seetaa back from the custody of Raavan, a Dravae*r*d (Dravidian) king, described as a highly literate human-demon.

The higher "caste" status of Aarya used metaphysical rationalism to create a self-serving bourgeois society to take over social and emotional control of the less privileged native tribes by infusing fear of supernatural powers in their minds. Guru Nanak Dev, himself of a high "caste," and many before him, did realize the nature of age-old Aarya socio-religious and political game playing. However, it was Nanak and other saints like Kabeer Daas, son of a weaver, and Naam Dev, son of a dyer and textile printer, who seriously took up the cause of enlightening the common people. The people engaged in similar occupations still form a major proportion of the existing lower "castes," and many others have been ground down into still lower classes as Dalit ("to grind"). The effect of the maltreatment of Dalit, lowest of low, to some extent is visible even today nationwide. They lack the motivation and ability to take on challenging roles to further their development and progress.

Guru Taeg Bahaadur, father of Guru Gobind Singh, made sure that his son would be fluent in all current languages in order to be able to read and understand ancient literature, and skilled in necessary techniques of warfare to withstand the opposition of the Hill Chiefs and the ruling Mughals. What is striking and more important to understand about the Gurus is that they were living under Mughal dominion, and their objectives were to bring freedom of social and religious practices for the well-being of all the citizens and denizens of Bhaaratvarsh, whether Aarya-born Sanaatan, non-Aarya Sanaatan, Dravae*r*d Sanaatan, followers of Shiv or Vishnu, or recently converted lower Hindu classes to Islam of Mughal Hindostaan. Unfortunately, because of the torture and death of two Sikh gurus and many accompanying Sikhs, Guru Hargobind Rai and Guru Gobind Singh were forced to empower and arm willing members of the communities suffering at the hands of Mughals.

Technically, the preaching of equality was never meant to be a wedge instrument intended to divide the nation into further sectors. The notions of the Gurus were noble, to meet the needs of their times rather than uncovering mythical facts of the ancient Bhaaratvarsh, to reveal hidden truths or expound systemic oppressive phenomena in Vedic literature and Puraanic epics, to govern and maintain the fears of the underprivileged classes. On that front, the Gurus made a sharp distinction between myth and reality, which were intimately tied together in the spiritual experience of the Sanaatan ideology. They propagated the philosophy of a single Supreme entity without any titles such as Raam or Raheem (Allah). Guru Nanak Dev introduced a very clear, fascinating, and thought-provoking concept of a timeless

(Akaal) and nameless Being (Purush) as the "Naam" (the Nameless Saint), leaving it to the imagination of each individual thinker to fill in the blank. It was an open-ended concept. The Gurus were more interested in what actually happened during one's lifetime, than what it meant to idol worshippers of ancient Vedic society. It was not to say that the fundamental facts of Vedic philosophy were characterized as false and misleading by the Gurus, as they did appreciate the underlying message as necessary for self-discipline, and to streamline the thoughts of a growing society. Originally, when Vedic philosophy was written, the governing royals, economists, and social scientists had serious long-term plans to logically offer a time-dependent and flexible rather than a rigid structure to suit their bourgeois lifestyle and people's behaviour at the time. It is perfectly normal to presume, and rightfully too, that the scholars (Rishis and Pundits) of advanced ancient Bhaaratvarsh told tales of gods, goddesses, and heroes of Puraanic tales in such a way that the portrayed characters and underlying morals would be seen as true models for listeners to emulate in daily life.

On the other hand, to protect the interests of every citizen the scholarly Gurus were strung together in a thread of spirituality, to curb Mughal offences against innocent humanity. They did not want to defy laws of nature by bringing in a radically new paradigm that was incompatible with the existing and widespread Sanaatan way of life. Instead, all the Gurus developed concepts that would advance the path of humanity towards ultimate truth and hopefully social equality.

Social reformers and leaders with completely original thoughts operating at different periods in history with different paradigms live psychologically entirely in a different world. The world in which Manu and his proponents lived was different from that in which Guru Gobind Singh was living. The Guru's observations of the sufferings of ordinary people during the Mughal period demanded change to the whole social structure of the society. That is, to become proactive, get motivated to protect self-interests, and combat social evils to have a better quality of life.

Guru Gobind Singh did not want to be labeled as a prophet. He was a leader of his people, and was right to create the "Khalsaa force" with such cohesion that it attracted like-minded members of the society prepared to rise against the oppressive regime of the Mughal and to sacrifice unhesitatingly. It certainly integrated a fair number of people into the visible community of the Khalas Sikhs. However, in the modern world of Bhaaratvarsh, it still lacks consolidation of the original idea of one society and one "caste" for all its citizens. In the long run, Guru Gobind Singh's dream, to socially integrate future generations of the nation, has scarcely been realized. He sacrificed all his family and his own life to try to create a utopia for the people he was leaving behind. Undoubtedly, he succeeded in initiating and giving direction to his mission. However, lack of complete understanding of his objectives by the immediate governing followers of the newly formed Sikhism, misunderstanding by a majority of high "caste" Hindus at large and the innate human desire to dominate one another, have ultimately failed him.

The perusal of such a great life is an inspiration for anyone, a spiritual experience that certainly could have a long-lasting influence in one's life. Guru Gobind Singh succeeded in raising a protest against political tyranny and religious intolerance, arousing strong waves of patriotism and nationalism through social reform and military engagement. He became a role model and the embodiment for his followers, the Khalsaa and non-Khalsaa communities, to inculcate within them elements of strength, gentleness, courage, and graciousness. By establishing the brotherhood of "Khalas" beings Guru Gobind Singh attempted to erase social differences among the members of the Sikh community and the rest of humanity. This was meant to increase awareness among the people of Bhaaratvarsh in general, to encourage them to live beyond the perimeters of the narrow clannish clusters of the four "castes" in the future. In scientific terms, such clustering of people is harmful to physical and intellectual evolution, and the social integration of the human race. Shamefully, his dream has been curtailed largely because of continued opposition to the true philosophy of the Sikh Gurus since his passing away. The mean agendas of religious factions, with the modern-day neologism of guru-ships and the altered appearances of Sikhism, have created further distinctions and have increased the level of discrimination among people, rather than closing the gulf between "castes" and classes.

Guru Gobind Singh as a mortal being lived a life of absolute fearlessness in the face of imminent violent death. He dramatized in real flesh and blood the mythical high philosophy inherent in his life and yet did not wish to be a religious icon to be reincarnated in marble statues as a god, decorated and imprisoned within the high walls of temples. For him, only deities and celestial beings were immortals who lived in great mythological epics and in "wonderland or paradise." It is inaccurate to say that he is a divine immortal hero of the Punjab. Instead, he was a saint, a scholar, a philosopher and a very special human being. He was a public leader, rather than a God-sent religious prophet, with the very clear objective of bringing social and religious equality to all. His aim was to liberate the common folk from the shackles of "caste" and class, fight the battle for truth, justice and righteousness and the right to walk free in their own motherland, which is a fundamental right of all human beings. All the Gurus consumed their whole lifetimes to bring an end to the age-old Aarya philosophy of Manu. Yet the Sikh people as a community are still divided by the same "caste" system Guru Gobind Singh and his predecessors wanted to eliminate.

In many ways, Guru Gobind Singh succeeded in his endeavour to enlighten ordinary folk about their equal rights. He was versatile in his actions, becoming a great social innovator and a motivator, demonstrating his leadership and management skills in the way he organized his followers. He proved himself a poet without romance, a warrior without territorial interests, a saint without the stain of ochre, and a real man with the heart to endure the most unbearable pain of sacrificing his family through complete submission to the will of God. To perpetuate his ideology there is a dire need to verbalize his philosophy and to animate him in the minds of literate as well as illiterate people through modern multimedia techniques in all the national languages. This should not be done to cultivate Sikhism, but to promote his democratic principles of social justice of human equality by narrating tales of his virtue and character.

There is only one living planet known to us, for all small and large creatures; and nature has granted each one of us only one lifetime, not to be born again. All the resources of the planet and the wealth generated thereof are there to be shared evenly, to realize the idea of equality. Without such an ideology battles over religious differences and preservation of the planet earth can never be won. Who is pure at heart to be the "Khalas" being? Not a present day initiated "Khalsaa," but a newborn cub in the wilderness and a human baby in our society!

Finally, it is important to realize that, before wielding the strength of steel and fire, creating violence against humanity to achieve social and religious goals, spoken words and the pen of a scribe can be more powerful and influential over time, as envisioned initially by Guru Nanak Dev.

4. *Fatehnamah*
(Prelude to *Zafurnamah*)

It was only at the behest of his beloved "Khalsaa quintet" that Guru Gobind Singh decided to vacate the country mansion, a mud fortress at Chumkor. Through a hazardous and physically fatiguing journey across the jungles of Macchiwarda, constantly chased by the Mughal forces, he managed to reach the village of the friendly brothers, Ganny Khan and Nabbhy Khan.

During a short break here, in a relatively secure environment, Guru Gobind Singh decided to write a letter to Emperor Aurangzeb, to inform the emperor of treatment received at the hands of his generals, and the false oaths taken by them to trick the Guru in the name of Allah and the Qur'an. The letter, in Persian verse, was entitled "Namah Gobind Singh ba Aurangzeb," and was written on the 24th day of December, 1704. It was passed on to Sayyed Inayat Ali, his Persian teacher, through the Khan Brothers for safe custody. Later the letter was returned to him after reaching Ghulal and sent on to the emperor through Bhai Daya Singh.

The recent history of this letter began when it was first published in Nagari Parchaarni Patrika, of Varanasi. Then it was reproduced in "Makhaz-e-twarikh-e-Sikhan," by the Khalsa College, Amritsar, and by Ganda Singh in his book Sikh Itehaas Barey *("About the Sikh History"). In the Panjabi newspapers it made its first appearance in* Khalsa Samachar, *on the 16th day of July, 1942. Then in 1944, Sardar Kapur Singh published it in the Urdu newspaper* Ajit *of Lahore, under the heading of* Fatehnamah.

Fatehnamah *may be considered the prelude to his future communication of* Zafurnamah, *as it sets out entirely new thoughts of repugnance towards the emperor rather than venomous hatred in the mind of the Guru. It was about the dubious attitude of the emperor and his officers. Despite the uncouthness of his ruling enemy, the Guru maintains an attitude of good etiquette in addressing and greeting his equals as would be expected of a truly royal personality. The letter begins with the greetings to the emperor.*

In this letter the Guru, apart from inviting a dialogue to resolve the matter openly, challenges the emperor to a duel in the battlefield. He is very sure of his physical and spiritual strengths. Beyond doubt, it is very much evident from the reading of couplet number 14 below that he wrote this letter from Macchiwarda being unaware of the whereabouts and fate of his two younger children.

With greetings from Gobind Singh to Aurangzeb,
I hereby write this message in the name of God (addressed hereafter as "*It*"), Self-existing, Timeless, and Almighty, unborn and free from all the laws of nature.

1. In the name of the Saviour, to whom belongs sword and halberd,
    To that Self-existent, to whom belong arrows, spears, and shield.

2. To the Self-existent belong the fearless warriors to testify,
    To that Self-existent belong (galloping) horses with hooves in the air.

3. The One, who has granted you the kingship,
   It has given me the shield of religious-treasures.

4. You have looted through acts of deceit and hypocrisy, but
   I seek remedies via acts of contentment and sincerity.

5. "Aurangzeb" (*glory of throne*), what your name implies does not befit you,
   Glory of the throne (*the king*) does not acquire possessions through acts of deception.

6. (Your sins) are more like beads of the rosary on its string (*the life*), and
   Dropping of each bead further, is burying its thread (*the life*) further yourself.

7. You have rolled the esteem of your ancestors in dust with your ill deeds, and
   By spilling the blood of your brothers, you have kneaded all together irreversibly.

8. Upon that foundation you have built a weak establishment, and
   (You have) made a gateway in order to gather treasures for yourself.

9. I shall now, with the favours of the Timeless Being,
   Shower upon thee the metal rain (*weapons/Umrit*) like the Monsoon!

10. So that forever, the wall of ominous aura/halo built around you would vanish, and
    Exterminate you without any sign, out of this sacred land.

11. From the hills of the South you have returned discontented in your mission,
    And you have come back after a bitter experience in Maeward (*West*) too.

12. It is likely that now your eyes are upon this region (*North*).
    Would that resolve the acridness and bring satiety?

13. (I) would set alight such flames beneath (your) horses' shoes,
    Not letting you to even have a sip of water in Punjab!

14. So how does it matter, if the wily jackal by false means,
    Thus has killed two little cubs of a lion.

15. For there still remains the ferocious lion alive,
    Who would surely take revenge of thee!

16. I would no more pay attention to your false religious attitudes, now
    That (I) realize the kind of god and religious revelations (you believe).

17. I have no more faith in your sworn oaths,
    For me except to wield sword, (I) have no other means left.

GURU GOBIND SINGH JI'S *ZAFURNAMAH* • 69

18. Even if you may consider yourself a shrewd old wolf,
    Nevertheless, I would still keep "The Lion" out of your trap.

19. If we have an exchange of dialogue, I would hear you out,
    Then I would direct you upon the holy path of righteousness.

20. In the battlefield, if it happens so, that both armies file up, and
    Within sight at a distance (if we) happen to confront each other.

21. In the battlefield, both should remain at an interval of two furlongs,
    And when, such an arrangement is set in this battlefield.

22. Thereafter in the space left in the middle of the field,
    I will approach, closing the gap, and two horsemen may flank you.

23. Up to now, you have lived in luxury, enjoying fruits of pleasure,
    And have never confronted a soldier in battle (for a duel yourself).

24. Descend upon the field in person with sword and axes set in hand,
    Thus, check the slaughter of God's people brutally under force.

Thus comes to an abrupt end the extant passage from Fatehnamah, *announcing his righteousness and possible frustration. It seems that it was his instinctual and reactive response to all the events that had occurred so far. Whether it is complete in itself or not is simply impossible to judge from the available text. However, it is amply clear that when he wrote this he was unaware of the execution of his two younger sons in the custody of the authorities of Sarhind. He only makes reference to the loss of his two older sons, during the battle of Chumkor. Exactly where he was stationed at the time he wrote* Fatehnamah *is also not clear, as he had not received any news about his younger sons so far. Neither is there in the letter any mention of the death of his mother at the hands of Muslim officials. The evidence is only circumstantial, as he may have recorded the message to Aurangzeb before reaching the village of Deenae.*

Guru Gobind Singh gives a hint of his escape from the trap in Chumkor, laid by the huge armed forces of Aurangzeb and the alliance of the Hill Chiefs. Despite the loss of his two older sons and his arduous and fatiguing journey through harsh woodlands, he demonstrates his confidence and persistence in achieving the goals of his followers. He advances an open challenge to Aurangzeb to come in person to have a dialogue with him and to confront him in the battlefield.

5. *Zafurnamah*

*To begin with, in his letter addressed to the Mughal emperor, Aurangzeb, Guru Gobind Singh praises first the Unbeknownst Energy, an Entity or a Being, which everybody presumes to be the Almighty Creator, and the Saviour, commonly known as God in the English language. To make Aurangzeb realize his minuscule status in this world, Guru Gobind Singh salutes God to sermonize the emperor, and starts by saying that the Unbeknownst God (addressed hereafter as "**It**") is—*

1. Miraculously perfect, forever eternal, is merciful,
   Grants us pleasures and provisions; redeemer of all; is compassionate.

2. Brings us peace, is forgiving and offers a helping hand to all;
   Forgives our mistakes, provides daily bread, and touches our heart.

3. That benevolent King of kings like a beacon guides us all,
   Despite the lack of material properties, even being invisible, is incomparable.

4. Those that have no treasures; neither have hawks, nor have armies and palaces,
   Still that Self-existent protects and offers them heavenly pleasures.

5. Upon this chaste world, is displaying *Its* influence, and
   Grants boon to the deserving as if *It* is present in person.

6. That true Preserver bring gifts to us all,
   It is merciful and provides daily bread at all places.

7. Isn't the Lord of the Universe mightiest of the mighty?
   Does *It* not have unimaginable beauty, bring contentment, and bless us all?

8. Doesn't that very understanding Lord, take care and help the poor?
   Bring glory to the meek, and make pulp out of the enemy.

9. Abiding the (book*)* of "True law" *(Sharia)* is central to one's supremacy.
   To realize the ultimate truth, know that Holy Book (Qur'an).

10. Would you not search for wisdom in the Lord who is wisest of all?
    The evidence of reality lies in *Its* omniscience and influence.

11. Only that Self-existent knows all the secrets of the universe,
    Runs it, and carries out all the activities of this world.

12. That conductor of all the activities is supreme in the Universe, (who is)
    Knowledgeable, and fully aware of it, is the Commander of the cosmos.

The fourth couplet indicates that the Guru acquired a hawk after he had defeated the Mughal and Afghaan hordes in the battle of Khidraney-dee-Dhaab. He established his sovereignty during his respite in Damdama Sahib. The reason the Guru Gobind Singh started to carry the hawk was to establish his military prowess and reconnaissance capability. It was in contrast to a dove, which demonstrates compromise and conciliation with an enemy. Thereafter, he was not styled only the Sikh Guru but also the military Khalsaa commander. Even Muazzam Shah believed in his military might and seems to have submitted to the strength of the Khalsaa when he sought his collaboration to accede the throne of Dilli. In return, Muazzam Shah demonstrated his gratitude by honouring the Guru with an appropriate gift of an aigrette and Khillat.

THE LEGEND

In his usual literary style, after appraising the supreme and unique qualities of God, the Guru begins to address the emperor Aurangzeb, by bringing to his attention all the false promises sworn upon a copy of the Qur'an by Aurangzeb's officials. The Guru is aware of the extraordinary strength of the armed forces made up of well-trained and equipped Mongols and Turks. He has lost trust in their promises and oaths taken upon the Qur'an. He believes in his physical strength and mental resolve to be "The Lion" under the aegis of "Huma," "The Powerful" Supreme Being.

13. Neither do I have faith in your sworn oaths anymore,
    The Almighty, the one and only Divine is witness to this fact.

14. Nor have (I) even a little trust in one like (you).
    Isn't it (true), that your defence personnel and civil officers have spoken lies (to me)?

15. Whosoever trusts the oaths taken upon the Qur'an?
    One day, ultimately that very person will endure.

16. When a person comes under the shadow of the "Huma" (*The Powerful*),
    Then not even the bravest of crows could (dare) lay its talons upon the (blessed).

17. When any one walks alongside a "He lion" in one's company, then
    No passer-by can just pounce upon the (meek like) goats, sheep, or deer.

18. If this is the way of deceit, taking oath upon a holy scripture, then
    One should never lend one's dear forces to even a minutest measure of such torture.

It is recorded that the battle of Chumkor was fought sometime during mid-December of 1704. In the following verses, Guru Gobind Singh described to Aurang-

zeb the balance of armed forces and resources, given that he and his small battalion of "Khalsaa" were forced to leave Anandpur based on a false oath. Secondly, he was chased by enormous numbers of Aurangzeb's soldiers. Then the Guru goes on to describe the bravery of his men despite their poor physical plight, due to hunger, fatigue, and the cold weather. Also a reader can note and enjoy the descriptive flare of the Guru, the way he expresses the events and his emotions, using his proverbial and dialectal linguistic skills. In the entire body of his literary works, the sense of rhyming is very strong and the displacement of first and third person occurs easily in order to maintain the rhyming of the couplets throughout. It must be appreciated that most of the linguistic play of the original author is lost almost completely in any translation, in an attempt to keep it simple and meaningful.

19. (Imagine) what forty famished men could do,
    When upon them leapt "one million" men unexpectedly.

20. That the promise-breakers descended out of the blue,
    Amid us was their descent with swords, arrows, and guns.

21. Out of obligation forced to plunge amid all, and
    (We were) strained to strategically deploy arrows and bullets.

22. When all (peaceful) acts and strategies are exhausted,
    Then it is legitimate to brandish the sword in hand.

23. Now that I did trust the oath upon the Qur'an!
    Otherwise, you tell me what purpose I had to tread upon this route.

24. (I) wasn't aware that these men are crafty like a fox,
    Otherwise, (I) would have never come this way at all.

25. Whoever becomes prey, trusting an oath upon the Qur'an?
    Should never ever be attacked, taken as prisoners, or killed.

Now, continue to experience the way the Guru further unfolds the scenes of the encounter between the large Mughal army and his famished forty brave men, descending upon the battle ground of Chumkor from within the "fortress" of unbaked bricks. The Guru and his sons sat themselves in the attic of the building, giving cover to each of the advancing company of five Khalsaa men, rushing out to the battlefield to take part in duels. In his letter, Guru Gobind Singh does not hesitate to praise the courage and bravery of Mughal soldiers as well.

26. Like the dark (*honeybee swarm*) they (*Mughal*) descended clad in black.
    Suddenly, all at once, (they) leapt in to cause bedlam.

27. Any person who came out from behind the shielding wall,
    At once received an arrow and was drenched in blood.

28. Any person who didn't come out from behind that wall,
    Neither received arrows nor that wretched death.

29. The moment (I) saw that Nahar Khan was advancing for a duel
    (He) tasted one of my arrows at once (to become still instantly).

30. At the end many fled the place instead of getting in to combat,
    The majority of Pathaans, so audacious, were hit and chased off too.

31. Still more Afghans descended into the field to battle,
    Entering like a speeding flood among the arrows and bullets.

32. Many of their strikes were certainly like that of a brave man,
    Some were in their full senses, while others were like those of a crazy (man).

33. Attempting many strikes, and receiving multiple wounds;
    (They) struck down two (Singh)-soldiers to death, likewise entrusted (their) life to us.

34. What about that coward Khwajah, shadowed by the wall,
    (He) dared not descend to the battlefield to strike like a warrior.

35. Alas! Only if his face would have become visible,
    That very instant (I) would have offered (him) a desperate arrow.

36. Finally, the majority were wounded with arrows and bullets;
    On either side, many met their death in a short time.

37. Many arrows (were deployed). It was like shower of arrows and bullets,
    Making the field appear as if covered in "Laleh" (*red coloured flowers*).

38. All over, an abundance of heads and legs were (scattered) in such a way,
    As if the field was filled with balls and hook-sticks (*like hockey-sticks*).

39. Tinkering sounds of arrows and strumming of the bows,
    It generated hell, panic and cries all over that day.

40. The other intense sounds were those of weapons and of the vengeful enemy,
    It was beyond the comprehension of even the bravest of all the braves.

41. After all, what could mere bravery do in battle?
    When upon the corpus of forty (men) innumerable lunged.

42. When the luminary of the universe (*the Sun*) had set itself within the veil,
    Then, the king of darkness (*the Moon*) pitched (*arrived*) in its full glory.

Although the foregoing verse clearly depicts the end of the first day in the battlefield of Chumkor followed by arrival of night time, but there is controversy over the meaning of "the king of darkness," whether "night" or "Moon." Here again, as in many other verses, the difficulty arises because of the use of metaphors and proverbial language, which was a very common way to bejewel poetry. Obviously, it was neither a full moon nor a moonless night, after the previous night and day of winter rain. It seems the climate and the atmosphere that evening was very conducive to the plan to allow a perfect escape for Guru Gobind Singh and his compatriots from the trap. Then again, metaphorically, it may be considered a linguistic play of words by the original author meaning that when the illuminating star, the "good" of the universe, pulls on the veil to rest, only then can the king of the darkness, the "evil," a deceitful person like Aurangzeb, come out in his full glory. After all, it is very hard to imagine the state of mind of the Guru and that of the soldiers on either side, following a day of bloodshed and scenes of violent death. At last, it was the end of a horrible day and the time for the Guru to plan the next move.

After narrating the day at the battlefield, thereafter the Guru describes his thoughts about the character of Aurangzeb in an attempt to make the tyrannical emperor realize that his acts and those of his officials were amoral and irresponsible. It seems that there is a missing verse or few verses, as the next verse does not connect very well with the last, abruptly going on to describe the character of Aurangzeb.

43. Any person who believes in an oath on the Qur'an to act upon it,
    That one would come only under the guidance of the Supreme Being.

44. (That is why) neither has a tangle in hair nor a bruise on the body,
    That very Self-existent pulls to safety and vanquishes the enemy.

45. None was aware that this exultant ruler is a promise breaker!
    That (he) is a worshipper of wealth and has thrown away (his) religious conscience.

46. (You) neither have religious commitment or knowledge of its principles,
    Nor recognize the Supreme Lord or have faith in Mohammad.

47. Any person who is truly committed to his religion,
    Never with his promise will play games, and go back and forth.

48. (Imagine), what is a man that cannot be trusted even a little?
    How could his oath upon the Qur'an or faith in Divine Unity be believed?

49. (Hereafter), anyone may responsibly swear scores of times upon the Qur'an,
    Even then, I would not have a drop of trust in any one of them.

50. (Yes), if at all you did trust and had visited (me),
    (Then) with all readiness (I would) have come forward to welcome (you in person).

51. Now it becomes an obligatory duty upon your "head" to fulfill the good word.
    That the oath taken in the name of the Self-existent was saying "I hereby promise."

52. If the "good lord" himself would have (presented) or stood here in person,
    Then (we) would have spoken to clarify and know the heart of the matter.

53. Whatever, now it becomes your duty that you do act upon it,
    Be reasonable, and you do reckon to focus on what you have written.

54. (We) did receive the written message and were told verbally (as well),
    (Preferably) this matter should have been done patiently to a peaceful end.

55. (We) men of status should become more eloquent (*in keeping our word*),
    Not (*differ in real motives*), to have one in-stomach and the other on the lips.

56. (If) what the Qazi said to me (is true), then still I am not outside of the promise, and
    If it is the truth, then (you) yourself take the necessary friendly step forward.

57. (However), if you should have that very copy of the Qur'an with the written oath,
    Then, I shall (gladly) get that very delivered for you to see.

In the following four couplets, the Guru is making an invitation to Aurangzeb for a bilateral talk in a summit at Kangard village. He promises the emperor safe passage, and expects to resolve "territorial" disputes. At the same time, the Guru displays his cynicism by saying that he has full control over the region, and encourages a subtle challenge to Aurangzeb to come and acquire the region through fair means. Guru Gobind Singh is putting up the challenge to Aurangzeb in a traditional way of asking to send out an "Ashvmeydh," a "Sacrificial War Horse" ahead of him (Aurangzeb) and his royal caravan of armed forces. Unlike "Ashvmeydh", which was considered emblazonry emblem as an explicit challenge to the other rulers in ancient Bhaaratvarsh, the Mongols and Turks sent out a fully armoured horse as a sign of submission. If the disposed sent an old horse it meant weakness, while a young horse meant an element of challenge or submission with strength. The Guru is expecting if not an "Ashvmeydh" worth thousand horses, he at least expects a horse no more than one thousand days old. So, the couplet 61 definitely carries implicit challenge to Aurangzeb. The Guru, while maintaining a defensive stance, is not being offensive in his attitude here. At the same time, he is not ready to part with the territory, as a gift, in his submission to the emperor.

If Aurangzeb must have this region, then he must follow certain royal traditions of acquiring any new territory without dispute. The Guru says—

58. That (if) the honourable do pay a visit to the town of Kangard,
    Then, out of that a (significant) meeting between (us) could happen.

59. Not even a little danger would befall upon you en route,
    The whole tribe of Birards (in the region) is subject to my command.

60. You do come this far, here to express in your own words, and
    Right there in your own presence you will experience my empathy.

61. Bring along a "War horse" (*an Ashvmeydh*) worth one thousand (horses), and
    Come this far to acquire from me this territory!

Guru Gobind Singh seems to be very sure of his military capabilities, despite his recent losses. He is not prepared to let Aurangzeb acquire any piece of land he puts his foot on, to maintain the dignity and integrity of his men. He is ready to face the challenge rather than fold and ask for a mere thousand horses or any other reward, to sacrifice his camping territory in return. He does not have any personal territorial interests. He just cannot let his men down and discourage them from continuing their fight against the Mughals, particularly as he had already lost all his family to their oppressive regime. As a leader he had the great responsibility of leading the way for the newly formed united front of all "castes" and classes, to their chosen destination against the Hill Chiefs and bigoted Islamic rulers. He would not abandon his men midstream. The Guru and his men had the right to socio-religious equality. Under the circumstances, the Guru continued to encourage and recruit more armed men to maintain his military strength and leadership, to protect and defend the interests of the downtrodden.

The Guru was not naïve in believing an invitation written on unofficial stationery like the cover of a copy of the Qur'an. He knew that it was an Islamic tradition to make oaths by writing on a copy of the Qur'an, to convince others of its authenticity. One might like to ask how an astute soldier and a leader of his calibre wouldn't suspect it to be a dirty trick, and why he did not carefully reconsider it. Especially as he had been cheated once before, and knew of inhuman cruelties committed upon his family, predecessors, and other members of society. Maybe he was under pressure from his mother and fellow men. The only other overpowering reason to evacuate the fort of Anandpur might have been to end the stalemate through a referendum of the Khalsaa force, or economic sanctions imposed by the allied forces blocking the supplies and threatening the survival of the trapped men, women and children. Probably it was these circumstances, which forced him to make the most difficult decision to evacuate his hometown and to proceed towards the district of Malwa. He might have felt that there was greater wisdom in accepting the written promise and taking the opportunity to remove his entrapped men to safety, rather than allow them to die without supplies within the fort or expose his weakened men to the Mughal war machinery and cause unnecessary bloodshed. On the other hand, he did not want to injure the admirable strength of the Khalsaa force either.

Once again the Guru returns to his briefly abandoned original thought process of what the characteristics of an honest king should be. He continues to hammer away at his feelings and give opinions without considering Aurangzeb's royal status as if he was speaking to his equal. He continues to say—

62. I am enslaved only to the beck and call of that King of kings,
    If (***It***) commanded the summons, (I) would be in attendance as a living soul.

63. If ever so, I do receive a "heavenly" message, an honest invitation,
    I would come with all (my) body and soul in the presence of his Excellency.

64. If you certainly do worship the Supreme Being,
    Then do carry out this affair of mine (to meet me), and do not show any laziness.

65. You should certainly recognize the supremacy of the Almighty, and
    Do not believe in what people say, and stop hurting others.

66. (I realize)! You are sitting on the throne as master of a large empire,
    However, your justice is rather strange and so are your other attributes.

67. That it is a strange kind of justice, (unexpected) of a guardian of the faith,
    How sad, it is one hundred percent shameful for a head of the state.

68. Strangest of all are your religious declarations (*the Fatwa*),
    Know only the truthful words, all the rest of the talk is deceit.

69. (Beware), to wield the sword against people, to spill their blood ruthlessly;
    Your own blood would also be made to flow by the "Cyclical Sword"* of time.

70. Don't be an ignorant man, have some fear of the Almighty,
    (Know) that ***It*** is without aspirations and above all kinds of admiration.

71. (Let it be known) that ***It*** is the only fearless King of kings, and
    It is also the (true) Lord of all the earth and skies.

In the following verses, the Guru does not want to reveal his own pride as a soldier and a great chevalier. Neither does he want the emperor to feel that he is expecting sympathy from any mortal being. Yet the Guru cannot display indifference to the loss of his family members. There is subtle sarcasm, with an element of resentment and natural signs of challenge, revealing his courage, which must be appreciated with applause.

*He is not an arrogant self-conceited strongman in his thoughts and feelings, but he wants to create an aura of supremacy of the Almighty God around Aurangzeb, through the process of self-realization, to experience **Its** greatness. In addition, he continues repeatedly to impress and stress the value of an oath, and keeps on reminding Aurangzeb of his diplomatic and spiritual failures.*

72. That Self-existent is the Master of the earth and skies,
    It has created for all the beings, whether little or large.

73. Also, from the harmless (tiny) insect to the ones with enormous bodies,
    It is a humble friend of all and destroys the ignorance of the naïve.

74. That when *Its* very "Name" is known as "Dear friend" of the meek, then
    That raises *It* above all the adorations and any expectations (in return).

75. That *It* is without any physical properties, as well as without any solid form, and
    Still, *It* is the pathfinder to lead and the guide upon the way.

76. That, still on your head is the "debt" of the oath taken upon the Qur'an.
    As per your statement, now act gracefully to deliver it.

77. You should certainly seek wisdom of self-counsel, and
    Take the matter in your own skillful hands to do it.

78. So what, as it has (already) happened that four children had been killed, but
    (Remember) that there is still a remainder in balance coiled up, to strike hard.

79. What a big man! That you did extinguish little sparklers,
    (However), that you did fuel a tiny fire into a volcano.

80. How well said by "Firdausee," and expressed appropriately,
    That, "An impatient act is the work of a devil's mind."

81. If and when I visit the court of your "highness,"
    That very day you shall witness the truth yourself.

82. On the contrary, (if) you do deny it (*the oath*) as a forgotten event,
    Then you too would also be ignored by the Almighty eventually.

83. If you undertake this as an act of duty with full determination, then
    The Self-existent would reward you with an appropriate boon.

84. That to carry out this good deed would be (like) religious nourishment,
    Since recognizing the Supreme Being would be for the betterment of (your life.

85. I don't think you have knowledge of the Supreme Being, from
    Which emerges the (reason) of your hurtful activities.

86. You do not recognize that the Supreme Being is generous; therefore
    You are not admirable despite having enormous wealth.

87. (Now) if upon a hundred (copies) of Qur'an you do take an oath,
    I would not trust even one of them for a little moment.

88. Neither would (I) come in your presence nor would take this route,
    (Even) if "Shah" (the King) desires so I would not come over there.

In many of the following verses, in his sarcastic way, Guru Gobind Singh did not hesitate to describe the virtues and military capabilities of Aurangzeb. He warned Aurangzeb to be aware of changing beliefs and attitudes of the people. He also tried to convince the emperor that, as in Islam, he does not favour the practice of idol worship. Guru Gobind Singh was very clear about his monotheistic beliefs. In "Shabad Hazarey" he wrote, "Do not recognize any except the One Lord." He actively denounced the idol worship of the multitude of gods and goddesses. In "Bachittrr Naatak" he gave his reason and said, "All deities are time bound and reach an end point in time. Only God is timeless." In addition he wrote, "Throughout the ages and at present, one has to rely greatly on the Sword as the most powerful extension of one's arm." The Guru had unfailing faith in the strength and support of the Supreme Being.

The subjective reality of idol worship had always been based on the belief of a worshipper. Idols were the most tangible and visual aids for illiterate people to have a representation in their imaginations of an ideal person of their choice, from epic and Puraanic tales, as role models in the form of gods and goddesses, to follow in life. Religious idols were not greatly different from the present-day iconic figures of the modern media world, for fans to copy and adore as their heroes. Similarly, over many centuries, idol worship, dances and dramas came into everyday practice with the development of the Sanaatan (ancient Hindu) way of life. Idols were the only mode of intimate relationship with the material image of a god or a goddess. Idol worship in the form of dolls, pictures, and a variety of other forms of images is still very common and popular among all the communities. For example, the shape, form, and the very stature of Shri Ganesh* bearing the trunk of an elephant, is the perfect picture of a gigantic, wealthy, affluent, well-fed, and content being, with some extra food at the disposal of other less significant creatures in the vicinity, so as to share his abundant wealth. For this very reason this idol frequently adorns almost all Hindu businesses. However, in this modern day and age, where there is plenty of food to consume, a similar kind of physique, with a high body mass index in *a health-conscious society, would be considered unhealthy and grotesque compared to that of well-built action heroes like Shree Raam and Shree Krishan. It could be acceptable as long as these idols are symbols of worship and a source of inspiration to achieve real goals, with firm faith in the One, and belief only in one Supreme Being, whatever Its name. That is where Guru Nanak's open-ended philosophy of **"Naam"** (nameless impersonal Supreme Being or energy) fits into all the debates on theology.*

The Guru continues to address Aurangzeb—

89. (You) are the glory of the throne and fortunate to be king upon many lords,
    You are clever in your handiwork and brisk in stirrups.

90. You are an elegant and handsome man with bright intelligence, but
    The Self-existent has given the kingdom and made you master of all the chiefs.

91. You may be a talented strategist and possess skillful swordsmanship, but
    The Self-existent Being is the provider and *It* is the strength of (your) sword.

92. You have a brilliant mind and elegant appearance, but
    The Self-existent Being has bestowed upon you the Empire and treasures.

93. (You) are a great philanthropist and like a mountain in the battlefield,
    Possess characteristics of an angel, and have the grandeur of "Sur-Rayaa."

94. You are an emperor and the glory of the throne of a large Empire, and
    These are epochal times of the wealthy that have distanced them from religion.

95. I am also a critic of the people living in the Hills, who worship idols,
    They are the idolaters and I rebuke idol worship (like you).

96. Look at this ever-changing unfaithful world,
    It so happens that as one turns around one may receive injury.

97. Look at the fairness of Nature and the holy Supreme Being,
    That from (*Its*) one strike, one million may get killed.

98. What can an enemy do, to the one who has befriended the kind Lord?
    Its affair is being generous and forgiving.

99. *It* liberates all, and guides us on the path of righteousness, and
    Acquaints us to speak gracefully and praise all (mankind).

100. Since the enemies are rendered "blind" by *Its* timely action, thus
    It pulls out the helpless (to safety) without even a thorn prick.

101. Any person who is upright and deals fairly,
    The kind Lord treats them with compassion.

102. Anyone who comes to serve wholeheartedly,
    The Self-existent Being grants them peace.

103. What kind of enemy can cheat and deceive a person,
    To whom the Self-existent has provided the protection.

104. Even if upon one descends tens and thousands
    The Creator (***Itself***) becomes the guardian.

105. If your apparition seeks armed forces and immense treasures,
    Then my vision extends to gratitude of the Supreme Being.

*At each stage, Guru Gobind Singh is trying to remind Aurangzeb of the dynamic role of the Self-existent Supreme Being in the running of the Universe. He is trying to make Aurangzeb realize **Its** total control and influence on mortal beings. In the following verses he is reminding Aurangzeb of the stern fact of mortal human life. Like Aurangzeb's own ancestors as well as the mortal Prophet Mohammad, no one has ever escaped the wrath of time, and everyone must ultimately break away from the phenomenon of life to reach the end point of their time, called death.*

The Guru continues to place his gentle pride in being a soldier under the aegis of the Almighty, Saviour of all humanity, who protects all from the challenges of evil human beings. A reader may feel an element of subtle challenge thrown at Aurangzeb by Guru Gobind Singh. Right to the end, the Guru displays his confidence in the magic spell of God.

106. Whilst your pride rests upon the vast Empire and its treasures,
    Well, I have the protection of the Timeless Supreme Being.

107. Don't be an ignorant fool; the inning here is of three to five days only,
    That in this world each "head" is trespassing turn-by-turn in exchange.

108. Where have gone the big lords, Khusaro, and other renowned personalities?
    Where have gone the noble Adam and the passed-away Mohammad?

109. Farundoo has gone; so have left Bahamun, Asfund and the friends;
    Neither are Daaraab, Daraa nor Daraamd anymore.

110. Gone are the zealous Sikander (*Alexander**) and Shaer Shah, and
    None of them are living any more to be seen.

111. Where has disappeared Shah Temoor; Babr too has gone,
     Humayoon has vanished and Akbar has departed too.

112. Look at the betraying cyclical events of this Universe,
     That, each and every one is trespassing on others' little and large territories.

113. You may be powerful, but please do not injure poor folk,
     Do not try to axe and erode (dignity) by making worthless promises.

114. When righteousness becomes the ally, then what can the foe do,
     Even, if the enmity does appear in the form of hundreds of bodies.

115. Even if the enemy demonstrates animosity, a thousandfold,
     Still it cannot bring any harm to even a "single hair."

The Guru concluded his letter to Aurangzeb by enumerating the non-elemental and non-atomic properties of the Unbeknown almighty creative force in Nature. It was to provoke Aurangzeb's human mental faculties, to make him realize and understand his own minute mortal self, made of physical elements, and to make him appreciate the timeless absolute force beyond ordinary human intelligence. That Unbeknown Being is—

116. Unidentifiable, indestructible, and featureless without an outline,
     Fathomless, autonomous, for the believers *It* is indescribable.

117. Non-metrical, formless, without contours, does not have specific complexion.
     Unborn, racially indistinct, that non-elemental is indivisible.

118. Impenetrable that cannot be cut, without human attribute and inert.
     Without repentance, indiscriminate, that indubitable force is unbidden.

119. Without an outline, undisguised, ineffable exists as a unity.
     That Self-existent Saviour has such a spectrum of properties.

Thus this famous epistle from Guru Gobind Singh to the emperor Aurangzeb comes to its conclusion. Whether the letter had any influence on Aurangzeb's thoughts and attitudes towards other religions may be appraised by perusing the letter to his son Azam, written from his deathbed. It is unlikely that the ninety-one-year-old Aurangzeb, born in 1616, died because of his repentance or penance to avoid the fires of hell in the court of Allah, or to enter paradise! Considering his age, it seems he died of the natural causes of aging, from the usual degenerative physiological changes rather than mental distress. At the end, he may have felt some remorse for causing injuries to the innocent. This he did realize and expressed his repentance while dictating his final will. The following excerpt is from his last testament and will, handwritten in Persian, recorded by Maulvi Hamid Uddin in chapter 8 of his account of the life of Aurangzeb. It does indicate the regrets of the Emperor for committing atrocities against the Hindus.

"There is no doubt that I have been an Emperor of Hindostaan, and I have ruled over this country. But I am sorry to say that I have not been able to do a good deed in my life. My inner soul is cursing me as a sinner. But now it is of no avail. It is my wish that my last rites be performed by my dear son Azam.... Allah should not make anyone an Emperor. The most unfortunate person is he who is an Emperor. My sins should not be mentioned in any social gathering. No story of my life should be narrated to anyone." *(This was published in an article by Ajmer Singh, M.A. in the weekly Fateh on November 7, 1976.)*

Still, his regrets had no specific influence on the attitudes of Bahaadur Shah (Muazzam) and his successors towards the Hindus.

Unfortunately like politics, religion too can become a malignant social ailment having secondary affects. An uncontrolled proliferation of fundamental ideals and misconstrued religious doctrines, when spread amongst illiterate, innocent people through the distorted views of a few, can have maleficent influence on the lives of common people. Ultimately, it can cause serious conflict, leading to hatred among various groups and sectarian violence intended to demonstrate supremacy of one over the other.

No doubt, the Guru did make a supreme effort to direct all towards the one and only "Supreme Being," the almighty King of kings. This included the awakening of the emasculated three-quarters of the non-kShatriya Hindu population and inspiring them to fight for their social rights through self-sacrifice. The Guru's sacrifices were no less; his whole family and ultimately his own life. Unfortunately, still there were not long-lasting effects bringing positive social changes, even among the people of his own province.

6. *Fatehnamah* in Prose

With greetings from (Guru) Gobind Singh to Aurangzeb

I hereby write this message in the name of the God (***It***), Self-existent, and Almighty to the Emperor of Hindostaan.

The swords and axes; arrows, spears, and shields all belong to that Self-existing Saviour of all. To the same belong all fearless warriors and galloping horses to testify ***Its*** guardianship. The Almighty, who has granted you the kingship; the same would shield me with the religious treasure ***It*** has given. You are a hypocrite and have looted all your wealth through acts of deceit. However, sincerity and contentment are my means to make headway.

Aurangzeb, the glitter of the throne, what your name implies, does not befit you. A king is the glory of the throne. He does not acquire treasures through acts of deception. Your sins are like beads of a rosary strung on the thread of your life. Each new sin you commit is like dropping of another bead trapping the thread deeper, burying your life under more sins. With your ill deeds, not only you have rolled the esteem of your ancestors, *not that they were any better*, in the dust, but you have also kneaded it irreversibly in the blood of your brothers. On such a foundation, you have built a weak empire, *based on misconstrued Islamic philosophy*, to open a door for gathering huge wealth for yourself.

Now you watch, how with the favours of the Timeless Being (Akaal Purush), I would rain upon you the shower of steel weapons like the monsoon rains. [*This sentence can also mean that he would rain upon him the shower of "the holy water from the iron bowl," the Umrit, like the monsoon rains, to absolve his sins*). It will wash away all the clouds of ominous aura built around you, to force you out of this sacred land and leave it pristine forever.

I do understand that you have returned discontented in your mission from the hills of the South, and had a bitter experience with warriors of Maeward *in the western desert province of Rajasthaan*. It is very likely that your eyes are now upon this region *in the North*. Let us see if that would resolve your acridness and bring satiety *to your ego. I warn thee*, I would set aflame such a "fire" in the path of your cavalry *that they would race out*, without having even a sip of water in Punjab.

So what if a wily jackal has killed two little cubs of a lion by deceitful means? Remember, there still remains the ferocious lion to take revenge. I would not pay any more attention to your false religious beliefs. Now I truly realize what kind of god and religious commandments you follow. I do not have any faith in your sworn oaths. I have been left with no other suitable means other than to wield my sword. Even if you think yourself a clever and experienced wolf, still I will not let "the lion" fall into your trap.

If ever we have an opportunity for an exchange of dialogue, I would certainly hear you out. At that moment, I would direct you upon the holy path of righteousness. On the contrary, if we happen to be on a battlefield, with our armies set in lines at a distance in confrontation within sight of each other, I would recommend that initially we should station our men at a distance of at least two furlongs. Once such an arrangement is set on the battlefield, with space left in the middle of the field of action, I will approach alone closing the gap, and you may come toward me flanked by two horsemen.

So far, you have lived in the lap of luxury and enjoyed the fruits of pleasure. You have never confronted a real warrior in a battle. *I am bringing you the honour,* to descend on the field in person with a sword and other weapons in hand for a duel. That way, you can stop the slaughter of God's people under your brutal rule.

7. *Zafurnamah* in Prose

With greetings from (Guru) Gobind Singh to Maharaja (Samraat) Aurangzeb,

I hereby write this message to "The Emperor" of Hindostaan, in the name of the God (*It*).

The Lord is the personification of perfection. *It* is eternal and manifests through its miracles. *It* generously grants all the bounties, and mercifully liberates us from this world. *It* grants peace upon us, is forgiving, and holds our hands to guide us. *It* excuses all our sins, and pleases us by providing sustenance. Only that King of kings, full of kindness, provides guidance. *It* is without any physical characteristics and incomparable since *It* cannot be traced.

It has neither material possession nor does *It* bear a mark of power; it is without armies and has no land to claim. Still that Self-existent grants us heavenly pleasures. Upon this chaste worldly creation *Its* apparent presence is found everywhere. *It* fulfills all needs as if *It* is present in person. That very provider without discrimination brings forth mercifully daily bread in offerings to all places. That very Master of all the regions is superbly great, is of incomparable "beauty," and sustains us all mercifully. That very Master takes care of the poor as well as the helpless, so that even the meek can defeat and destroy their enemies.

The person who follows the law of "Sharia," and knows its virtues, truly understands the real meaning of the "Book" of the prophet. Only those who search for knowledge receive the Master's word, and become familiar with the reality of *Its* apparent presence. Those who are versed in the worldly affairs of the Self-existent would perform worldly duties according to *Its* wishes. The one who regulates the workings of this world is the greatest, and he who has complete knowledge of its secrets is the commander.

Aurangzeb, my trust does not rest any more on oaths. The only witness to my belief is the Supreme One *Itself*. I do not have even a drop of trust in you, and what to say of all the lying generals and advisors in your service! Anyone who does trust the promises made upon the Qur'an, that very man one day would become the most wretched at the end. An object or anybody who comes under the shadow of "Huma," *"The Powerful,"* not even the bravest of crows can lay its talon upon it. A passerby cannot dare to pounce upon goats, sheep and deer when they are in company of a "He-lion." If this is the way of deceit, taking an oath upon the Qur'an, then one should not lend one's dear forces to be hurt and sacrificed.

You tell me, what vigour and contest forty hungry men could display when tens and thousands descend upon them without any warning. Those promise-breakers suddenly descended with their unsheathed swords, arrows, and guns. Out of sheer helplessness in the middle of all this, I intervened with as much tactfulness as possible with our bows and arrows. When all the dialogue and other strategies had been exhausted, it becomes legitimate to take a sword in hand. I trusted the oath written upon the Qur'an as an *authentic royal promise*, and left behind the territory of Anandpur. Otherwise, you tell me for what reason would I ever take this route? If I had realized that you and your men are cunning like foxes, I would have never taken this path at all. Any person who does act believing the oath upon the Qur'an, should neither be struck nor taken prisoner, and must not be killed. However, your men came like common flies in dark uniforms, and all of them landed suddenly at the same time creating uproar. Nevertheless, every single person who came out from behind the shelter became the target of an arrow, to be drenched in blood. Fortunately, the person who did not come outside the shelter was neither pierced by an arrow nor met his wretched death. When I saw Nahar come out for a duel, he immediately tasted one of my arrows.

Many fled from the battlefield, and many of the "Khans" who made idle talk, they too had the "taste" of our arrows. However, some of the Afghans did plunge into the battlefield among a flood of flying arrows and bullets. Many of their attacks were launched bravely. Some were attempted in their full senses, while others were complete madness. Many of their attacks were such that they experienced injuries. Some of them, who entrusted their life to us, got killed. What about that shameless coward Khwajah, who took shelter behind the wall and did not enter the field like a real warrior. Alas! If I had seen his face, I would have at once granted him a desperate arrow.

At the end many were injured by the arrows and bullets. And on both sides many were to be killed fairly quickly. Many bows rained arrows and so did the bullets make the earth like a field covered in red Laleh flowers. There was an abundance of heads and innumerable lower extremities. They were so many that the field appeared filled with balls and hook sticks. Along with the sharp whizzing sounds of the arrows and the vibrations of the bowstrings, came random senseless cries filling the world around us. Other intense sounds of the weapons were so dreadful that even the bravest of the brave men lost their senses. After all, in the end what can the bravery of a man do in a combat when innumerable numbers descend upon those forty bodies? At the end of that day when the Sun had set in its veil, the bloodshed stopped with the falling of the night. The murky nebulous Moon, king of the night, appeared in the sky.

Remember, every single person who comes believing the promised oath taken upon the Qur'an has come under the guidance and leadership of the Supreme Being. That is why he neither gets a tangle in his hair nor any bodily harm. *It* helps him by destroying the enemy. I was not aware that you are a promise-breaker, a worshipper of wealth, and have such feeble religious integrity. You neither have any understanding of human integrity nor knowledge of religion. You neither have any understanding about the nature of the Master nor truly believe in Mohammad. Each and every person who does know the value of human integrity does not back out and bring forth the promise himself. The man that cannot be trusted even a little; how he can take an oath upon the Qur'an and of the Supreme Being at the same moment? Now even if you take an oath responsibly written upon hundreds of Qur'ans, I would not have even a drop of trust in it, coming from you.

However, if you have had trust in me, as I came, you would have come well-prepared to meet me as well. It still is your duty and responsibility to keep your "word," as a promise given to the Self-existent that "I promise," taking an oath. If "his majesty" (Aurangzeb) himself had been present in person, in flesh and blood, then the matters of the heart would have been much clearer. Still, it becomes your objective responsibility and affair, to be reasonable and reckon with what you have written. I have received the written message as well as being told verbally. Now you should act in such a manner that it brings tranquility. Be an eloquent man and keep your word, rather than have one thing in your "stomach" and something else on your tongue (*be honest and truthful*). I was acting entirely according to what the "Qazi" promised me. However, if the truth is to be known, then you yourself step forward in a friendly manner. If you want to see the promise as written on the Qur'an, then it can be provided for your closer look.

If the "honourable one" does want to visit the district of Kanga*r*d, then out of that a face-to-face meeting could happen. There would not be even a minutest danger to you on the way, since the people of "Bira*r*d" are under my command. Do come thus far yourself to have a dialogue in person. You will experience in person my compassion and hospitality. Send ahead of you one "war horse," *an Ashvmeydh*, equivalent in strength and prowess to one thousand horses, *to demonstrate your challenge, instead a cavalry of thousand men*. And come this far to capture from me this territory. I am an enslaved subject, and a servant only to that King of kings, *who is the Supreme Being*. If the order comes from *It* then I can only present myself as a living soul. However, if I receive an honourable invitation from your Excellency, I will consider coming over complete in body and soul. If you do worship the Almighty at all, then in this affair of mine you should not act lazily. As you do recognize the Almighty, you should not allow your officials to talk you into harming ordinary people. You sit upon a throne as a saviour of this huge territory, but your ways of justice are strange when they should be praiseworthy. Your way of justice is bizarre, and so is the way you nourish your religiousness. What a pity it is, and a hundred times more pitiable is your lordship. Strangest of all is your religious proclamation. To use anything but truthful words is to tell lies and be deceitful. Please do not strike the sword to freely drain the blood of the people. With "*Charkho Taeg,*"* the sword of time, your blood will flow too.

Do not be ignorant and be a man without fear of the Almighty. *It* is free of all desires and does not seek praises. That King of kings is without fear and is the true Emperor of the earth and heavens. That very Self-existent has created these earth and heavens, and is maker of every little and large dwelling. Also from time immemorial *It* has created all the creatures from the humble little ant to the ones with large bodies. *It* is kind to the poor and helpless; and eradicates ignorance. When *Its* very title signifies kindness towards the poor and helpless, then *It* does not seek self-praise and is free from any desires. *It* does not have any discriminatory colour and is without a form. *It* becomes our guide *without disguise* and leads the way.

The oath upon the Qur'an is a liability on your head. It is your job to speak out and serve it in the best way. You should demonstrate your wisdom by carrying out this act skillfully by taking the matter in your own hands. So what if you have killed four children, there still remain the rest of us, like a coiled-up, *snake* to strike back. Is it manliness *on your part* that you have extinguished young sparklers? Haven't you made the fire furious and brighter? In what a nice manner it has been said by sweet-tongued Firdausee, "a hasty act is the work of a devil." The day I happen to come to the court of your Excellency, that very day you will witness the truth all by yourself. If you disregard me even a little bit now, then you will also be overlooked and ignored by the Almighty. If you are prepared well at this task, the Self-existent will grant you prosperity. This kind of act will be like religious nourishment to you, since recognizing the Almighty will be for the betterment of your life. I do not know how much faith you have in the Almighty, it appears you have done too many hurtful acts. You do not recognize that the Almighty is very generous. *It* does not want this magnificent wealth of yours. Now, even if you take hundreds of little oaths upon the Qur'an, I shall not have any trust even for the smallest moment. Neither I will ever come in your presence nor let it so happen that I have to take this route again. I will not set upon a journey in that direction even if the Shah [*whether the Guru is referring to Aurangzeb or Muazzam Shah is unclear, otherwise Shah is a generic term in Persian to mean a king*] wants me to.

You are the Emperor, ruling over other kings and embodying the glitter of the throne. You are clever in your handiwork and a good horseman. You are handsome, charming, and of bright intelligence. You have the kingdom and lordship over all the Chiefs. You may be well-organized and knowledgeable, with skillful swordsmanship, but the Self-existent is the provider and *It* carries the ultimate "Sword." Remember, it is the Self-existent that have given you the bright intelligence and handsome elegant looks that you possess. The same Self-existent has also given you the kingdom and all the riches.

You may make great contributions and stand strong like a mountain in war, and have the attributes of a celestial being and may be glorious like "*Sur-Rayaa*" [likely referring to the Pleiades, a group of hundreds of stars in the constellation of Taurus, of which only six can be seen with the naked eye]. You may feel Emperor among kings, and an enthroned jewel of the universe. Despite living in these great times you are remote from righteousness. Like you, I may be a critic of idol-worshipping people living in the hills. They are simply idol worshippers, and I only want to defeat their idolism. *I am not an iconoclast, destroying religious monuments and idols.*

Watch out in this ever-changing, unfaithful world; it may reach out to cause hurt after you happen to turn around. Notice the goodness of nature and the kind Almighty. However, *It* can reach out to cause death of millions with a single strike. What can the enemy do against an affectionate friend of the Almighty? *Its* job is to be kind and to forgive. *It* delivers us and offers guidance. *It* acquaints us to utter praises. *It* blinds the enemy in difficult times and pulls out the most helpless, thus defending even from a thorn prick.

Each and every person who is upright and fair does get treated mercifully and with compassion. A person who comes to serve completely with heart and soul the Self-existent grants peace upon them. Then how can an enemy or any other person cheat them when there is protection of the Almighty? Even if tens and thousands attack at once the Creator becomes the guardian. If your motivation is a huge army and wealth, then my eye is upon the gratitude of the Almighty. The empire and wealth is your pride, but I have the protection of that timeless Almighty.

You do not realize that you are only here "three to five days" at this "inn" [meaning a short period in this world]. In this passing world the exchange of heads is taking place constantly. Tell me, where have all the big lords, Khusaro, and other legendary personalities gone? Where have gone the noble Adam and the passed-away Mohammad? Farnundoo has gone; so have left Bahamun, Asfund, and all the friends. Neither are Daraab, Darah nor Daraamd left any more. Gone are the eminent Sikander (*Alexander*) and Shaer Shah. Isn't it true that none of them are still living to be seen? And, where has disappeared Shah Temoor; Babr too has gone. Humayoon has vanished and Akbar has departed too.

Be on the lookout in this changing, distrusting world where each is trespassing on others' small and large territories. With your oppressive and cruel regime do not maim and torture people. And do not devise promises in a scheming way. What can an enemy do to the one who befriends the "Righteousness," even if hundreds of bodies do appear as an enemy? Even if the adversary applies thousands of different strategies to show animosity, it may not able to harm a single hair.

Let me remind you, the Almighty Lord is unmarked, eternal, and featureless without an outline. *It* is fathomless, independent, non-divisible, and indestructible. *It* is non-metrical, formless, without contours; it does not have specific complexion. Unborn, racially indistinct, that non-elemental is indivisible. *It* is impenetrable and cannot be cut; is without human attributes and inert. *It* is untraceable, undisguised, ineffable, and exists as a unity. That self-existent Saviour has such a spectrum of properties.

> May the Almighty bless the Emperor of Hindostaan
> (Guru) Gobind Singh,
> The Sikh Guru at Anandpur

8. Aftermath: The Rise and Fall of Banda Singh Bahaadur

The Mughal power prevailed upon the political scene of Bhaaratvarsh after the victory of Babr, in the battle of Panipat, after many attempts, in the year 1526. This was the true beginning of the rape of "Mother India." It ripped apart and destroyed the socio-religious fabric of the nation further, during multiple invasions across the northwestern frontier. Babr was a hybrid of the fierce Mongol Chengez Khan and the Turk Shah Temoor, of Turkestaan. Each one of his descendants had separate religious agendas. For Babr, during the time of Guru Nanak Dev, it was war against the Afghaans and the Hindus. There were periods of better relationships between Raajpoot* and Mughal during the existence of the state of Akbar, which brought the softening of religious and tax policies. Such mutual regard was wiped away instantaneously with the ascendancy of Nour Uddin Jahangeer, targeting the Sikhs, as evident from the martyrdom of Guru Arjan Dev. Seeing increasing intolerance against the Hindus, Guru Hargobind Rai, the son of the martyred Guru, took up sword against the new ruler Shihab Uddin Shah Jahaan, to oppose the relentless policies of inequality towards citizens practicing religions other than Islam and other social injustices.

These bigoted policies reached a critical state when Aurangzeb came to power. He was a staunch Sunni Muslim, who wished to eliminate Hinduism within his empire. The petty Raajpoot Hill Rajas were still maintaining the hereditary allegiance of their forefathers as the emperor's royal slaves. It was the sacrifice of Guru Taeg Bahaadur that once again inspired consolidation of Sikh military activities, this time led by Guru Gobind Singh. The Mughals were already faced with long drawn-out battles against Maraatha* in the south and Raajpoot in the west.

In the winter of 1705, following the evacuation of Guru Gobind Singh and his family from Anandpur, the Hill Chiefs eyed the region nervously, because of their past defeats at the hands of the Sikhs. Ajmer Chand and other Hill Rajas were bitterly conditioned to the electrifying boldness of the Sikh soldiers and their ability to reorganize rapidly. However, some of the vagabond soldiers of the Hill armies had the courage to invade the undefended town of Anandpur and the surrounding villages. They looted and caused structural damage to the forts. Thereafter, the town was deserted and left ungoverned, as nobody dared to establish any authority over the region. It was only after the passing away of the Guru, following the monsoons of 1708 that Ajmer Chand took control and retained it, until he surrendered to Banda Singh Bahaadur at the end of 1710. By then, Banda Singh Bahaadur had already won over the towns of Samanaa and Sadhaurda, as well as Sarhind, which, apart from Lahore, was a major stronghold of the Mughals in the province of Punjab.

The rise of the Khalsaa in Punjab and their display of religious spirit led them to make sacrifices for the goals established by Guru Gobind Singh. The Sikhs left behind during the time when the Guru was in the south suffered hardships under the local landlords. However, the smouldering courage of the Sikhs, working in the fields and other manual jobs, was fuelled with arrival of the Banda Singh Bahaadur. The mandate of the Khalsaa Sikhs was to destroy the unjust rule of the provincial

Vazeers and to destabilize the Mughal Empire. The destruction of the Empire in the north was accelerated by the hot-footed and violent approach of the new Khalsaa leader, Banda Singh Bahaadur. Even before the death of Guru Gobind Singh, the message of a crusade against the Mughals had already spread around the province. The Guru had the vision of dismantling the Mughal rule, under the military leadership of Banda Singh Bahaadur, to prevent further atrocities against Hindu and Sikh communities. The Guru blessed Banda Singh Bahaadur by giving him five of his own arrows and chosen Khalsaa men at Nanderd. Thousands of troubled Sikhs in Punjab were waiting to join Banda Singh in the fight against the Mughal.

The compatriots of Banda Singh Bahaadur were local peasants, filled with rage and passion, wanting to liberate themselves from forced hardships. The fast-moving forces of Banda Singh attacked the Vazeers of Punjab, one by one, storming like a wildfire through the region, destroying all the structural symbols of Islam and ransacking the mansions of the rich landlords, while advancing toward victory. The Sikh peasants put the large landholders in the region to the sword. They captured and occupied their properties. Banda Singh incited the enraged peasantry further with promises to share the loot from the rich Muslim chiefs and farmers. This lit a fire of opportunity and enflamed hope for the peasants to become owners of big landholdings, between the river Yamuna* and Sarhind.

When Banda Singh Bahaadur reached Sarhind,* the northernmost principal city of Mughal Hindostaan, the regional capital of the province, he encountered a well-trained and organized regular Mughal army. The unorganized peasants and the self-motivated Khalsaa force, although full of zest, were without modern weapons when facing the army of Vazeer Khan of Sarhind at Shapperd Chirhi. Despite the odds against them, the show of Sikh unity in this fierce battle managed to overcome the devastated Sarhind. This victory was crucial for Banda Singh Bahaadur for historical reasons related to the personal life events of the Guru. With Sarhind under his rule, he had full influence over the region extending between the borders of Dilli and the river Satluj.

The confidence following the miraculous victory steered Banda Singh Bahaadur and his well-motivated Sikhs across Yamuna to Saharunpur and its surrounding areas. This victory took him further northwest of Satluj, past Beas to the Majha region of Punjab. As these expeditions of Banda Singh caused havoc, the Mughal forces were preparing to launch counterattacks and capture him. Muazzam Bahaadur Shah, leading an imperial army, chased Banda Singh Bahaadur towards Lahore. However, during these attempts, Muazzam was killed in 1712. Mughal forces were bent upon smothering the fire of unrest caused by the Khalsaa men. Finally, Abdus Khan and his son Zakarya Khan managed to capture Banda Singh Bahaadur alive. Hundreds of battling comrades were also caught and humiliated in the vicinity of the town Gurdaaspur. As expected, the fatigued, frustrated and bruised Mughal ruler, with fear of further battles, ordered the most severe and torturous death penalties for Banda Singh Bahaadur, his young son and close associates.

However transient, Banda Singh Bahaadur may be called the first Sikh ruler of Punjab. On the foundation of the Khalsaa Sikh establishment of Guru Gobind Singh, the ambitious Hindu Tantric Madhodas, now known as Banda Singh Bahaadur, was as a Khalsaa warrior steadfast in his mission, who raged aggressively all over Punjab to draw the territorial boundaries of a Sikh kingdom. The powerful Sikhs, to fulfill their ambitions, forcefully acquired many tiny kingdoms, creating a number of "Misl" states in the region. Finally, from among them appeared the one-eyed warrior, Maharaja Runjeet Singh,* to establish Sikh rule in Punjab.

The Afghan tribes inhabiting the region of Khyber Pass at the northwestern frontier of Bhaaratvarsh were insensible to law and order. The Sultans of Dilli and Mughals, like their predecessors, failed to control these unruly tribes. Soon after taking the throne Maharaja Runjeet Singh adopted the policy of subjugating the smaller Misl states at the first instance. Then he reached out to conquer the more formidable enemies. He was faced with constant attempts not only by the Mughal but also by Afghans to take firm hold of frontier territories. He used the Akaali, the staunch among the Khalsaa, against the Afghan tribes, who fought fanatically and relentlessly. Ultimately, his general, Hari Singh "Nalwa,"* blocked the chronic trouble caused by invaders from the frontier borders. Maharaja soon realized the difficulties of administering a large geographic region. In order to maintain peace within the newly acquired territories he set up a system of regional autonomy, and was content with receiving taxes in one form or the other.

Maharaja Runjeet Singh successfully used the Afghans to his advantage by accepting them as administrators of conquered territories for a number of years. During this period he strengthened his resources, and pitted adversaries against each other. Thus, Maharaja Runjeet Singh managed to extend his benevolent rule to the northwestern frontier. According to the British Treaty of Amritsar, the Maharaja was prevented from expanding southward. Therefore, it became natural for him to divert his forces towards other northern territories. He looked upon West Punjab, the natural preserve, as his territory.

The Sikh empire extended from Satluj to the northwestern frontier. Maharaja Runjeet Singh built a strong, centralized administration. He effectively controlled the military system by amalgamating the best elements found in the local warriors and European advisors. One of the conspicuous and typical features of his administration was that he encouraged setting up a composite Punjabi culture and Punjabi nationalism. He achieved this by bringing together the religious traditions of Hinduism, Sikhism, and Islam into a common platform and forum. To give life to the dream of Guru Gobind Singh, Maharaja Runjeet Singh himself showed a tendency to respect the sentiments of the people of all religions, "castes," and creeds in various ways in the realm of his kingdom. In principle, it meant that Maharaja Runjeet Singh provided opportunities to the subjects believing in nascent Punjabi nationalism, rather than individual religious dominance.

To this end, Hari Singh "Nalwa" too showed broadmindedness, curbing unwanted communal motives among various religious factions. When Hari Singh "Nalwa" was appointed governor of Kashmir, all restrictions on Brahmans concerning individual practices of worship were lifted. Hindu converts to Islam were set at liberty to re-convert themselves to their original faith. Like the Maharaja, Hari Singh "Nalwa" also built a number of Gurudwaras at places associated with the Sikh Gurus. He helped to set up united Hindu, Muslim and Sikh townships in Kashmir. Maharaja Runjeet Singh was considered a benevolent suzerain, who would never enforce oppression upon his subjects. Moreover, he made sure that the governors in his territory showed no negligence in the affairs of administration. Apart from building new Gurudwaras, temples, and mosques, he gilded the dome of Har Mandir Sahib in gold, hence the name "the Golden Temple," and many of the already existing renowned places of worship were renovated to enable Sikh, Hindu and Muslim communities to live peacefully with each other.

9. Conclusion: A Critical Review

Every human being has a divine origin within the womb of a woman. In this respect, Gobind Rai was born no different than other human beings. During his childhood, history and circumstance were such that the divine spark galvanized his mind and body, filling him with courage and spiritualism at a very early age. He believed in the Wahey Guru, an invisible and indivisible entity, as the Supreme Being, and experienced *"Its"* manifestation in his mortal body. He understood the basic elemental nature of all living and non-living matter that constitutes physical form, and provides strength to the human body.

Throughout his formative years, the growth of his intrinsic powers helped him to reveal and demonstrate the strengths of a leader and a soldier. He grew up no less than a royal child, surrounded by the best available teachers and trainers who transformed him into a strong, multifaceted person. His strength, courage, intellectual abilities and leadership qualities were driven by the power of knowledge, the capability to motivate his followers, timely responsive action, and mindfulness as part of the spiritual environment that had surrounded him since childhood.

The model of spirituality had already existed in Sikhism established by the preceding Gurus, with a huge following of faithful disciples. The development of the Sikh Gurus' philosophy followed the principle of "cause and effect" that had come to exist as a result of intense relationship between the invaders and indigenous people of Bhaaratvarsh. With increasing influence of Islam over several centuries, the imperial overlords tightened their grip through physical violence, economic sanctions, and the discriminatory taxation system. To establish Islam in Hindostaan, the rulers used all possible means to undermine the socio-religious activities of the indigenous people.

Guru Nanak Dev was a contemporary of the first Temoori (Mughal) ruler Babr. He had experienced the atrocities committed by the invading forces firsthand. The Mughals took advantage of the socially divided society and underprivileged to impose Islam easily through a variety of incentives. He acted wisely and prudently to avoid direct confrontation with Mughal authorities. However, as Sikhism evolved under the spiritual tutelage of its Gurus, the philosophical "takeaway" message for its followers was very different from that of Sanaatan Dharam.

The concept of Sikhism was rooted in monotheism. The Gurus attempted to eliminate a well-established and extensive social classification system by educating the Hindu masses, advising them to stop performing misunderstood and modified Vedic rituals. They clearly understood the harsh religious environment that existed, and acted appropriately to prevent further injury to the spirit of the nation. The Hindus had to consciously overcome the influence of Islam, which was being forced upon them by the Mughal rulers. Upon resisting Mughal policies, Guru Arjan Dev and Guru Taeg Bahaadur were severely tortured and finally put to death.

With this in mind, Guru Har Gobind Rai, son of Guru Arjan Dev, purposefully took up two swords, fulfilling his role as a soldier to deter the Mughal and at the same time continuing to serve the Sikhs as their spiritual leader by following in the footsteps of his predecessors. He erected "Akaal Takht," the timeless throne, within the premises of Har Mandir Sahib (the Golden Temple), as the seat of sovereignty, in order to act on his political concerns. It was on this foundation that, in order to militarize the Sikhs, his grandson Guru Gobind Singh fashioned the Khalsaa force under a completely new ideology of self-sacrifice, creating a military-style uniformed saint-soldier Sikh community, something that had never been done before. The creation of the Khalsaa encouraged both the higher and lower "castes" to rise against social injustice, calling on them first to establish social equality among themselves before confronting the Mughal.

Guru Gobind Singh made use of all that was available from the experience of past Gurus. Following the execution of his father and great-grandfather, who had defended Hinduism, as well as facing the escalating threat posed by Aurangzeb, it was time for the tenth Guru to change the rules of the game to protect his self-interest and check the aggression of the Mughals. For these reasons he was forced to establish a new order of "Khalas-knighthood," within the enclave of Sikhism. The Khalas-knighthood or the Khalsaa Panth became a distinct unit of initiated eminent members of Sikhism, frequently referred to as soldier-saints or Nihung Singh. Selfless, ready to sacrifice for the cause, voluntarily recruited Sikh and Hindus were trained in the ways of warfare to raise a distinctive military force.

It was on Baisaakhi day in 1699 CE that Guru Gobind Singh brought together ordinary members of different "castes" from all over the nation. During this gathering his leadership qualities and ability to motivate people of all denominations were evident. He staged a display of the self-sacrificing potential of the Sikhs, not for his sake per se but to rise against the Mughal rule under his leadership. The majority of those present were already spiritual followers of Sikhism from all walks of life. The first five men, who responded of their own free will to his call, were united, erasing their "caste" differences by drinking the "Umrit" from the same bowl. The newly formed unit of five initiated men then initiated Guru Gobind Rai, who became one of them and affirmed his willingness to sacrifice himself and his family for the chosen cause. Thus, Guru Gobind Rai became Guru Gobind Singh, and introduced a new concept of shared leadership and responsibility in all political and spiritual activities. By doing so he had lifted up all his Khalsaa followers to the same level—onto the same pedestal, so to speak—eliminating all social and religious differences. Hereafter, all the Khalsaa and even the non-Khalsaa followers of Sikhism became part of one large family and accepted the common name "Singh" for men and "Kaur" for women, shedding their "caste"-distinguishing family nomenclature. The outcome was a congregation of truly brave and courageous men and women, good at heart and sincere, willing to sacrifice their lives for social and religious equality within the diverse Hindu society. He invoked in them the spirit of self-pride and self-esteem, thus creating a true social integration. This was the beginning of the "Khalas-knighthood," the Khalsaa warriors, who became the military force needed to advance his campaign against the Mughal rule.

The practice of idol worship was firmly embedded in the mind of every Hindu. The God-anointed soldier Guru Gobind Singh only believed in rightful actions and well-minded sacrifice. The concept that an inanimate pacifying god made of stone could bring socio-religious freedom to the people seemed impossible to believe. To show his opposition to the practice of idol worship, Guru Gobind Singh reiterated the philosophy of iconoclasm, which had already been established by the predecessors of Sikhism. Baba Naam Dev said:

"The worship of idols of gods and goddesses, and the practice of the caste system has rendered the Hindu spiritually blind in both eyes, whereas the bigoted Muslim, who worships one God, is blind of one eye. Wiser than both is the one who sees God in all. Temples are sacred to the Hindu, and mosques are sacred to the Muslims, while Naam Dev focuses on his mind where lives the One and only, who is not restricted either to the temple or mosque." —Guru Granth Sahib, *page 875, verse //4//3//7.*

In the mind of an idolater, a statue of stone is a great teacher and a role model, while for others the Lord resides only in one's heart. It was Ek Lavaya,* in the epic tale of *Mahabhaarat*, who understood the true value of an idol, not as an object of worship but as his inspiring mentor. He sculpted a doll in the form of his chosen guru, learnt the art of archery and practiced in front of the idol to become a proficient archer. Metaphorically speaking, the faithful Hanumaan* displayed his deep and true servile devotion by revealing the iconic image of his much-loved Shree Raam and Seetaa by "ripping apart" his breast bone. For a believer, these very well-known examples are enough to show the significance of idols and icons. Idols should be viewed as objects of inspiration and focus.

The heritage of all Sikh Gurus was rooted in Sanaatan Dharam. They never destroyed the Hindu icons physically as the Mughals did. They certainly objected to the blind faith and ritualistic practices designed to please these static caricatures, and the seeking of material wealth and physical support by posing inert and lifeless in front of them. The objective value of these idols is to serve as role models to make positive changes in one's life and remain on the chosen path to the final destination. In the following verse, for self-encouragement and that of his "Khalas Knights," Guru Gobind Singh is praying to the Supreme Being in his composition of *Chandee Charitrr*, Dasam Granth.

"Deh Siva bur moh ehai subh karman te kabhuN na taro
Na daro arr sau jub jaaye laro, nischey kar apni jeet Karo."

"Do grant me the boon of Shiv\ (Shiv.h) so as never to retract from a righteous deed,
Never be afraid as and when engaging in a combat to firmly assert your victory."

As commonly interpreted, here Guru Gobind Singh is not asking for physical and spiritual assistance from the lord ShivaH. The name ShivaH in Sanskrit is written with visarg (:) dots at the end of the word, forming a personal noun, while Shiv.h with a halant (\), a stroke at the bottom of the last letter of the word, is an adjective, describing the lord's discipline, strength and calmness for his "Khalas Knights." It is not the same as posing in front of an idol. He is creating a mental and spiritual sojourn with the Supreme Being, seeking boon not from Shiv:, but Shiv\ characteristics for his "Khalas Knights," so as to attain valour and a steadfast nature and remain upon the path of righteousness.

Guru Gobind Singh wanted to encourage not only the Hindus divided by "caste", but every citizen of the nation, including Muslims, to detach themselves from inanimate stone objects and time-wasting rituals. He expected them to become visionaries, to understand the gravity of the oppressive Mughal regime. The Guru taught them to raise themselves with pride instead of kowtowing, and to earn the much-deserved human freedom required to live a dignified life. It was part of his strategy to raise all his disciples to the same level as himself, so as to drive them forward with their own strength. He managed his role as a leader in a miraculous way, changing the façade of the province and the lands beyond its borders with a new kind of military discipline.

At the age of nine, the violent death of his father, Guru Taeg Bahaadur, must have pained his pre-adolescent heart immeasurably. Knowing that his own grandfather, Guru Hargobind Rai, had donned the swords of Miri and Piri (sovereignty and spirituality), Guru Gobind Singh did not hesitate to raise his sword to continue the struggle against imperial injustice. Inherited wisdom had taught him to be courageous and to fight for righteousness. He believed in survival through life force rather than wasteful sacrifice.

With saintly intent, he became a warrior without anger and duplicity. He was a brave soldier free of the lust for power, with no desire to control a state; a royal figure without arrogance, even though he could have conquered a kingdom if he so wanted. He relinquished all comforts, and never surrendered to the greed for material wealth. He achieved his goals by living life according to his creed of social and religious equality for all. For Hindus, the religious intolerance and fanaticism of Aurangzeb had brought desperate times. The Khalsaa soldier-saints were never promised a special place in heaven, but were simply asked to fight the bigoted emperor to achieve a high quality life in their own motherland. They were initiated to become defenders of humanity rather than shields of the effete and weak-hearted to stave off the oppressor's sword.

It would be unwise to criticize the Guru, because one who did not live during his time can never truly understand the hardships and grief he faced. He succeeded in his mission to bring together members of the four "castes" of the Sanaatan Hindu community. The "Khalas-Knights" of Guru Gobind Singh boldly met their death fighting against the emperor Aurangzeb for all the Hindus of the nation. The question is not whether he succeeded or failed in achieving the objectives of his mission. Instead we must ask whether Hindu citizens from all "castes" and provinces collaborated to defend themselves against the Mughals. Did the fundamental disciples and future followers, the "Khalas-knights," pure at heart, called Khalsaa, succeed in creating a society with equal rights? And did they practice righteousness among themselves in the Sikh community at large, after the passing away of Guru Gobind Singh?

The answer to all these questions is no.

Unfortunately, they became a divided and different sort of Khalsaa over time. There is still a lack of social and political will for truly progressive democratic governance to fulfill the need for education and character building, to strengthen and develop all the communities equally in Bhaaratvarsh. The neo-Khalsaa and Sikh society are enmeshed in deprecated rituals and power-driven with a lack of political intelligence to act righteously and become a progressive society. Many "leaders" are filled with greed for personal gains, unlike the leadership and integrity of spirit hailed by the Guru.

To realize the dream of Guru Gobind Singh, one must include not just the turbaned Sikhs and the elite "Khalsaa," but also the modern trimmed and clean-shaven Sikh, the willing Hindu of today's Bhaaratvarsh, and the coerced Hindus who converted to Islam during the Mughal rule. All must only be courageous and pure at heart to become a true "Khalas" human being. Equality for all, not just a privileged few, was his dream. A true "Khalas knight" of Guru Gobind Singh would never seek the shelter of forts and temple walls, blemishing the Guru's name like a coward, because cowards do not deserve to be residents of the land of the *"pure at heart"* that the Guru fought and died for. He excelled in his leadership role as a "Khalas" human being. Those who do not share the same beliefs as him are neither *"pure at heart"* nor can be called "martyrs" without the sacrificing spirit of a true saint-soldier.

Guru Gobind Singh certainly succeeded in his campaigns against the Mughals, but suggesting the contrary should not be taken as anti-Sikh. It was a shared responsibility of the newly erected saint-soldier force made up of citizens of Bhaaratvarsh to empower themselves and prevent the tractable Hindus slipping out of the fold of Sanaatan Dharam. The Guru entered Chumkor, *"the village of death,"* famished and fatigued in cold winter rains, along with his 40 men and two older sons. He did not fully realize intensity of the danger he was in. Despite limited resources and the short time available to prepare, the fearless and brave "Khalas-Knights" raced their horses into the *"fire of hell"* without hesitation, swords flashing, willing to do or die. All the 40 nobles, including his sons, fought to their final glory. It was as if these intrepid warriors were merged as one, carrying the head and heart of their Guru without any thought of retreat. Guru Gobind Singh's military successor Banda Singh Bahaadur successfully continued his crusade to dismantle the Mughal Empire. Thereafter, it was up to the Hindu citizens and the silenced royal elites of the nation to rise in defense of their interests and land.

It was neither a holy war, nor a power struggle for his family, as none were left at the end. It was a war for the socio-religious freedom of the whole nation. His failures and successes were tied up with the attitude and attributes of all citizens. The Guru addressed and demanded a united front from all concerned. He sacrificed his parents and all his sons. He sacrificed innumerable "Khalas knights" close to his heart. Finally, he met the same fate himself. He sacrificed his life for the sake of equality for both the elite Brahmans and the oppressed kShuderr: (kShudraH, meaning insignificant and weak). If he seemed to fail in his mission, it was only because of the cowardice of the Hill Chiefs and the majority of the elite members of the Hindu community, who lacked his courage. They feared losing their comforts and were concerned that lower "castes" would become their equals, and thus cease being subservient to them. Guru Gobind Singh tackled the problem of inequality and demonstrated his opposition directly by mobilizing the vital force of the people.

The principal aim of the Guru's movement was the brotherhood of all humankind, regardless of religion and social position. He wanted to create a pathway for everyone, to provoke the divine spark, to manifest the invisible "Supreme Entity" within everyone, rather than seek *It* externally through prescribed solemn ceremonies meant to invoke the "Entity" in non-living materials. His thoughts, philosophy and finally actions corresponded to the experiences of his own life and those of his predecessors. As a visionary Guru and a noble citizen he became an example of courage and strength, which he passed down to his disciples, through his acts and writings.

Guru Gobind Singh brought to life the very basic philosophy of the first Guru, Guru Nanak Dev, but with a difference. For both, there was neither Hindu nor Muslim (or even Sikh, Christian or any other religious denomination in today's terms), but only "Khalas" human beings, loyal Shishaye (disciples) of the Supreme Being true at heart and pure in mind. Guru Nanak Dev was a saint, a wise and prudent citizen, who travelled the world and engaged in philosophical discourses, sharing his experiences. On the other hand, Guru Gobind Singh was a military leader and an astute soldier rather than a crafty statesman. He achieved his mandate by example, providing means to unify society. Whether the "Khalas" human beings he fashioned continued in his footsteps, without personal gain, is a different matter altogether.

Guru Gobind Singh tried to further cement the message of Guru Nanak Dev, that the Supreme Being is neither a Hindu nor a Muslim, or a representation of any other man-made religious denomination. No one religion possesses absolute knowledge, only self-serving doctrines and distinctions. We are all human beings, creations of the same Supreme Being. The first step to human equality is reason, not religion. Only reason can serve as the basis of correct and righteous human behaviour. Guru Gobind Singh understood the meaning of Guru Nanak's remark, and also recognized the dark side of Manu's idea of fragmenting the society of Sanaatan Dharam into variety of "Varn.h." Originally, during the Vedic period, the term Varn.h (attributes and virtues) was used to describe an individual's distinguishing qualities, vitality, interests and skills, to further define the functions and workings of the society. However, the meaning of the word Varn.h was twisted by the social scientists on the basis of physiognomy and the skin pigment of the population. The assailing and exploiting authorities capitalized the concept to divide the society formally into a social system to limit intellectual development, as an instrument to subjugate those of distinctive and dissimilar outward appearance. Outsiders took full advantage of the social system based on a misunderstood meaning of the term Varn.h as meaning complexion and colour due to geographic evolution. They found easy to manipulate the divided society, to rule not only the commoners but the royals too. The term Varn.h is what has been referred to as "caste" system since the arrival of the Portuguese on the soil of Bhaaratvarsh and which was formalized by the British. After independence it was applied to nation's constitution to make provision for growth and development of the underprivileged citizens.

The Mughals invaded during the fifteenth century through the Khyber Pass, engaged in fierce battles against the already ruling Afghans, and settled in to impose their own rule and religion. Throughout their regime, they wasted the wealth and natural resources of the land, fighting provincial rulers, recruiting native people, killing hundreds and thousands to expand their empire. Mughal rulers did very little for the indigenous people. To glorify Islam and the Mughal presence in Hindostaan (Bhaaratvarsh), they built palaces and gardens for their own pleasure, and created wonders in marble as mausoleums to entomb their loved ones. They did not lay even a single brick in remembrance of thousands of sacrificed artisans who had labored to erect these buildings. These elaborate and fancy structures were of no practical value in bettering the lives of ordinary working class people. Neither did the Temoori rulers hold up social and religious values of Hindus and indigenous tribes.

Overlapping the period of Mughal rule, the pirates of Portugal anchored on the western coast. The elementary goal of these enterprising sea-wolves was to seize seaports across the Indian Ocean (see appendix). They accepted indigenous hospitality, obliged their hosts to join their religious system, and intervened in the pre-existing established trades to take control of an already well-organized market, even if it meant the deaths of hundreds and thousands of people. The British and French, not far behind the Portuguese, found a battleground in Tamil Naidu (Madras/Chennai) to fight over the natural resources and products of the subcontinent, killing the local inhabitants in the process. The Portuguese also sowed the seeds of the African slave trade, transporting millions of human beings by force out of Africa. They bartered slaves in exchange for pirated imports from Bhaaratvarsh and rest of the Asia. The British, searching along the eastern coast of Bhaaratvarsh, beginning in Bengal, robbed local rulers of their wealth, taxed the peasantry, and armed impoverished natives dressed in red coats and blue trousers to kill their own countrymen. Once established, they touted lofty self-serving principles of civilizing the people of the country, having been versed during their own subjugation first under the Romans and then the Normans. Barefaced and brazenly, they stole from the golden platter that not only fed their needs living in Bhaaratvarsh, but also to celebrate "Maharani" Victoria as they brought wealth to her subjects back home. They financed their own industrialization by stealing twice over, first by shipping cotton, silk, and spices out of Bhaaratvarsh as raw materials and then selling them back as imported manufactured goods at a premium price. They robbed the nation for well over a century, and completely ignored the basic needs of the people, preventing their development as Europe itself was rapidly industrializing and growing wealthier, to finally become the developed "first world." British civil servants, at all levels, served with racist attitudes, wearing white collar and dark mind, trying to civilize the already civilized Dravaerd, Aarya and other races of Bhaaratvarsh in their own ways. The British "Raaj" was a game played by pirates as privateers, traders as traitors, governing the land as brutes. The traders of East India Company behaved and acted like pseudo-royals presiding over Durbars playing Rajas and Maharajas dressed-up in costumes made by the London theatrical society.

In the end the British Empire was no more than a "British Theatre."

After the dismantling of Mughal rule and British dramaturgy, centuries of oppression of the underprivileged from both within and outside the nation, as well as the forceful subjugation of the privileged, had left behind a chronic state of social inequality, economic insecurity and lack of national loyalty among a divided multicultural society of diverse lineage, destroying the virtue of honesty at all levels. After the independence of the divided Bhaaratvarsh from British rule what had been left behind was an irreparable degradation of civil services at all levels that tarnished the social character of the citizens from footpath to the parliament house in the capital, New Delhi, an expanded version of old Mughal Dilli.* Whatever kind of political discipline instituted by the British was meant to manage provincial rulers, silence social and religious upheavals and educate the middle classes to meet the clerical needs of the government. They constructed the transport system to link seaports both to enhance trade and to rapidly deploy forces around the nation and other parts of the Empire. The limited infrastructure was developed to facilitate day-to-day governance of the natives, export national resources and meet their own leisure lifestyle.

At the time of pulling down of the Union Jack, nothing except chaos in the whole nation was visible. The morning after the departure of the British, their coattails were immersed in the blood of nearly one million Punjabis, having the same culture and language but divided by religion, moving across a new border dividing the province of Greater Punjab and Bengal into west and east. The "British Empire Syndrome" of dividing nations and leaving behind chronic social and politically smouldering wounds, still seen frequently as explosive conflicts in places such as Palestine, Hong Kong and Jammu and Kashmir, and similar to what is also seen in Ireland, as a result of divided ancient lands and people. The signs of the syndrome are evident as the ongoing instability of these divided lands and military interventions among them. This was inflicted deliberately by the incumbent British on all major states within British Empire.

The social and cultural divides in all the major states and the migration of human beings is generally considered a normal historical development due to natural disasters. But in the recent times the active invasion of Asia, Africa and the Americas led by the British and other European nations for more than five hundred years with a well-designed political ideology and "doctrine of discovery" (see appendix), left the people and their lands divided. This "British Empire Syndrome" has adversely affected the timely and parallel development and progress of the people, particularly that of powerless minority communities living in those independent states. Out of that chaos have grown deeper communal divisions, economic inequalities and enmity among neighbouring states, obstructing nation building. Wherever the British and other Europeans had left their footprints, whether the Indian subcontinent, Asia or Africa, they left behind a broken and underdeveloped so-called "Third World," building their own economies on the stolen wealth and physical strength of others. The British and other Europeans, who still feel proud of their forefathers having participated at any level in establishing colonial states, are a potential danger to the stability of the world, as they have economic interests and military power to master and manipulate the developing nations to their advantage.

After the curtain fell on the "British Theatre," "Mother India" was cruelly abused by a variety of her own citizens, from all walks of life. Its natural magnificence was eroded and left in ruins after being plundered by multiple foreign powers over the last thousand years. The nation has been further exploited by post-independence political leaders and government officials in the name of development and progress. Over more than 70 years, selfishness combined with bribery among low- and high-ranking British-styled civil servants together with a wage structure inadequate to meet daily needs has resulted in dishonesty, corruption, and economic inequality. Right down to this day, there is a belief strongly ingrained in the minds of the people that what has been inherited by the civil services and political leaders cannot be changed and that they are incorrigible.

Poor political leadership and the bureaucratic culture of "Babu jee" (meaning an office clerk who could write English, derived from middle English and the old French word babouin, meaning stupid person, obviously a derogatory term and still applied) left in the wake of self-serving British has depleted the energies of the nation, causing a lethargic attitude among the majority of people, who dream of succeeding without hard work. Instead of a well-trained leadership capable of managing a nation as large and diverse as Bhaaratvarsh, an extremely self-centred hierarchical political structure obstructs progress. False social pride and a feudalistic type of individual arrogance at street level impede the maintenance of the law and hamper everyday life. Despite constitutional measures intended to uproot inequality that have been in place now for nearly 70 years, the "caste" system and class discrimination are still rife in the society. Contrary to the expected outcome, these measures have consolidated the lethargic attitudes of the underprivileged. Furthermore, they have caused the prolongation of inappropriately administered "caste" reservations to bring about social and economic equality among all citizens without giving them much needed self-esteem and human dignity. Recent female empowerment at lower political levels in towns and cities has endowed collaborating men with a new instrument of privilege; in politics behind a victorious woman there may be a "front man," who could be her husband or father-in-law, carrying out her public duties and exercising their own political will, while she may still continue to be a mother and a householder.

All human beings are equally intelligent and capable; however there is a difference in acquired individual abilities needed to develop professional and vocational skills to be successful due to lack of equal opportunities for higher education and training. These limitations lead to underdevelopment of mental abilities and a growing gap in wealth and standard of living generation after generation relative to the privileged classes, something which has happened not only in Bhaaratvarsh but also in Europe and North America by social design and through the political will of some leaders. It results in the failure of a large segment of struggling citizens to create better opportunities for themselves. This lack of collective development of a divided people by design rather than destiny not only causes discord among citizens but can prevent the development of the whole nation. In general, the undermining of confidence over the centuries has caused apathy, dampening the motivation of the lower classes to further the progress of the nation as a united whole. On top of that, amongst the large majority of underprivileged citizens of the nation, there is an intense lack of an honest pro-active attitude, which has created indolence and a lack of desire to succeed without external encouragement. In many ways people undercut their own interests by not rising up against the current state of inequality or the way they have been oppressed based on their social status. Instead of embracing needed changes and taking up the challenge to improve the quality of life, many communities obstruct progress so as to highlight their past oppressed status. They use their lower social status as a privilege in order to obstruct many national projects for modernization and industrialization, showing passive aggression in the form of civil disobedience, behaviour established during the British presence, to disrupt day-to-day activities.

The success of democracy depends on social and economic equality, and national pride among all citizens. Primarily, it originates through unity of national identity as nationals of Bhaaratvarsh rather than Mughal Hindostaan/Hindustaan or British India, and through character-building as a nation. The growth of democracy depends on cultivating a homegrown intelligentsia, even if it means having to reinvent the wheel, without having to look up to Europe and English-speaking nations. True self-development promotes the ideology of social equality by braiding together all "castes" and classes into a single plait, so as to develop minds of their own and think outside the box, rather than seek solutions to problems at home somewhere else. Without self-motivation there will be neither individual development nor that of the nation. Sending the youth of the nation away for higher education in foreign universities in former British colonies such as Canada, Australia, New Zealand as well as the United Kingdom itself, and emigration and subsequent transfer of wealth, helps these nations' economies, with the influx of young workers bolstering the pension funds of their older citizens. Instead, Bhaaratvarsh has to grow her own "gardens" of young academics and innovators to become a more developed nation, peeling off the invasive foreign skin to return Bhaaratvarsh (Mother India) to her original glory.

The study of Guru Gobind Singh's philosophy and life teaches the need to become proactive through self-encouragement and self-help in order to end centuries of lassitude due to servility engendered by the social system developed by the Manu of Aarya society, and taken advantage of by outsiders. There is no hope until we all, underprivileged and very privileged alike, begin to think of the well-being of the entire nation, without trying to take rights away from other citizens.

The modern day failure of democracy as well as social injustice and corruption are all results of bad governance. Furthermore, failures of our society include the degradation of socio-political behaviour, which has given birth to thriving fake "gurus" and religious practices, and nepotism in administrative services. It has ruptured the rich fabric of our society by misleading the illiterate and blinding the educated, who lack basic skills for critical thinking and effective decision-making. It is not hopeless, however; all can be cured and made good through the intense practice of self-induced honesty, following the laws of nature to set principles of competent administration, as well as character building in a religious fashion.

The social history of the world is studded with intellectual revolutions that overturn long-standing conservatism to resolve current socio-religious conundrums. Even today, religious beliefs are blindly adhered to, with the acceptance of assumptions, doctrines, and practices imposed hundreds of years ago out of fear of uncertainty and natural calamities. Practices such as idol worship, outmoded social divisions and manufactured hierarchy are either irrelevant or serious social issues in the face of a changing environment. Only a person of immense intellectual understanding of the social machinery can question ongoing practices that further the oppression of illiterate parts of society, and debunk the accepted norms.

The altruism of Sikhism demands first preservation of self, then sacrifice for the sake of individuals ready to participate willingly and die for their cause too. The sacrifices of Guru Arjan Dev and Guru Taeg Bahaadur were not vainglorious, and the "Khalas knights" in the battle of Chumkor were not on a suicide mission. Ultimately, when all diplomatic measures had failed, the best option left for Guru

Gobind Singh was to fight and to continue to live a chivalrous life.

Guru Gobind Singh was an innovative leader who inspired people of the nation, and worked to address the weaknesses plaguing the socio-religious structure of the time. He worked as a facilitator to assist society to develop as individuals rather than members grouped together in segregated "castes." His dream was embedded in the dreams of the common folk. He had a dream of a society of people with complete socio-religious freedom, positive moral values, who could take control of their future. From this perspective the actions of Guru Gobind Singh were honourable and for the benefit of all citizens. He wished to bring in a judicious rule of equality by the Mughal ruler, Aurangzeb.

The victory of such social and religious reforms is not the consequence of a single lifetime. Instead, it is achieved through generations of unified collaborative actions by a society, adding up to a cumulative effect that unfolds in a subtle way as the free will of people, rather than the divine magical powers of a heavenly incarnation. It can never be realized through the irrational activities of corrupt men of politics and venal religious reformers. Therefore politics must free itself from religion and act independently to alleviate the miseries of the underprivileged to modernize Bhaaratvarsh.

Guru Gobind Singh instituted principles of democracy. By devising the system of the "Khalas quintet" and granting the "Adi Granth" the status of a Guru, he removed the privilege of a human successor who would follow after him. He successfully introduced the concept of self-governance through a collaborative process, to bring together all the citizens of the nation and to cherish each other. In addition, raising his sword for equal rights, and through the militarization of non-kShatriya "castes," Guru Gobind Singh shifted the whole paradigm of Sikhism, and became a warrior of democracy. He thoroughly believed in the collective voice of the people for better governance; if not heeded, the governing body would face the inevitable consequences, as is amply clear from the following simple message which he narrated to the poet Nandlal jee:

Khaliq khaliq kee jaan ke
Khaliq dukhavay nah
Khaliq dukhai Nandlal jee
Khaliq kopai tahan

Know well, the people are of God,
Do not hurt the people;
Nandlal jee, if the people are hurt,
That will anger God.

Guru Gobind Singh had a noble character and was a successful motivator. He made sincere efforts to revitalize and invigorate all classes of society through social equality free of corruption, and envisioned a true self-governing parliament based on democratic principles of the "Khalas Quintet." Now it is up to the people of the nation to re-ignite in the true sense the democratic principles and apply them to meet the modern needs of our society successfully. Elect only educated and well-trained persons with genuine leadership qualities, and hunt to extinction corrupt political tigers.

A SELECTION OF PHOTOGRAPHS

1 (top). A young Khalsaa enthusiast (centre) in an uncustomary turban with his parents. His father is wearing a regular-style turban.(top).
2 (bottom). Personal preference: A Khalsaa disciple wearing an impressively styled steeple-shaped turban decorated with columns of Khalsaa emblems and metal rings ("Chakrum"*). He is a shopkeeper in a village near Muktsar.

3 (top). The Gurudwara at Anandpur.
4 (bottom). Interior of Gurudwara Paonta Sahib.

5 (top). The Gurudwara Bhathaa (brick kiln) Sahib, Ropard.
6 (bottom). Interior artifacts at the Gurudwara Bhathaa Sahib, including the preserved part of the mud heap showing marks of hooves believed to be that of Guru Gobind Singh's horse.

7 (top). Gurudwara Fatehgard Sahib at daybreak, also the site of other Gurudwaras where the two younger sons of Guru Gobind Singh were bricked-in alive and his mother passed away in the Thanda Burj.
8 (bottom). The Gurudwara at Chumkor.

9 (top). The Gurudwara at the site of the battlefield, Chumkor, where once stood a mansion house made of mud bricks, often referred to as "mud fortress."

10 (bottom). Interior of the Gurudwara at Macchiwardaa, the likely site where Guru Gobind Singh rested in the forest after his escape from Chumkor.

11 (top). Gurudwara Tibee Sahib, Khidraney-Dee-Dhaab, where Khalsaa decisively defeated the Mughal forces.
12 (bottom). Gurudwara at Muktsar.

13 (top). Gurudwara Sabo-dee-Talwandee.
14 (bottom). Entrance to summer palace of Maharaja Runjeet Singh, Amritsar, with inset (left) showing the old spelling of the city's name, "Umritsur."

15 (top). A plaque at Gurudwara Tibee Sahib, Khidraney-Dee-Dhaab, describing the defeat of the Mughal Vazeer Khan of Sarhind by the Khalsaa, written in Gurumukhi script.

16 (left). A brief account of life and role of Mai Bhago at Khidraney-Dee-Dhaab, Muktsar, in Gurumukhi script.

Note: Many thanks to my chachajee, S. Sewa Singh Gandhi, and the driver S. Sukhwinder Singh for their company during our tour of historical places.

10. Descriptive Glossary

The descriptive glossary has been written for readers who may be less conversant with some of the terms, places, rivers, personalities, and ancient historical events that occurred during the 5,000 years antecedent to the Christian era in northwestern Bhaaratvarsh, the golden land of opportunities. Some of the material presented here is controversial. It is very difficult to establish the facts as complete written records from past centuries and millennia do not always exist. Sometimes what material has been discovered is difficult to date, and to attribute to a particular author. This is particularly true of the original Vedic and Puraanic literature. The writings did not become prevalent until after 500 BCE. Currently, available descriptions, interpretations, and annotations of such literature can vary significantly, as there is always another opinion leading to further research to establish the most plausible truth.

Much of the author's point of view and hypotheses may be perceived as complementary to what is already known. For example, Sanskrit terms like Hindu, Sindhu/Sindu, Kush, Aarya, and many others are crucial to the understanding of the evolution of the Sapt-Sindhavaa (Seven Rivers) valley civilization (Greater Punjab). In Sanskrit, the term Hindu is formed by "ha" meaning the Sun and "indu" meaning the Moon, together meaning the people of Suryavansh (the Sun Clan) and Chandervansh (the Moon Clan). In the epic Raamayan the name of the lead character Raam: (Ra + Aham is Light + that I am) once again refers to the Sun and means a representative of the Sun Clan (Suryavansh); Raavan (the Light + forest), the king of Lankaa, means light of the forest or wilderness, and Havan (the Sun + forest) refers to the fire-worship performed in the forest. Sindhu ("Sa" meaning body of water and "indu" meaning the Moon) refers to a large body of water which is brilliant like moonlight. Kush is from the word "Kusa," a kind of grass, which has long thin fine blades growing in the sunlit and moonlit valleys of Hindu Kush (Sun + Moon + Green pastures), Mountain range rich with green and fertile pasture lands. No wonder the region east of the Hindu Kush with numerous waterways originating from Hindu Kush and Himalaya became a haven for the prosperous natives of the rising civilization of Seven Rivers and the migrant nomads settling as traders and agriculturists. Their magnetic success attracted many more nomadic communities, as well as other foreigners from lands further west of the Hindu Kush in search of green pastures. These included people as far away as the Mediterranean seeking the land of "Golden Fleece," described in Greek mythology, which was found in the east as gold nuggets in the river Oxus. Many like Alexander of Macedon arrived with their military might killing people in large numbers, gathering wealth and precious resources on the way.

Zafurnamah, written by Guru Gobind Singh to Aurangzeb, explicitly highlights the issues arising as a result of power-hungry invaders, expressing the intense suffering of the native people. To elucidate this kind of ongoing history-making events even in the 21st century, the author has made numerous remarks to emphasize the ongoing oppression of many communities all over the world and the sufferings of human life. The criticism of the author in this regard is reasonable.

1. Aarya – Etymologically, the words "Aarya" and "Aaryaa", male and female gender respectively, have their origin in the Sanskrit language. But their exact contextual meaning is not easy to explain unless the origin of the Sanskrit language is established with certainty, including how the words of a language are coined out of uttered sounds and their representative alphabets are invented. The adjective or noun "Aryan" is definitely not a Sanskrit word, as adapted and written in English. The word "Aarya" first appears in the Rig Veda.

The currently accepted meaning of the word Aryan in English as "wise, civil or noble" does not apply to the Sanskrit word Aarya or Aaryaa. Neither does Aarya apply to a group of hypothetical prehistoric people migrating out of Central Asia to Sapt-Sindhavaa valley nor a non-Jewish person of European descent as assumed by some to be Nordic people of Northern Europe. Since the appearance of foreign language translations of the Vedic and other ancient literature of the Indian subcontinent, much has been modified and the meaning of many Sanskrit words has been lost in translation. Frequently, there are never exact equivalent words in other languages when it comes to translating hymns and poetry. Secondly, much of the work initially translated by German authors is greatly biased. They found the discovery of Aarya culture and Vedic and Puraanic literature so fascinating, enriching, and enlightening that they declared Germans and other Germanic tribes to be of Aarya origin. First, to acquire this mistaken identity as Aarya or Aryan and then hurt humanity immensely was greatly irrational, if not foolish, on their part. Seemingly, it was hard for European scholars to accept the grand nature and highly developed literary skills of the people of the Sapt-Sindhavaa (Seven Rivers) civilization, also called the Indus valley civilization. The grand, well-organized communities existed long before invasions of aggressive nomadic tribes from Central Asia, which is now divided into Turkmenistan, Uzbekistan, Kyrgyzstan, Tajikistan, and Kazakhstan. In the past, before the Russian occupation, the whole region across Oxus River, between Persia, Mongolia, China, and Afghanistan, had been referred to as Turkestaan, the land of the Turks (not the same the inhabitants of Turkey). Turks and Tartars are considered a hybrid race between the Europeans and Mongols. Now for more than a century, like the Russians, the Chinese have been seeking a pathway through Bhaaratvarsh to the Hind Mahasaagar (Indian Ocean). It will prove fatal to the Indian people and their economy if China ever encroaches upon the land and waterways of Bhaaratvarsh.

The Vedic literature has been transmitted orally by rote since the second millennium before the Common Era. The Vedic prayers were recited and rhymed through resonance of short and long vowels in unison with the oscillation of head and rest of the body in a specific manner to allow correct pronunciation of the words without paying attention to the meaning of each and every word. How well the sounds and rhythm were preserved in a religious sense over centuries, reproduced and transformed into written texts, is difficult to say, as there are natural individual variations in the structure and function of the sound-producing apparatus and articulation of the complex utterances. Therefore, over time it would have been extremely difficult to preserve the ancient oral version of Vedic incantation and almost impossible to exactly recreate the sounds into words and meaningful sentences as intended originally. On top of that, the later written versions were grossly interpolated and altered to suit the interests of the invaders. Originally, Dev Indra was not part of the peace-loving Sanaatan Dharam. Sanaatan Dharam was an eternal practice of personal duties and righteous daily living. It was not a religious concept about God, Satan, Hell, and Heaven. Sanaatan Dharam was a practice intended for individual development rather than mass public worship of a "God". It is unlikely Indra, the god of the sky, rain, lightning, materialism, and war ever existed in original Vedic incantations of the Dravaerd people. The peace-loving Dravaerd (Dravidian) never placed Indra alongside Brahma, Shiva, and Vishnu. He was the king of other Dev and existed in many parallel "worlds", seeking wealth, pomp, and glory. There is not a single temple dedicated to his worship, unlike many other gods and goddesses. It seems that the concept of Dev Indra arrived along with the migrating nomads and was only given significance by the Dravaerd in the later written versions of Vedic literature. It was intended to include the newly arrived nomadic residents without prejudice against their cultural practices and to make them feel secure and easily accept the Vedic way of life.

The presence of extensive description of Indra alongside Trimoortee, the three godheads of Sanaatan Dharam, Brahma, Shiva, and Vishnu, found in the written versions of Vedic literature, was probably a much later inclusion, created under the rule of foreign aggressors. However, with continued invasions and the drifting of the Dravaerd communities along with the original nomadic settlers southward in the post-Puraanic period, the significance of Indra diminished dramatically to near extinction, unlike that of Shiva and Vishnu.

It was arrogant and presumptuous of later invaders to call themselves "Aarya," as applied to earlier settlers arriving from the north and west sides of the Hindu Kush mountain range, spreading across the territories of the valley of Seven Rivers and rest of the subcontinent, later to be called Bhaaratvarsh. Bhaaratvarsh means "land and era of king Bharat," who is believed to be the ancestor of Pandav and Kaurav families, characterized in the epic Mahabhaarat.

The Latin alphabets are not at all like the Devnaagri alphabet of the Sanskrit language. However, over time Sanskrit likely accepted some of the common vocabularies of the Latinized languages of the new settlers gradually migrating from north of Oxus River and west of the Hindu Kush. The melding of people meant mixing of vocabulary too, just as present-day Hindi has been significantly contaminated by English words in the last two centuries with the occupation of the Indian subcontinent by the British.

The vowel "Aa" describes the adjectival function of the suffix –rya. To explain further, there are many similar Sanskrit words, such as Aa-tama, that which describes oneself; Aa-tmanaH, meaning that of the person; Aa-tamaa, meaning that of one's own living entity (often translated incorrectly as soul); Aa-chaarya, meaning that of one's pursuit or occupation, usually as a teacher; Aa-yudhaM, meaning that which is of the war, or weapon; and so on. Similarly, the word "Aa-rya," meaning that of one's attributes to become informed and enlightened. It simply describes the ability of the initial migrating nomadic people to modify their activities and attitudes to follow Vedic practices. "Aarya" was an appreciative title given to the nomadic settlers by the Dravaerd, upon becoming similar to them, long before violent savage clans invaded the valley of Seven Rivers. The migrant nomads overtime became the natives as Aarya merged with pre-existing ancient natives, the Dravaerd.

The reasons why the people from north of Oxus River and across the Hindu Kush range migrated is unclear. One of the overwhelming reasons could have been unfavourable environmental conditions in their homeland such as floods, drought, and failure of crops, or they possibly were driven out by invaders from other regions of Central Asia because of the same natural causes or to expand their economic base. Initial arrivals were illiterate nomadic migrants, who entered through accessible narrow valleys in the snow-laden Hindu Kush mountain range in small groups over a long period measured in centuries. Their livelihood was based on agriculture and cattle-rearing. They were seeking fertile green pastures to settle somewhere where they could live a safe and progressive lifestyle. Archaeological evidence suggests that the eastside of the Hindu Kush was inhabited by indigenous Dravaerd people in the fertile sub-Himalayan plateau of Greater Punjab, the land of five waters (rivers). At the time of the independence of India, Greater Punjab was divided into west and east Punjab, and East Punjab was further divided into three states, Punjab, Haryana, and Himachal Pradesh. Punjab in Bhaaratvarsh has two rivers, Beas and Satluj (Sutlej). The other three rivers in West Punjab in present-day Pakistan are Ravi, Chenab, and Jhelum, which finally merge to form the sixth, the Sindhu (Indus) river. All these geographical regions now divided were once irrigated by seven major waterways, including Saraswatee (now extinct), Sindhu, Jhelum, Chenab, Ravi, Beas, and Satluj (the seventh water), over almost 2,500 years before new migrants made their way into the valley around 1500 BCE. The origin and course of the river Saraswatee are still unexplored because it is believed by many to be an imaginary river. Nevertheless, it is possible that its extinct course could be lying somewhere between Peshawar and Kabul emanating from the snow-laden Hindu Kush mountain range.

The already existing inhabitants, Dravaerd, developed the valley of Seven Rivers into a prosperous, literate civilization and progressive culture as evident from archaeological excavations. Dravaerd had a well-organized social and spiritual practices embodied in Sanaatan Dharam. It was not a religion as commonly understood and described in European literature. Over the last five centuries, most of the cultural practices of the world have been manipulated by the Europeans because of their well-honed "doctrine of discovery" (see appendix), to destroy indigenous religions, cultures, and languages of newly found lands. Sanaatan Dharam was an ancestral self-generative embodiment streaming from one generation to the next, following the embedded principles of righteousness and discipline during one's lifespan. The Sanaatan Dharam aimed to direct the society to practice and acquire the higher wisdom of ancient Vedic literature through oral tradition, to advance and achieve higher levels of physical and spiritual development. The ideology was transmitted orally in Sanskrit, which over time developed into daily Vedic orations like a prayer, and was later written down in its Devnaagri (metropolis of the Dev) script. Recent local excavations do not suggest any man-made cataclysmic destruction in the region of the valley. The finds suggest that the inhabitants formed a highly organized society, and lived a peaceful life marked by equal rights instead of multiple tiers of the rigid structure of social classes, which came much later with invasions from the north and west sides of the Hindu Kush mountain range.

Dravaerd were very accepting of productive immigrants, and they believed that the whole Prithvee Devi (the goddess Earth) and her natural resources were the shared wealth of all humanity. Large numbers of the natives were agriculturists and dairy farmers. Many of the nomadic migrants later also became agriculturists and still later travelling traders. They became enlightened practitioners of Sanaatan Dharam following in the footsteps of the hosting Dravaerd community. The Dravaerd called the new immigrants "Aarya," because they developed varied occupational interests similar to the natives without difficulty, becoming enlightened in the Dravaerd social practices, amalgamating with the various indigenous communities, and accepting their social and spiritual practices. Over time nomads adopted and learned Sanskrit. It is likely that the mother tongue of the nomadic migrants was one of the Latinized languages and they used it fluently alongside Sanskrit in their everyday communication. In this respect, the Dravaerd were not any different. Among a variety of Dravaerd communities, there were numerous dialects and distinct mother tongues spoken alongside the formally taught and learned Sanskrit as a language of the literate. It is not surprising that over the following generations some of the common vocabularies of Latinized dialects and vocabulary of the immigrants began to reflect in the literary works written in Sanskrit by the nomadic settlers.

It is highly likely that nomadic immigrants from across the Hindu Kush continued with their own religious and social practices, which developed into a variety of schools of thought, partially merging into the culture of Sanaatan Dharam. Sanaatan Dharam had a well-established vast, descriptive literature describing the hierarchy from the divine Supreme Being Brahma, the creator of the universe, to the stratification of numerous Vedic gods, Dev and Devi such as Shiva, Vishnu, Mitra, Prithvee, Surya, Agni, Varuna, Vayu, Yama, Usha, Aditi, etc. The hierarchy was based on their divine powers. Although the number 33 (3x3=9) and number nine is pervasive in the Hindu numerology system, it is unclear how the suggested number of 333 million Dev (masculine gods) and Devi (feminine goddesses), even if it is a metaphor, came into being, and there is no list of their names to author's knowledge. One possible hypothesis could be that the elite members of the society who held highly revered positions based on their social status by birth, level of education, divine intellect, government ranks, and amount of wealth they acquired the titles of Dev and Devi, spread over hundreds of years just like present-day lords, ladies, Nobel Laureates and other titled and prominent people. For ease of understanding, the stratification of the titles as Dev and Devi is inaptly translated into the English language as gods, goddesses, demigods, and deities. It was only much later that greater numbers of arriving migrants associated greater significance to Indra, who otherwise did not have much role in the Sanaatan Dharam practiced by the peace-loving and non-violent Dravaerd. However, as the settlers started to meld with them socially, to give continued equal social and spiritual rights Dev Indra was established alongside the concept of "Trimoortee," the four-faceted emblem of Brahma, Shiva, and Vishnu. Indra lived a life of luxury in paradise but was never revered as Shiva and Vishnu because he had a highly sensuous nature and was constantly at war, misusing his powers against humanity. The supposed Supreme Being Brahma was believed to be the source of "Light" and the creator of the universe. There were many other intermediaries and minor Dev and Devi of the Dravaerd origin, a concept rooted in

Sanaatan Dharam, before the arrival of the nomadic tribes. It was only later on that the list grew to millions when the subsequent Aarya took over the administrative roles. The titles of Dev and Devi were mostly conferred upon kShatriya, Brahman, and other accomplished members of the society.

As the newly arrived immigrants were from regions of higher altitudes and colder climates, they were of lighter complexion compared to the people of the northwestern valley of the Seven Rivers with its longer days, mostly sunny and warm climate year-round, and outdoor occupations. With the passage of time, the immigrants organized their life alongside the natives amicably and happily without distinction. As the immigrants mixed further with the indigenous Dravaerd population through marriages they too came to be called Hindu, as well as Aarya. These immigrants and their accepting hosts, socially woven together through marriages and trade relationships, ultimately merged genetically. The concept of Brahma, Shiva, Vishnu, and Indra strengthened the Sanaatan establishment, cemented the newly formed society, and over centuries the new ideology emerged as a culture popularly known as Hinduism.

The nomads might have emigrated from the land beyond the Hindu Kush, but the term "Aarya" as a complimentary title given to them by the Dravaerd has its roots in Sanskrit, the language of the people living on the south and east of the Hindu Kush. During the development and evolution of a peaceful and content society, the natural environmental cycles involving the extinction of the river Saraswatee and with periods of flood and drought, the population started to drift towards the basin of the rivers Ganga* and Yamuna*, into the main expanse of the Indian subcontinent.

Seeing the continued success of the first immigrants, over the following centuries, opportunists using aggressive tactics started to invade Bhaaratvarsh instead of heading towards less fertile and rough terrains west of their homelands. These invaders took over the lands and governance of the people who were already living there peacefully. This changed the whole social and cultural structure of the region and altered the landscape forever with frequent invasions occurring thereafter. The natives living there for centuries were driven south and east along with a majority of the original immigrants who were already living happily as Sanaatan. The violent invaders and remaining settlers living in the northwestern territories seeking a respectable status also acquired the epithet of "Aarya" unlike the earlier migrants, inaccurately trying to portray themselves as a noble ruling class. As they did not have any other god except Indra, like their predecessors, they too followed the tradition of the original immigrants and accepted the practices of Hinduism. This also changed the platform of administration and their socio-religious practices. The progeny of the ruling class over the next few generations became sons of the soil. It is possible that so as not to stigmatize their newly acquired higher civil status, they completely severed their roots from their violent past. This could be a possible reason why there is no definite mention of their origins in the available Vedic literature. If they were migrants from Central Asia, as commonly believed, proud of their deeds and roots, they had no reason not to freely expound their origin, at least in later versions of Vedic and Puraanic literature. It is more likely that they were not foreigners at all, but just another distinctive community that had always lived alongside Dravaerd in the valley of the Seven Rivers, had adventurous nature, and it was these high spirited people who assailed across to west of the Hindu Kush.

Within the newly consolidated society, the higher-ranking Aarya through acts of violence became Rajas and Maharajas. This marked the dawn of a new era with the rise of a new culture. In addition to the existing Vedic establishment, there was the beginning of new schools of thought. Very likely, the Vedic literature was also modified and expanded to create newer spiritual treatises such as The Upanishads (800–400 BCE) and much later The Vedanta, to conclude the Vedic System. The new scholars compiled numerous semi-fictional epic tales known as Puraan (ancient texts). The Puraanic texts presented a purposeful exposition of recent history with layers of fiction designed to bio-mythologize the characters of the current and past rulers and their ancestors. It comprised a network of moral tales about royal characters, their feats and follies, and their intimate social and spiritual relationship with both ancient Vedic and newly created gods and goddesses. The object was to develop indelible popular psychology encouraging trust, faith, and loyalty among the citizens towards the rulers and the administrators, making those fictitious characters immortal religious figureheads.

Much of the oral tradition learned by rote and disseminated among the citizens as "Shrutee" (a transcendental revelation or an experience perceived by the ears) started to be preserved as written manuscripts to pass down through generations in the form of hard copies, as writing became a routine media of communication by 300 BCE. It should not come as a surprise to anybody that during this period the ruling class may have used its authority to make changes to the Vedic literature and interpolated material of historical interest in their favour, expressing their heroic and humanitarian deeds. During these prosperous times also appeared the infamous everyday reference compendium of "Manu-Smriti," a legal social and religious memorandum, for the common citizens to civilize (regulate and organize) the society to serve the interests of the high-ranking citizens and, to establish a decision-making algorithm through the social hierarchy.

There was already in existence a social hierarchy within the Sanaatan social practices among the Dravaerd based on skills and level of education without bonds of hierarchical categorization. The ancient Dravaerd community was divided into four groups:

(1) Rishi-Muni were writers, scientists, philosophers, and mentors to Brahman, royal families, and other prospective citizens. Rishi-Muni residing outside the city boundaries operated centres of education called Gurukul. Without discrimination, the pupils were resident scholars throughout their juvenile, adolescent and early adult years up to the age of 25, and served as a family to the presiding guru.

(2) Brahman had advanced knowledge specializing in two or more of the Vedic texts, performing religious rites for all members of the society, including the royal families.

(3) Vaishya formed a class of traders, merchants, skilled workers; and

(4) kShuderr meaning insignificant citizens, below the poverty line, of partial or compromised mental abilities, engaged as cattle-herders and in other semiskilled and menial activities, such as working in the fields and everyday environmental maintenance.

The entitlement was based on the level of education and skills rather than familial hierarchy, although due to heterogeneity of financial status and lack of self-driven enthusiasm there was a rise and fall of social status within these categories. It was only in the post-Vedic period that the ruling class defined themselves as warriors and acquired the title of kShatriya (meaning bearer of the battlefield; which is different from the current term Khatree, which was very likely introduced during the Mughal period, meaning a bookkeeper in a treasury or a business), and became the torchbearer and protector of the other three ranks of the society, acting as the guardian of the civilization. In the existing classification, the new rulers could not place themselves above their gurus, mentors, and priests as superiors; therefore they interpolated their position between Brahman and Vaishya. During the post-Vedic period, the community of Rishi-Muni was not considered as a regular citizenry. They did not participate actively in the everyday life of society. The Brahman carried out everyday rituals for royals and other citizens. As the educational structure changed over time, the class of Rishi-Muni completely disappeared, leaving four of the five social classes for ritualistic, legal administrative, business, and communal purposes.

By the fourth and fifth millennia BCE, Aarya over multiple generations altered much of their lifestyle significantly but did not change some of their social behaviours such as eating and drinking habits to adopt indigenous vegetarianism and the avoidance of intoxicants, including the famous Soma drink. The governance practices of the ruling Aarya brought long-lasting changes within the northwestern communities of Bhaaratvarsh. The earlier nomadic migrants had easily accepted the social, cultural, and legal practices of the hosting Dravaerd, unlike later hostile assailants from across the Hindu Kush who entered directly via well-carved-out routes and the Khyber Pass. The defending native Dravaerd lacked the necessary fighting skills to defend their interests. They considered intense social oppression, cultural differences, and the rigid social divides obstructive to their prosperity and an ever-increasing threat to the longstanding autonomous indigenous society. They were ultimately forced to move further to the south and east of the civilization they had built in the land of Greater Punjab, to maintain peace with the co-existing aggressive class of Aarya and escape from seasonal invaders on the northwestern frontier, a process that continued until the reign of Maharaja Runjeet Singh, which extended over most of ancient Punjab, from Khyber Pass to Satluj River.

The Sanskrit language and its dialects spoken all over the northwestern sub-Himalayan plateau were not those of migrant communities out of Central Asia and further west. In their homeland, they may have had either Latin or other Latinized spoken languages and similar scripts. However, it is unlikely that the original nomadic settlers were literate. These landless herding communities were only interested in regions where they could develop and practice their survival skills. They could not have found a better place than what they discovered in the fertile valley of the Seven Rivers.

It is possible that Norse had its roots in Central Asia. The Nordic adventurers and aggressors considered themselves warriors and started to spread westward across the deserts of Central Asia and Asia Minor. They finally reached the northern coast of the European mainland in Scandinavia, to continue their violent adventures as Vikings across Europe. In addition to being skillful traders and master craftsmen able to cross large expanses of ocean, the Norse Vikings were also bloodthirsty, killing, raping, and pillaging regions extending from the eastern coast of North America to the Black Sea and Constantinople. The remaining mixed communities that settled in the Persian region became the people of present-day Iran. Neither the Nordic people nor the Iranians are "Aarya" in the true sense of its meaning in Sanskrit. The Devnaagri script is related neither to Latin nor Persian, Arabic, Cyrillic, or existing languages of Turkestaan. The same can be said of currently prevalent Dravaerd languages. Sanskrit was very distinct as a language of the literate during the Vedic period. In this respect, the Devnaagri script is unique and had always been a language of the elite and literate few of the valley of the Seven Rivers civilization, reserved for academic and Vedic literature. Over time, with the introduction of a rigid system of ranks and classification in society and the loss of the oral tradition, poorly educated and uneducated citizens became completely ignorant and lost the use of Sanskrit. They remained in the dark once daily incantation of the Vedic hymns receded into written and printed versions available only to those educated in the Sanskrit language.

As mentioned above, the reason certain words found in Sanskrit are similar to that of Latinized languages is the result of its development as a language of educated host and migrant communities. The reason many languages that are spoken in Bhaaratvarsh as well as Sanskrit, Persian, Latin, Greek, English, and German, all with very different alphabets and spoken words, have been lumped into a single group as Indo-European or Indo-Germanic by scholars is because of some similarities in their grammar rather than the script, and their origin on either side of the Hindu Kush range. The inclusion of Latinized vocabulary in Sanskrit is not surprising, given that throughout history the immigrant and the hosting communities over time do tend to merge socially and share languages. The most recent such example is the English language. This does not mean that in another thousand years many of the languages of the Indian subcontinent could be lumped together as Anglo-Indian with British English the origin of the included languages.

Once the hospitable Dravaerd and other communities of the Seven Rivers were separated from the Aarya by divisive administrative policies and social segregation, the Dravaerd also developed a very rigid social classification to exclude communities of mixed marriages. What was noticed by later invaders of the subcontinent was a deep divide between the diverse population extending from north to south and east to west. It became very easy for the new invaders, traders, and settlers like the Huns, Afghans, Mughals, and British, to take full advantage of people driven by socio-religious divisions. This social chaos has continued to this day obstructing the growth and prosperity of the united yet not very united independent Bhaaratvarsh.

It would be inappropriate to celebrate the alien tribes of men-at-war out of Central Asia (Turkestan) or further afield as "Aarya," and to erroneously describe them as wise, civil, or noble. The word "bruubraaH" in Sanskrit, meaning stammering or gibberish, does sound similar to the word barbarian, which in Greek means people whose language is difficult to understand. In this respect, the term barbarianism is not a misleading expression to describe aggressive invaders speaking a foreign language. All non-Romans, Greeks, and non-Christians were called barbarians. The Huns, a notorious fighting tribe coming from the east, reached the banks of river Danube. The Huns' Empire paralleled the Roman Empire in its power and strength.

The Vandals, the wanderers, were Germanic farmers who willfully destroyed anything beautiful, venerable, or worthy of preservation. They were pushed out of Europe by the Goths, who were nomadic fierce men-at-war. These nomadic tribes had a travelling existence. The Goths too were a Germanic tribe, who invaded the Roman Empire. They were split into two, east and west of the Danube by the Huns as Ostrogoth and Visigoth respectively. The Vandals and the Goths, who converted to Christianity in the fourth century, were the followers of the priest Arius, who was not a Catholic. These Germanic tribes came to be called Arian, a homophone of the word Aryan. They were Arian or Aryan, not Aarya, as Hitler and many German scholars liked to believe. The Arians believed in the doctrine of Arius of Alexandria, who taught that Jesus Christ was not of the same substance as God the Father, but certainly a superior human being rather than a divine as believed by the Catholics. The Sanskrit term "Aarya" does not fit even remotely given the context in relation to the Germanic tribes assailing into Europe against the Roman.

The chance finding of the horse as an animal of strength and speed was not a godsend for the savages from Central Asia, who used it as a war machine. Iron embedded in asteroids striking the Earth was not a godsend to make weapons and kill other human beings. The discovery of radioactive material does not mean it should be used as a weapon for mass human destruction and believing that war is a means to hasten material and scientific progress indicates the poor intellectual nature of human beings with such thoughts. To brutally kill human beings is a pathological behaviour that pertains to a lack of natural social or moral responsibility to demonstrate a friendly association with other human beings as well as other living creatures. Aggressive invasions by humans of foreign lands cannot be considered analogous to the natural survival instincts of animals, who rush out in search of salt licks, such as buffalo across the American continent. The ultimate goal of an invading force is to strike fear and inflict inhuman physical injury. The invaders kill to conquer lands in a lust for power and material wealth under the pretext of bringing in a new era of their kind of organized civilization (see appendix). All invaders oppress and try to educate the natives about the wrong and right ways of their own culture and to destroy the culture and language of the indigenous peoples. All the entitled nobles and royals, without exception, were terrorists and bloodthirsty, and their descendants have their roots in such pathological behaviours. Warriors were primarily trained to wage war against others to serve their self-interest, not for the betterment of humanity.

The same is true even today of nations with highly organized systems of annihilating weapons and collaborative militarized multi-national security machinery. Astonishingly, human beings possessing highly developed intellects have failed to understand the very simple principle of non-violence. The rivalry among violent people is motivated by with material wealth, which defines their religious and moral values and causes them to hurt each other physically and mentally. Even more interesting is to learn about the chaos caused by the so-called civilized and developed nations of Europe and North America that have created huge economic differentials around the world through enforced slavery, resource transfer, and oppressive colonialism. The simple chemistry of gunpowder used to make firecrackers by the Chinese has been transformed into lethal missiles and sophisticated instruments are designed to deliver it. After nearly 500 years of causing irreparable chaos and misdeeds, they are now busy apologizing and reconciling. They work with both a hammer (political and military force) and an anvil (human aid) to drive in their nails (supply of weapons) to feed and create new conflicts, the purpose not to mend but to mend and break time and again the world they broke in the first place.

At the same time, to prevent equitable global growth, they hold the economic reins tightly, paralyzing the physical and mental ability of the broken peoples through an organized system of global aid, and perpetuating economic globalism predominantly to their own benefit in every aspect of life. The highly paid foreign-aid workers, non-governmental organizations, charity employees, and volunteers are members of a new breed of political functionaries whose goal is to serve poor nations. It is an act of penance for the cruel and domineering behaviour of their ancestors over the last five centuries, but one which is proving deleterious to the development of these very same nations.

2. Alexander of Macedonia – Alexander was famous for his "amazing" capability of organizing a well-trained army. He besieged and plundered the most prosperous parts of northern Africa and Central Asia. The roots of his courage and cruel enthusiasm lay in his ambitious mother, Olympia, who called him the son of Zeus, to retaliate against his father Philip II, the ruler of Macedonia and parts of Asia Minor. The idea that Alexander was indestructible was embedded in his mind by the declaration of Delphi—"You are invincible, my son"—and these words of wisdom led him to terrorize and kill human beings not only in his homeland of Macedonia but across Asia up to the province of Punjab in Bhaaratvarsh. At the time, the Persian Empire extended from Greece to Sogdia (Tajikistan) and Bactria (Afghanistan). It was the creation of an Empire at the cost of human lives that brought Alexander the title of "the Great". Another terrorizing king, Cyrus I, who ruled between 548 and 529 BCE, is often glorified with the spurious title of "the Great," and it was further extended to his descendants. The genesis of such an ideology lay in the Akkadian (Acadian) king, Sargon the Great, the world's first emperor, who raised a huge army to conquer his neighbours, rule over their lands and peoples and demanded part of their hard-earned wealth as taxes.

The time was right for Alexander to take command of the large, well-trained standing army of 25,000 built up by Philip II to take over Greece, the rest of Asia Minor, and Persia. The gift of armed forces in waiting provided Alexander momentum to fulfill his dream to conquer the known world. Alexander was one of several children of Philip II, schooled as a pupil of Aristotle. Not content with the throne of his father and Greek territories, in 334 BCE he made thrusting advances across Asia Minor, Syria, and Egypt, following the assassination of Philip II. By the age of 25, he had conquered central regions of Persia. He marched along the Oxus River, and via the Wakhan corridor between Pamir and the Hindu Kush Mountains reached the Sindhu River extending his reach nearly 11,000 miles from home. He and his fighting men, trained to kill, rape, and pillage, acquired enormous experience in strategically mounting fresh attacks to cause human and material destruction of invaded territories. Each victory empowered him further, which encouraged him and his "well-oiled" military force to frighten and coerce humanity across three continents.

Alexander's regime began close to home, butchering 6,000 Thebans, selling 20,000 of them as slaves, and razing Thebes to ground. Upon reaching the far end of the Persian Empire, his campaigns on either side of the Wakhshu (Oxus) River resulted in the massacre of more than 150,000 troops of Bactria and Sogdia. These kinds of massacres continued, killing hundreds and thousands, probably amounting to a million or even more by the time he died in Babylonia, in 323 BCE. He launched his final assault in May 326 BCE on the east bank of river Sindhu, slaughtering more than 20,000 infantry and 3,000 cavalries and killing two sons of King Purus/Porus of the northwestern frontier kingdom of Bhaaratvarsh.

Does this make Alexander great? It does not. He felt no remorse for killing human beings. Monuments were erected and conquered cities renamed as Alexandria in his honour. All this was built upon the pointless sacrifice of human beings and the sweat and blood of indigenous people. Upon the death of his favourite commander Hephaestion, the embittered Alexander demonstrated his labile psyche by razing Asclepius, being upset with medical men. However, it was the death of his horse Bucephalus ("ox head") that plunged him into grief for the love of his animal rather than his own kind. His advances into Bhaaratvarsh were stalled by heavy monsoons and the swollen Beas River in Punjab. The proliferation of mosquitoes and malaria defeated him, forcing his return to Persia. Plutarch states that "the battle of the River Jhelum had blunted their courage and made them determined not to advance any further into India." His forces were also deterred by large, fierce elephants in the kingdoms beyond Beas that shattered the prospect of Alexander, a cruel being in human skin, of reaching the east coast of Bhaaratvarsh.

There was great relief among his soldiers who hoped to return home alive to their families. Alexander took a U-turn back to Persia via the River Sindhu, abandoning plans to reach the farthest end of Bhaaratvarsh, and headed towards Babylonia to attack Arabia. When Alexander reached Susa in 324 BCE, he married Barsine, the eldest daughter of Darius, and Parysatis, the youngest daughter of Artaxerxes III. Earlier in the spring of 327 BCE, he had married Roxanne (Rukhshana from Wakhshana, origin from Wakhshu) of Sogdia. These marriages and those of his commanders and Greek soldiers were not true signs of human and cultural affinities but worldly-wise acts, political demonstrations meant to link the Greeks to the Persian bloodline. While Roxanne was pregnant with his child, Alexander at the age of 33, on June 10, 323 BCE, died not as a warrior or a hero in a battle but of illness. It is very likely that he had cerebral malaria, as it is said that during preparations to attack Arabia he developed a fever and lost the power of speech. Roxanne, carrying his legal heir, ordered the extermination of his other wives and all possible contenders to the throne in Greece. In August 323 BCE, she gave birth to Alexander IV. During the struggle of succession, murderous rivalries spread all over Greece, Persia, Egypt, Syria, and Asia Minor. For almost 40 years, the legacy of violence generated by the evil-spirited Alexander led to further loss of human life throughout his fragmented empire, leaving behind devastation like a sad senseless terrorist.

Antipater, who ruled Greece and Asia Minor, died in 319 BCE, and his son Cassander acquired regency and executed Olympia, the mother of Alexander, in 317 BCE, then imprisoned Alexander IV and executed him and Roxanne. Alexander and his well-trained mobile and violent military force had woven a brittle empire that was bound to crumble, and so it did. He did not contribute anything to the development and progress of humanity. All those cities renamed Alexandria are lying in heaps of dust without any believable traces of Greek architecture. These already well-established cities were no more than campsites to launch future invasions further east, in search of greater wealth and the mythological land of "Golden Fleece." One ambitious person's aggression and violence born at the behest of a vicious mother caused untold atrocities for more than fifty years on three continents with the fall and rise of his power-hungry generals, and finally death of his own family. The carnage also included the death of a blameless unaccountable number of horses and elephants.

The embalmed body of Alexander was finally put to rest in the capital of Macedonia, Agae, with grandeur under the crushing weight of precious objects stolen from the conquered lands. The famed visitors to the remnants of his funerary were none other than future terror-striking kings and commanders, including Julius Caesar. They came to pay homage and fuel their ambitions to perturb thriving humanity and to become great like the prototype, Alexander the Great! The ambition and frenzy of Alexander taught likeminded men that they could take away the land and freedom of peace-loving and enduring people. Romans went out to kill and civilize others in their ways. Norse Vikings invaded Europe to gather wealth and, Normans invaded England to capture land and rule upon the English. British left their homes as seafarers and traders to be where the Sun was shining, with the same dream as Romans to civilize and indoctrinate others and deceive natives with their diplomatic policies to tax and steal resources to develop their homeland. Others to join these ranks were the Spanish conquistadors, Portuguese, Dutch, French, Germans, Mongol Genghis Khan, Ottomans, and the Mughals. Most recently among others is Hitler of Germany, who created the Second World War and holocaust, Japan invaded China and China invaded Tibet at the cost of human life and the USA used a nuclear weapon to cause human destruction and immense misery. Unfortunately, wars and the building of empires fill the pages of world history at the cost of human life and other carnage. The leading commanders and generals of these nations can be easily classified as psychopaths, suffering from extreme mental eccentricity to kill humans, animals, destroy other nations, and plunder wealth. None of them can be glorified with the title "Great." The only human beings who deserve to be called "Great" are Mohandas Karam Chand Gandhi of Bhaaratvarsh and Nelson Mandela of South Africa, who respectively fought the British and the Dutch for the freedom of their people without violence and weapons.

Guru Gobind Singh raised his sword out of necessity against the Mughals for the rights of the people of Bhaaratvarsh. He never had a dream to conquer a slice of his nation for the Sikhs. Unfortunately, violence begets violence and therefore he resorted to violence to curb the violent attitude of Aurangzeb. In retaliation, he lost his whole family and life. Guru Gobind Singh never attained the title "The Great," because his focus was to gain socio-religious rights for his fellow citizens rather than an empire. Of course, the sword he raised against the Mughals perpetuated further violence in Punjab under the command of Banda Singh Bahaadur, who too met violent death and the decapitation of his young son.

3. Ardaas – It means to make a request, petition, or beg the Supreme Being. In Sikhism, it is a set prayer at a closing congregational ceremony and daily worship in the Gurudwaras, the places of worship. The prayer is performed by one of the attending priests and the attendees stand up in a pleading poise. A standard structure of the Ardaas has three parts. The first part recites the virtues and glorious character of the ten Sikh Gurus, from Guru Nanak Dev to Guru Gobind Singh. The opening sentences are from Chandi-Ki-Vaar in the Dasam Granth (an extensive compilation of entire literary works of Guru Gobind Singh). The second segment enumerates the trials, tribulations, and triumphs of the Sikh people and the Khalsa soldiers. The third and concluding piece is a salutation to the Supreme Being, "Wahey Guru," and a joint appealing invocation by congregates. The tradition of Ardaas was ascribed by Guru Gobind Singh as a means of daily invocation of the Supreme Being, appraisal of the teachings of the Gurus, and remembrance of the martyred Khalsaa. It is possible that some of its narration has changed since it was first started by the tenth Guru; however, its opening couplet has remained strictly the same. Finally, at the very end, the priest announces individual petitions, blessings, celebrations, and disbursement of charities.

4. Ashoak of Patliputrr – In Sanskrit, "A-Shoak" means without remorse and grief. He was the grandson of Chandragupta Maurya, the founder of the Maurya Dynasty, who ruled most of the Indian subcontinent. The Chandragupta Maurya was raised, mentored, and trained to be an emperor by Chanakya (Kautilya) about the same time Alexander was heading towards Persia. The Ashoak killed his half-brother Susima, eldest son and apparent heir to their father Bindusara, and ruled a well-established empire between 288 and 232 BCE. Buddhist literature describes the Ashoak as a person of bad temper, a wicked nature, and someone bloodthirsty for power. To include in his empire the land of Kalingaa, the present-day eastern coast state of Odisha, Bhaaratvarsh, he mounted a fierce attack and conquered it in 260 BCE. The war of Kalingaa resulted in nearly 200,000 deaths and immense destruction. Despite what his name and nature mean, seeing the loss of human life he felt great empathy and self-reproach. Observing the virulent power of war to cause such destruction transformed the brute in him into a benevolent patron of Buddhism. He became a protagonist of non-violence, and his patronage led him to send his son Mahinda and daughter Sanghamitra as missionaries of Buddhism to the southern part of the Indian subcontinent and Sri Lanka. At the same time with his support, the Buddhist monks travelled wide and far, which led to the expansion of Buddhism outside the Indian subcontinent into Central Asia and China.

The Ashoak is remembered for erecting pillars and edicts all over his empire. The inscriptions carved on these pillars are the only authentic sources depicting the way he changed completely after the lethal war of Kalingaa. He maintained strong armed forces to defend his territories, developed cordial relations with kingdoms of the south, and the post-Alexandrian kingdoms in the north-west part of Bhaaratvarsh. He continued to possess a dynamic temperament, living a subdued lifestyle, and resolved to serve his subjects kindly. He founded hospitals for his people and also for animals. He stopped cruelty against all animals and preached compassion and moral virtues as part of his civil administrative principles. As a practicing Buddhist, he built commemorative mounds, Stupas, and monasteries. This dramatic change brought in a new era of benevolence and non-violence but it became very complicated to control the political administration of a vast and diverse empire. Slowly new internal political and foreign policy ideologies undermined the strength of his armed forces, and all active armed conquests were stopped. He died in 238 BCE.

Atop every pillar, now called an Ashoaka Pillar, was a sculpture of four heads of Asiatic lions back to back, facing in four geographical directions, representing imperial rule and the kingship of Siddharth, the Gautam Budh, the founder of Buddhism. After the exit of the British, the Republic of India, Bhaaratvarsh, adopted the four-lion-headed apex of the Ashoaka pillar as her national emblem. At the base of it on the right is a bull and on the left a horse. In the centre is a wheel with 24 spokes to represent the day and night cycle, called Ashoak Chakker.

5. Babr Mirza (1483–1530) – Zahir Uddin (defender of the Faith) Muhammad Babr (meaning lion or tiger in Persian) Mirza was among the slayers of the human race. He proved no less than the tyrant Temoor-lang, "the lame." Babr was born in Andijan, Fergana valley (Uzbekistan) on 14 February 1483. He was the fourth-generation grandson of Temoor.

Despite the 800-mile-long Hindu Kush Mountain range with its peaks exceeding 7000 metres that separated the rich fertile valleys of Amu Darya (Oxus River) and Sind Darya (Indus River), it was the civilization, culture, and wealth of Bhaaratvarsh that appealed to both the famished nomads and ambitious warring clans for thousands of years. Temoor, a Sunni Muslim, who governed a tribal confederacy between 1347 to1360, was not one of the Mughal Khans of Mongolia. Mughals were fundamentally Shamanists and were extremely slow to accept Islam and Sharia. He was a puppet to the ruling Chagatai Khan of Mughalistan, however, and in the late 1360s he took over the lands across both sides of the Amu Darya. Temoor called himself the "sword of Islam". He began the holy war as a jihad to expand his territory and prevailed over the royal Mughal Khan women in forced marriages. Despite these criminal marital relationships, he could not acquire the title of Khan, as he was not from the same lineage as Chengez Khan. As a child, he raided travelers, and during 35 years of invasive expeditions, he and his forces killed 17 million people, which testifies to his lifetime of psychopathic behaviour. His expeditions extended into China, Tibet, and serious incursions into Hindostaan. It was in 1398 that he captured Dilli (Delhi), ruled by Sultan Naseer Uddin Mahmood Shah Tughlaq. Before entering Dilli he executed 100,000 captive Hindus. His army built towers out of heads of the killed to celebrate his victory. He succeeded in looting one of the richest cities in the world to fill his bags and carts. He left behind chaos and suffering, a nation consumed by emotional, mental, and physical exhaustion for the next one hundred years. He returned home to continue his expedition into Christian Armenia and Georgia. He declared himself a ghazi, "warrior of Islam."

After the mid-fifteenth century, most of the territories of Turkestan, Khorasan, and Kabul, on either side of the Hindu Kush Mountain range were battlefields for gangster-style skirmishes between half-a-dozen ruling descendants of Chagatai Khan and Temoor Mirza. These two tightly knit clans had consanguineous relations to concentrate their corrupt psychopathic behaviour. Babr was born to Omar Shaikh Mirza and Qultuq Nigar Khanum. He joined the struggle to regain the Samarkand and Fergana valleys ruled by his ancestors during his adolescence. In 1501, immediately after gaining them, Babr lost them again to Muhammad Shaibani Khan, an Uzbek, and as a fugitive crossed the Hindu Kush Mountains. In 1504, with the help of his close family, loyal Baegs and warriors, Mughal hordes, and other tribes, he practically walked into Kabul. He could only get Samarkand back after Shaibani Khan was killed by Shah Ismail Safavi in 1510. In 1526, Babr turned his attention towards Hindostaan, his final frontier, and ultimate lifetime dream, after Samarkand. At the time, Greater Punjab and the plains of Ganga were ruled by Ibrahim Lodi and Rana Sangha, a Hindu Raajpoot, who ruled Raajputanaa (Rajasthan). Babr defeated Ibrahim Lodi and captured Dilli in the first battle of Panipat to establish his rule. The dithering and confused Rana Sangha first decided to align with Babr, and later with the Afghans to force Babr out of Hindostaan. However, the Raajpoot were uprooted in 1527 and Rana Sangha was allegedly poisoned by his own men.

Babr Mirza as a patriarch and believing his Temoor lineage disapproved of and refused to be recognized as a Mughal. This indicates the flaw in the historical label of Mughal Hindostaan and that it would be wrong to continue to call the rule of the Temoor Dynasty the Mughal dynasty. To the north and west of the Hindu Kush Mountains were Mongols, Persians, and Europeans and in the East were the Dravaerd, Arya, and other tribes of Bhaaratvarsh. Tartars and Turks were hybrid of Mongols and Europeans; Mongols and Persians bred into Tajiks, and descendent of Turks and Persians became the Uzbeks. The people on the east side had completely different physiognomy from that of the west side. The army of Babr consisted of Barlas and Chagatai Mongols, Persians, Arabs, and Afghaans. The reason for his success was good relations with Mughal Ottomans, who provided him matchlocks and cannons, which gave his forces extra confidence to scare the Afghaans and the Hindus. He was brutal and tyrannical and so were his loyal Baegs and commanders. In his biography, "Babur Nama," he exposes his psychopathic behaviour, the way he graphically illustrates the massacre of combatants and benign civilians. He praised and held Allah accountable by saying, "Out of His own favour and Mercy, the Most High has made a day of triumph for us." As if he was the torch bearer of Allah and graciously given the right to act against humanity to secure a special place in Paradise as a reward. By their very nature Turks, Mongols and other tribes were distrusting of each other and disloyal to their siblings. Frequently, they behaved like a pack of street dogs, fighting and killing each other to gain small territories. There is no man more evil than one who has the name of God or Allah on his tongue with Satan residing in his heart; and there is no person more corrupt than a political leader who takes the counsel of a religious leader to govern a nation.

Guru Nanak Dev, in 1526, witnessed the invasion and massacre caused by Babr. He described crisply the current and aftermath state of the Hindus in his hymns (Guru Granth Sahib on pages 360, 417, and 722). In "Tuzak-i-Babari" is found the description of Babr's invasion of Punjab and violence against Hindus and Sikhs; making towers out of skulls atop the mounds and hillocks in the province. The inhuman atrocities committed by the invaders led to introspection and it took nearly a century for the pacifism of the Sikhs to revolutionize the nation in the northwest and to develop the concept of Miri and Piri, sovereignty and sainthood. The situation forced the sixth Guru Har Gobind to militarize the Sikhs. The Zafurnamah of Guru Gobind Singh provides ample evidence of the insensitive behaviour of the Muslim occupying forces beginning in the eleventh century with the Afghaans and carrying on relentlessly for six centuries.

In October 2003, the Archaeological Survey of India undertook the excavation of Babari Masjid, in Ayodhaya, which revealed 1360 artifacts from a tenth-century Hindu temple and human activity that dates back to 1300 BCE. Despite the knowledge that their ancestors as citizens of Greater Punjab suffered enormously at the hands of Babr, in October 2005, the Pakistan government named its cruise missile "Babur" to honour him. He is a national hero in Uzbekistan. Temoor and Babr were war criminals; and to uphold as national heroes and honour them is a criminal act. All their works of art, whether literary or built of stone, are smeared in the blood of benign human beings, and are not worth even a mound of dirt. To acclaim them is to give the second life and to encourage the modern military to continue the manufacture and spread of destructive weapons.

A hardworking ant that carries a load and climbs the wall of a fort, falling sixty-nine times only to succeed at the seventieth attempt to feed other hungry ants (John C. Johnson, "Tamerlane and the ant," Stories, 2011) is not the same lesson of dedication as making multiple attempts to invade, kill and loot the wealth and natural resources of others. Such is the disgraceful history of this world, kept alive by annual celebrations and remembrances, instead of curbing the ongoing thoughts of violence and greed, through daily acts of meditation and prayer.

6. Bachitrr Naatak – It literally means an astonishing and enigmatic drama. This volume is considered a biographical portrayal of previous incarnations of Guru Gobind Singh, but there is a lot of doubt in the minds of scholars of its authenticity because it contains contradictory accounts related to the Guru. It is written in the literary style of Braj Bhasha, one of the northwestern dialects prevalent during his time. It describes the ancestral lineage of "Bedi" professing that the first Guru, Guru Nanak Dev, was a descendant of Vedic authorities. The sub-clan of "Sodhi" relates directly to Guru Gobind Singh, connecting him to mythological character Shree Raam Chander, and his sons Luv and Kush of the epic Raamayan, making him a direct descendant of royal kShatriya blood. The whole narrative is illogical and designed to establish in the mind of the readers that Guru Gobind Singh was the reincarnation of a Hindu god of a bygone era.

A careful perusal will reveal that the anonymous author of the script is motivated by Puraanic philosophy to bio-mythologize not only the life of the tenth Guru only but the whole hierarchy of Sikh Gurus in order to generate the impression in the mind of the readers that their writings are recent segments of Vedic literature. Acceptance of such a notion would mean falsifying the Sikh philosophy. For example, it describes that in his previous incarnation Guru Gobind Singh retreated to the Hemkunt (snow-laden) mountain range, a part of the Himalaya (Him-alaya) mountain range, where he meditated upon Shiv: and other gods and goddesses to acquire the gift of divine weapons.

After the passing of Guru Nanak Dev, the following nine Gurus always considered themselves enlightened souls as a result of his philosophy of how to live a better quality of life. Therefore, to merge and become one with Nanak they pronounced themselves as Nanak II, Nanak III, Nanak IV, and so on. This does not mean that they were transmutations or reincarnations of Guru Nanak Dev. It was simply to establish in the minds of the Sikh followers that they together formed a single corpus and believed in the same philosophy so as to direct the future institution of Sikhism to follow the same path as directed by Guru Nanak Dev without divisions within their community. To write such a bio-mythical account means fictionalizing the truth by transforming the reality of the Sikh history into what amounts to the latest chapter of Hindu mythology.

7. Bhanganee, Battle of – Bhanganee is approximately six miles north of the township of Paonta. In September 1688, the men of Guru Gobind Singh were ambushed by the joint forces of Hindu Hill Chiefs Raja Bheem Chand and Fateh Shah. This event is frequently referred to as the "Battle of Bhanganee." Guru's men defeated the organized preplanned ambuscade and returned to their camp victorious without much loss of life against a large force of the Hill Chiefs. The Battle of Bhanganee is given historical importance because it was the first encounter and decisive victory of the Guru over the Hill Chiefs. It raised the dignity and self-esteem of his meagerly equipped but courageous men. At the same time, it helped the Guru to understand the capability and loyalty of his men in the campaign against the Mughals.

8. Charkho taeg, Cyclical sword of time, and Sudarshan Chakker – All these terms more or less mean the same and refer to the unceasing concept of time since the beginning of the Universe in the form of the cycle of day and night and the passage of the seasons. Sudarshan Chakker has its origin in Sanskrit. Its literal meaning is "divinatory wheel or cycle (Chakker) of ideal foresight (Sudarshan)" leading to peaceful times ahead. The word "taeg" means a deeply curved sword. In Zafurnamah Guru Gobind Singh used the term "Charkho taeg" to represent the fast-moving cyclical pace of time and a circular weapon with a razor-sharp cutting edge as a defense against evil times and destructive human power. In Rig Veda, the use of the term Chakker symbolizes the wheel of changing times. For hopeful beings time takes care of the duality of good and bad, and has attributes to automatically destroy evil among humans.

The Sudarshan Chakker was originally described in reference to the god Vishnu. In the epic tale of Mahabhaarat, it was the sole weapon possessed by Shree Krishan, believed to be a reincarnation of the god Vishnu. The weapon operated as a fast-spinning missile, released only under dire circumstances with adequate warning to the struck individual. The instrument had self-returning capability like a boomerang. In Sanskrit, a ruler whose empire encompasses a very large landmass is given the title of Chakkervarty emperor, and major coins of such an empire had the imprint of a wheel with 16 spokes representing the number of subunits to add up to its total value. For this reason, one Indian rupee had sixteen Anna as its subunits.

The Khalsaa soldiers carried similar circular weapons called Chakkerum, 15 to 30 cm in diameter, with sharp outer borders, to throw at the enemy. The Khalsaa wore multiples of these ring instruments around their traditional tall-peaked conical turbans. Several Chakkerum(s) are still worn by some of the traditional Khalsaa members called Nihung Singh. They are always seen wearing the originally fashioned uniform of a soldier-saint, trained in traditional warfare techniques for demonstration during organized religious fairs and annual festivals in Anandpur. At present, seeing some of them with very tall and immense royal blue and saffron turbans seems to suggest more of a competitive spirit and the characteristics of a soldier-saint. They have regular families and participate in daily household and business activities while living in small towns and villages. They follow the Sikh principle of "live earnestly by the labour of two hands." The practice of begging and idleness was strongly condemned by all the Sikh Gurus. Guru Nanak Dev, following his self-directed long adventurous journeys finally settled in Kartaarpur, now in Pakistan. He returned to the life of a householder and cultivated his land until the end of life.

9. Dilli – Dilli is the original name of Delhi, which was a major city throughout the Mughal period. It has continued to be so as the capital of Bhaaratvarsh (India) after independence in August 1947. The older Mughal part of the city is called Old Dilli, which includes Laal Quilaa (red fort) and Jamia Masjid (mosque). The new extension of the city built during the British presence is called New Delhi. New Delhi includes the parliament houses, government buildings, administrative civil offices, and modern shopping centres. The origin of the name Dilli is uncertain. The root word is "Dil" meaning heart, so Dilli could mean "of the heart" or city with a heart. The ancient name of the region was Inderprasth, the capital of Pandav.

10. Ek-Lavaya – Ek-Lavaya is a less famed personality, who appears in the epic tale of Mahabhaarat symbolically as a sincere and plain character. His name stands for "focused single-mindedness." He was of a prodigious and undeviating nature. He was treated with prejudice by Aachaarya Drona, the mentor, and trainer of the royal princes of the ruling Pandav and Kaurav families. Ek-Lavaya was an aboriginal from Nishaadha clan and belonged to a Bheel tribal family. Fishing and hunting were their main occupations. However, his father Vyatraaj Hiranyadhanush was chief of the clan and a soldier in the army of regional king Jarasandh. The name of his mother was Sulekha.

Ek-Lavaya had heard about Aachaarya Drona and his tutelary ability as an enlightened instructor in high-ranking archery. When this proactive young man came of age, he decided to visit the school of Aacharya Drona. Ek-Lavaya was denied and rebuked on the ground that he was not a kShatriya and as an aboriginal person could not be accepted to learn the art of archery alongside the princes. He was not the only one to be rejected on the basis of his social status. Another character in the epic text of Mahabhaarat was Karan, born of an unmarried princess, Kuntee, later to be the mother of Pandav princes, who was also denied lessons by the Aacharya Drona because Karan after being abandoned was brought up in the family of an underprivileged chariot driver. Ek-Lavaya, dejected but not defeated by the discriminatory practice, possessed of a tenacious and resolute temperament returned to settle down in nearby woodlands. For him, Aachaarya Drona was still the best and most learned teacher of archery, even in absentia. As he had accepted Aachaarya Drona as his sworn guru, he built a mud sculpture of him and prepared his practice ground in front of it. He would sincerely meditate upon his chosen guru every morning before starting his practice. He was fully motivated and practiced hard to achieve his set goals.

One fine morning a barking dog interrupted his practice. Exasperated, Ek-Lavaya turned around from his target, shot half-a-dozen arrows at the dog, and filled its mouth with them to simply shut up the animal. Soon from behind the tall hedge appeared Aachaarya Drona and his princely pupils. All of them stood still, stunned by the demonstration of fine archery without actually hurting the dog permanently. Arjun, one of the Pandav princes, stepped forward to examine the mouth of the dog and was taken aback noticing that the mouth of the dog was free of any bleeding from the arrows. Ek-Lavaya instantaneously recognized the guru and the party of his princely pupils. He quickly posed himself in front of the guru in complete obeisance. Aachaarya Drona raised him on his feet and asked who his guru was. Ek-Lavaya replied pointing back at him, saying "you are my guru." Ek-Lavaya directed the guru towards the mud sculpture. The Aachaarya Drona and the princes were amazed because Arjun was considered the best archer in the kingdom. Arjun was taken aback because the guru had promised Arjun that he would be second to none, and as the royal trainer he would never divulge the divine knowledge of archery to anyone else.

Arjun felt challenged and Aachaarya Drona was concerned over the skills of Ek-Lavaya. The guru could not tolerate the challenge Arjun faced at the hand of an aboriginal. Aachaarya Drona told Ek-Lavaya that having accepted him as the guru for his inspiration and discipline to become proficient and adept in archery, accordingly he must be paid an honorarium as the proprietor of the talent in the form of this idol. According to Aachaarya Drona, Ek-Lavaya was in breach of his intellectual property and he must receive an appropriate emolument in return. Ek-Lavaya agreed to the request of his personal guru who had encouraged him, even in the form of an icon. In return, Aachaarya Drona demanded the right thumb of Ek-Lavaya to disable him, so that he could not hold and fire an arrow from his bow. Without reluctance, Ek-Lavaya pulled-out his dagger and amputated his right thumb, delivering it into the hand of his guru. The whole scenario left the kShatriya princes dumbfounded at the genuineness of Ek-Lavaya. Despite his disability, he turned out to be a master archer.

With his proactive nature, ability to teach himself, and absolute faith in the sculpted idol of his guru, Ek-Lavaya cultivated strength and ability to reach his defined goals. Beyond doubt, even if it is only a mythological tale, it demonstrates the potential of an idol to inspire and discipline a well-motivated person. In Bhaaratvarsh, according to the 2011 census, the descendants of "Adivaasi" (ancient inhabitants of the southeast tribes) formed 9 percent of the population of the country. In honour of Ek-Lavaya, the national government runs Ek-Lavaya Model Schools and the Karnataka State government confers the Ek-Lavaya award upon an outstanding sportsperson every year.

11. Five K's – The letters refer to five wearable items on one's person that signify a communal relationship to Sikhism. These were introduced in 1699 CE, on the day of Baisaakhi, when Guru Gobind Singh initiated the first five recruits of the Khalsaa force. To introduce uniformity within the ranks of the Khalsaa force, the Khalsaa men were asked to have unshorn beards and scalp hair covered with large royal blue turbans topped with one or more Chakkerum, wear a loose navy blue top shirt, a pair of white half-pantaloons, an iron wristlet, and a Kripaan, essentially a sword, as a weapon. This created uniformity and distinctiveness among the militarized Khalsaa soldiers in comparison to the Mughal forces, which were dressed in black with a hard skull cap underneath a headband. The Muslim soldiers frequently wore a trimmed chin beard without a moustache. However, wearing five items on one's person beginning with the letter K—Kaesh, Kaccherah, Kanghaa, Kardaa, and Kripaan/Kirpaan—is now uniformly accepted within Umritdhaaree (initiated) Sikh community. More frequently only one or more of these items are worn by almost every individual born into a Sikh family, whether boy or girl. But what exactly each item signifies and means to the wearer was not clearly defined and recorded for non-Umritdhaaree Sikhs in the long run. Wearing one of these items, particularly the wristlet, has become an outstanding external identifying marker even among Sikhs who are clean-shaven and do not wear turbans. However, the turban is not one of these five items. The turban with an aigrette was acquired as a regular feature of everyday dressage by Guru Gobind Singh to challenge the authority of the crown bearers and other royals. Since that time all Sikhs wore a turban to establish their prerogative over higher castes. Nevertheless, the turban remains the most readily visible part of everyday dress for men; and Umritdhaaree women too are seen wearing it.

The five items beginning with the Gurumukhi letter "Kka" or simply "K" are:
(1) Kaesh, naturally grown unshorn scalp and facial hair including other body hair.
(2) Kaccherah or kacchaa, a pair of loose-fitting knee-long pantaloons, made of white cotton material tied around the waist with a drawstring. It is a specially fashioned unisex design, worn by Umritdhaaree men and women. Originally, it was a regular garment for the Khalsaa soldiers designed for ease of lunging during combat and suited to regional weather conditions instead of Persian-Mongolian-style paejamah trousers. Now instead of traditional external bottoms, the present-day Umritdhaaree Sikh wears it as an undergarment in place of underwear.
(3) Kanghaa is a small traditional wooden comb usually kept engaged in the scalp hair under the turban after combing. In principle, its design allowed ease of its application so as to keep the Khalsaa hair tidy in a tress knot to prevent them from getting matted like that of ascetics when camping in the battlefield for long periods away from home. Now, apart from an Umritdhaaree, it is rarely carried by other members of the Sikh community.
(4) Kardaa is an iron wristlet worn by almost every Sikh man, woman, and child from the time of birth as a basic symbol of Sikhism. What exactly it signifies is not very clear but it is very popular, and pretty much a fixed wearable feature, despite the absence of other accepted items on one's person. Iron is a strong metal and represents strength. The intention behind introducing it was to bind the brotherhood of Khalsaa into a unified force. Secondly, as it was made to be worn on the right wrist, it reminded the Khalsaa soldier to raise his or her sword in the battle to strike only upon the enemy, and never against children, women, and the unarmed.

(5) Kirpaan is the Gurumukhi transformation of the Sanskrit word kripaan (kripa+aan), and means an instrument of pride and kindness, as opposed to its synonym talvaar (tal+vaar) which means a leveled strike or an equalizing vengeful strike in retaliation. For Khalsaa soldier it was not provided with the sole purpose to kill. The word "Kripa" means to shower kindness upon others, and "Aan" means pride free of ego. Guru Gobind Singh expected his Khalsaa to employ Kirpaan/kripaan to preserve life and to carry it formally was a matter of pride and honour for a Khalsaa.

12. Ganesh/Ganapati – Ganesh, the most worshipped chimerical divinity in Bhaaratvarsh, is an image of prosperity. An elephant head is an identifying feature, usually sitting on a stool with servings of fruits, flowers, and sweets indicative of contentment, good health, and prosperity. The presence of rats within the frame of the image suggests that they too freely enjoy the prosperity of the master and householder. The elephant is a vegetarian and does not have natural predators. It is associated with royals and represents a good life and a progressive economy. Lakshmi Devi, the goddess of wealth, is usually seen flanked by elephants on either side, performing a welcome shower for a rich harvest. A female elephant is called Gaja-Gamini. As the name suggests, she is a symbol of a matriarch, gender freedom, and sexuality.

No wonder the elephant head Ganesh is considered auspicious and holds a special place on the mantelpiece of most Hindu businesses and homes, wherever the Hindu community lives. This godhood represents multiple talents as an advocate of learning, numeracy, art, science, and writing skills. This masculine divine emblem is honoured at all kinds of initiations, particularly business ventures, to erase impediments, expel evil hindrances, and encourage entrepreneurs.

Ganesh does not exist in the Vedic texts of the Dravaerd during the time of the Seven River Civilization. The chimerical human figure Gajanar (male elephant) has an elephant head. It is believed to have first appeared during frequent alien assaults not much before the beginning of the Common Era. There was a need for an enormous and strong deterrent with a pleasant countenance to inculcate courage and intellectualism. At the time an elephant cavalry often led the army during an assault on invading forces, and the elephant face became an obvious choice of its original creator.

The stone carvings of Gajanar first discovered belonged to the second- and third-century Kushan dynasty. The concept was fully exploited as a means to encourage and empower society during the Gupta period (240–590 CE). This period marked the most prosperous period after the Seven River Civilization in Bhaaratvarsh, frequently referred to as the "Golden Age." There was a dire need of a matching icon depicting excellence, intellect, and wisdom for the furtherance of the new society on the rise. Prosperity and affluence were accompanied by plenty of wealth and charity, and with it came obesity and vanity among the progressive population. Ganesh became the ultimate iconic embodiment of all these human attributes. Ganesh acquired multiple appellations to honour the prosperity of the rich in society. Ganapati had a complete facelift with additional elements added to its appearance, raising the already revered icon to new eminence with the nickname of Lambodera, meaning hanging pot belly. Not surprisingly, the image transmuted to adapt to the needs of the society time after time. Otherwise, the most dominant designation is Ganesh, meaning lord of numeracy; Gana refers to the system of numeracy such as arithmetic (Ganit) and accounting and Ish means lord. Similarly, Ganapati means master of the numerical system. Ganesh or Ganapati is an inspiration and guide to numeracy, hence its great reverence in the Hindu business community.

According to Puraanic literature, Ganesh was a progeny of Dev Shiv, who resided in the snow-clad Kailaash Mountains, and his wife Perwatee, which means the Devi of highlands. This genealogical connection put Ganesh among the higher ranks of the Dev and Devi lineage. Ganesh even as a child was plump and chubby, much attached to his mother. He had a half-brother named Kartikay, son of a forest-virgin, Krittika. Once Kartikay teased Ganesh to compete with him to see who could go round the Earth faster, to which Ganesh agreed happily. They started together standing beside their mother Perwatee. Kartikay took off quickly at the final call by their mother to run. When Kartikay returned he found Ganesh already waiting beside the mother smiling at him. Obviously, Kartikay got very upset that how a chubby little child could beat him. Ganesh said very politely, "Brother, my whole world belongs where my mother is. Therefore, I only had to walk around her to win the race. In the process, you travelled around the whole earth. You must have acquired a wealth of wisdom and have returned home knowledgeable to start your new enterprise." Kartikay instead of feeling being cheated appreciated the wisdom of his younger brother.

Ganapati is known to be a Brahamachaari (an enlightened pupil), meaning a seeker of wisdom to become enlightened. This Sanskrit word had been inappropriately translated in English as meaning a celibate. Ganesh, other than his elephant head and neck, has four upper extremities, holding in each an elephant tusk (symbol of wealth), a food delicacy where the trunk is pointing (symbol of prosperity and satisfaction), with the third hand holding an axe (a weapon for self-protection) and the fourth hand an Ankush (an instrument with a spike and a hook to mind the elephant by its mahaut/mahout is an instrument of self-restraint) and a noose (symbolizing self-directed discipline and control to follow the path of righteousness). A serpent is variously placed around his neck symbolizing alliance with his father Shiv, around his belly representing insatiability, around the throne as stability, and around the ankle demonstrating unperturbed, peaceful, and even-tempered mobility. A variety of vehicles for the Ganapati are also well-thought-out by the designers to tie to individual levels of social status. It can be a snake, mouse, tortoise, ram, horse, lion, peacock, and even an elephant, representative of an individual's nature, speed, and glamorous standing in the community.

Ganesh is espoused to Buddhi, Siddhi, and Riddhi, meaning intellect, spirituality, and analytical logic respectively. Other associates represented in his consortium are Saraswatee (maiden excellence, goddess of learning, and music), Lakshamee (goddess of material wealth), and his mother Perwatee (Devi of mountains). As a result, the offspring are Keshav (prosperity), Labh (profit), Subha (auspicious dawn), and Santoshee (happiness and contentment). As Ganesh is endowed with a multitude of attributes, therefore his propinquity to disciples seeking all-round prosperity should not be surprising to anyone. It is a perfect and most versatile icon to possess, even if it does not leave the vicinity of his alma mater, the bounteous mother as a source of education and discipline. He was born of Devi of mountains to touch the peak of life.

It is important that the value of iconographic representation of God, Bhagwaan,

Ishwar, Dev, and Devi be fully understood by an adherent of religion who is not fooled by contrived religious practices. Icons are powerful instruments, not designed for the blind disciples of faith. It was because of the blind faith of the Hindus, fallen off the righteous path of Sanaatan Dharam, that Guru Nanak Dev was opposed to iconography, and Guru Gobind Singh like the other Sikh Gurus grew in favour of iconoclasm.

13. Ganga – Ganges, as written in English, is a corrupted pluralism of the name of the river Ganga. It has numerous streaming tributaries and drains a basin of about one million square kilometres as it flows in a southeasterly direction to the Bay of Bengal. Before emptying into the ocean, it finally bifurcates into two major distributaries, Hoogly and Padma Rivers, running through West Bengal and Bangladesh respectively. It remains a single large body of water dancing down the northern plains of Bhaaratvarsh. This enormous river has served inhabitants of the region since humanity first settled on its banks. The river has been revered as a female in gender and addressed as Ganga Devi. It has been given numerous names during its existence due to the abundance of historical developments along its course. Searching its bed would reveal enormous historical information and wealth.

Its lofty origin is 13,451 feet (4,100 metres) above sea level. Thousands of years ago, without aerial reconnaissance, it must have seemed to an observer to be falling out of the misty fog of the Himalaya Mountains as if descending from the heavens. The origin of Ganga at the Gangotri glacier, Gaumukh (face/mouth of a cow), has been known since before the Vedic period. These names better describe the character and importance of the river for those inhabiting her banks than what can be discerned now looking at her indescribably polluted fate. The cow was holy to the region's inhabitants long before the origin of Ganga Devi was discovered. The cow was important for providing her milk to the people and to name the origin of this enormous body of crystal-clear water emanating from the glacier Gaumukh was only appropriate. During her long course from the point of origin to discharge into the sea, her waters are tamed naturally. The water drops into a bucket-like receptacle underneath, which seems to be hung from the rainbow handle formed by its water sprays with sun rays shining through it, giving it the name of Kaman-dolu (rainbow-receptacle). Thereafter, to reduce the fluid pressure further, the multiple streams seem to be kissing the feet of Vishnu, rushing between his toes and controlling her frantic flow. Finally, her water is ejected, funneling through the spiraling tress-knot of the Shiv, winding around a mountain peak and celebrating her birth in the cool glow of the newly born crescent moon, then pouring out upon the northern plains of Bhaaratvarsh.

Thankless corrupt humanity filled with greed certainly reveres her, washes in her waters to get rid of their sins, and in return poisons her waters with all kinds of wastes. Does humanity take good care of the river? Of course it does not. The same humanity, numbering in the millions, which reveres her as a Devi, fills her 2,620-kilometre-long course (1630 miles including Bhagirathi at its origin to the Bay of Bengal) with feces, urine, wastewater, and in modern times suffocating plastic garbage. The ashes and cadavers of her disciples are then drowned in her holy waters to escape from the cycle of death and rebirth to achieve freedom from the earthly hell they leave behind and merge into her "heavenly" flow.

Despite the mind-cringing assaults Ganga Devi has to tolerate, she has survived because of her built-in biotechnical processes managed by fish, amphibians, and microbes. Her surface is graced by an abundance of solar power, and fast-moving currents at many places in the river all year round clear the dregs and detritus collected along the banks into the sea. Since the mid-1980s there have been plans to cleanse her waters but so far the project has been stalled by political players and religious masters acting in their own interests. Cleansing the holy waters of Ganga Devi from beginning to end and surface to riverbed is a colossal task, and without a well-thought-out scientific process, half-hearted attempts are a waste of financial resources. However, with human lockdown during the Covid-19 pandemic of the year 2020, the environment and the Ganga cleansed itself within a few weeks, without high-tech human intervention. Such is the power of nature. As long as the people of Bhaaratvarsh consider their terrestrial existence a Karmic punishment with their permanent abode on some divine planet, they will never able to achieve their goal to manage the environment around them. Immersing oneself in the polluted water of Ganga Devi is not a sure way to escape the phenomenon of death and rebirth or to prevent them from falling back to an earthly hell they have created themselves.

This divine river has suffered enough from the paradox of religious reverence acting in parallel to religious abuse. She has been suffocated by her beholders with their everyday waste. Ganga Devi desperately needs respite now and then to cleanse her polluted waters and prevent water-borne illnesses among her devotees and visitors.

One way to transform the fate of this significant waterway would be to transfer the management to multiple private developers to create a variety of water-based recreational activities and river cruises. To clean up the banks, all religious hubs need to be redesigned as private indoor crematoria. In addition, arrangements need to be made for the provision of piped water from the river for final ceremonies and religious bathing on special occasions in government-run or private low-maintenance indoor pools. The water thus used would only be released back into the lap of the Devi after treatment at water management centres along its banks. There is also a need for miles of green spaces and natural life with high-quality residential and business development along its banks from beginning to end. The revenue earned by each hosting state can be invested back into the inner city and suburban environmental development and recreational activities for the people. Nature will continue to cleanse her with built-in biotechnology.

14. Hanumaan – The name means imposing jaws. However, the appearance of Hanumaan is chimerical, with large jaws and blown-out cheeks filled with air, more or less looking like the face of a primate possessing a long tail. The first description of Hanumaan appears in the epic tale of *Raamayan*, when Shree Raam goes out in search of his wife Seetaa, abducted by the demon king Raavan of Lankaa, along with his younger brother Lakshman. Hanumaan and his brother form an alliance with them and recruit an army of forest primates, Vaaner (monkey), to help the two lone brothers get Seetaa back to Shree Raam.

There are many adventures of Hanumaan recounted in mythological texts. He was a child of a nymph, Anjana, and father Vayu, the Dev of wind. He had an inborn ability to fly and could metamorphose into a colossal stature or a tiny creature. During his childhood, once he tried to swallow the Sun when Dev Indra struck his jaw with lightning to cause irreparable injury. The injury left him with imposing jaws and his blown-out cheeks filled with air symbolize his desire to fly alongside his father Vayu. During the battle against Raavan, Lakshman sustained a grievous injury and lost consciousness. To revive him, Hanumaan flew from the southern tip of Bhaaratvarsh to Himalaya, to fetch a specific rejuvenating luminous fragrant herb requested by the attending Ayurvedic Vaidya (medical man). As he could not be sure of the specified herb, he returned carrying the whole mountain of luminous herbs. Hanumaan played a significant role in the battle between Shree Raam and Raavan. The impressed Hanumaan became a dedicated disciple of Shree Raam and Seetaa and a celebrated figure of devotion and reverence among the Hindus.

Hanumaan is one of the most worshipped religious celebrities in Hinduism. There are numerous temples dedicated to him in almost every town and city. He is usually seen kneeling in obeisance to Shree Raam and his wife Seetaa. He carries a large mace and is revered for his strength, courage, and celibacy. The idol of Hanumaan is held in high regard and worshipped by wrestlers as a source of inspiration and devotion to their sport. In temples his statues are painted red, demonstrating his unconditional spousal loyalty for Shree Raam and Seetaa, and he is seen holding his chest cage wide open, showing off their iconic image as a symbol of love for them in his heart. Hanumaan is a symbol of simplicity, devotion, servility, and strength.

15. Hari Singh "Nalwa" – Hari Singh was in the service of Maharaja Runjeet Singh from 1804 to 1837 CE. He was born in an Uppal family at Gujranwala in 1791. His father held a substantial estate there. Hari Singh was trained in horse riding and warfare techniques from an early age. Before the birth of Hari Singh, his grandfather, Hardas Singh from the town Majitha near Amritsar, was a recruit in the service of the Shuker-Chakia Misl, who lost his life in 1762 during combat. Hari Singh was initiated as a Khalsaa Sikh at the age of twelve and served Maharaja Runjeet Singh as a personal guard. The title of "Nalwa" was conferred upon him by the Maharaja as he had killed a tiger at an early age, as did the king Nal, as described in the Hindu Puraanic texts.

Hari Singh "Nalwa" established himself as a fearless soldier after a significant military campaign of 1807 to help incorporate the city of Kasoor, now in Pakistan, within the domain of Maharaja Runjeet Singh. Hari Singh under the command of Dewan Mokham Chand defeated Azim Khan; this was followed by a victory over the clans of Durrani and Barakzai. In 1813 he seized the fort of Attock, a major crossing over the river Sindhu (Indus), to subjugate its host Kutab Uddin Khan. He established himself as a leading soldier and got promoted to the rank of commander. After the death of Vazeer Shah Mohammad of Kabul in August 1818, Hari Singh arrived in time to occupy the territory between Peshawar and Kabul. He stayed back to consolidate his status in the region. After that Hari Singh "Nalwa" became a household name striking fear in Afghanistan as an invincible commander. He was portrayed as a symbol of terror among Afghan women and children. He founded the town of Haripur in present-day Pakistan. As commander-in-chief, he played a significant role in extending the borders of the Sikh Empire to the north beyond Kashmir including Ladhaakh, and the west up to Jamrud, next to the fortified entrance of the Khyber Pass. In his absence, Afghans always kept ready to return and strike back in order to acquire the fort of Jamrud and secure the Khyber Pass.

In 1837 Hari Singh, instead of being at the wedding of Nau Nihal, the son of Maharaja Runjeet Singh, stayed behind in Peshawar. Not realizing his presence in Peshawar, Shah Mohammad Khan of Kabul considered it an opportune time to attack Jamrud to take over the fort. Hari Singh quickly proceeded to Jamrud with his battalion stationed in Peshawar. During intense combat surrounded by Afghans, Hari Singh was badly wounded. Luckily, by that time reinforcements had already arrived from Lahore and managed to push back the Afghans towards Kabul. Hari Singh died at the Jamrud fort later that day. He died the death of a valiant soldier in action from his battle wounds. He was cremated in the Jamrud fort. Long after his death, in 1892, a resident of Peshawar, Babu Gujju Mal, built a memorial on the premises of the fort.

16. Kaashee – Also known by the names of Varanasi and Banaras or Benares. It is one of the oldest cities in the world and was a major centre of learning in the ancient land of Bhaaratvarsh. It is situated in the state of Uttar Pradesh, on the left bank of river Ganga, making it one of the most important sites of Hindu pilgrimages. This historical ancient city is now only a small part of Banaras and reference to it appears in *Rig Veda*. In Sanskrit the word Kas means "to shine," making Kaahsee the city of lights. The name Varanasi takes its origin from two tributaries called "Varuna" and "Assi," now barely flowing through the modern city's suburbs. The Bangla alphabet does not have the letter "V"; therefore people of the nearby state of Bengal called it Baranasi, which got contracted to Banaras. When the British first established themselves in Bengal, they pronounced and spelled the name Benares, corrupting the name of the city further.

17. Khalsaa – The root word is Khalis, via the Persian word Khalisah from the Arabic Kalis meaning pure or genuine. The category of Khalsaa among the Sikhs was organized by the tenth Guru Gobind Singh on Baisaakhi day in the year 1699 CE, at Anandpur. It was an act to encourage all "castes" and creeds to come together to rise and fight against Mughal imperialism. Those who willingly joined the organization were initiated into the theocratic militarized force, accepting his leadership as their Guru. The concept of the militarization of the Sikhs was originally conceived by his grandfather Guru Hargobind Rai following the martyrdom of his father Guru Arjan Dev under the rule of Mughal emperor Jahangir and disbanded following his death. The pioneering five Sikh men from various social ranks who entered Khalsaa Panth were Daya Singh, Dharam Singh, Himmat Singh, Mokham Singh, and Sahib Singh. Since that time the nature and function of this orthodox religious section of Sikhism have assumed a very different role. A subsection of it works as an active political party called Akaali in the state of Punjab, and many consider themselves part of an elite group within the Sikh community. The Akaali movement was started by Kartar Singh Jhabbar in the 1920s to reform and unify ritualistic practices in all the

Gurudwaras, including Golden Temple at Amritsar, under a single administrative body. The initiation ceremony of Khalsaa-hood is generally offered to both male and female adolescent Sikhs, and to non-Sikh persons who fully understand the purpose of becoming an Umritdhaaree. The participants must demonstrate the ability to learn and follow the tenets of the Khalsaa lifestyle, to live by five Sikh symbols, perform daily sets of prayers in the morning and evening, live lives of high morals, never consume intoxicants, and refuse to consume Halal meat.

18. Mai Bhago – In December 1705, Mai Bhago encouraged the Sikhs of her village, who had abandoned Guru Gobind Singh during the siege of the fort at Anandpur by the alliance of Mughal and Hill Chief forces, leading them to the village of Khidrana, now the town of Muktsar, where Guru Gobind Singh was waiting for the arrival of the Vazeer Khan of Sarhind with his forces. These men had abandoned the Guru due to the adverse physical and mental conditions facing the trapped Khalsaa soldiers because of inadequate supplies of water and rations. Before they could leave, the Guru had asked them to sign Bey-dawa, an indisputable memorandum of disloyalty and alienation under the circumstances.

Mai Bhago persuaded many other deserters encountered en route to accompany her to Khidrana. The Mughal forces had been hunting Guru Gobind Singh incessantly since he had left the mud fort at Chumkor. Upon reaching Khidrana, at the request of Mai Bhago, the Guru accepted the deserters back into the Khalsaa force and destroyed the memorandum of disloyalty. In the battle that followed on December 29, all of these men including her husband and two brothers were martyred to bring victory to the Khalsaa military that day. Ultimately, the defeated Mughal force of Vazeer Khan with heavy loss of life had to rapidly retreat, battered and thirsty, from the region. One can say that it was the courage and persuasive power of Mai Bhago that won the day for the Guru. Her forceful shaming taunts forced these apostate traitors to regain their honour as liberated human beings. Later that day, along with many other injured soldiers, her battle injuries were attended by the Guru and the Khalsaa.

Malo Shah, her father, was an enrolled soldier of Guru Hargobind Rai, grandfather of Guru Gobind Singh. It was her grandfather Pero Shah who had become a disciple to the teachings of Sikhism during the time of the fifth guru, Guru Arjan Dev. Mai Bhago was born in the village of Jhabhaalkalan, in the present-day district of Tarntaran, Punjab. She had visited Anandpur as a child and had become devout to the philosophy of Guru Gobind Singh. She was trained in horse riding and other Sikh martial arts growing up in the company of her brothers. She was married to Nidhaan Singh of the nearby village Patti. After the battle of Muktsar, she joined the Khalsaa force and remained in the service of the Guru following his entourage to Nanderd. She left Nanderd in 1708 after the death of the Guru, and headed further south to Janwaarda, in Karnataka, and lived there until her final days. At her station, there is a Gurudwara, and also at Nanderd Mai Bhago centre within the premises of Gurudwara Hazoor Sahib.

19. Manu – Etymologically, there is much controversy about what the word "Manu" means as well as its origin. Is "Manu" the name of a person who wrote the text *Ma-*

nu-Smriti or a Sanskrit noun, "Man," meaning mind, pronounced "mun" as in munch and not like "man" in English? It is likely that "Man" is also the root word for other Sanskrit words such as Maanushya and Maanav, both meaning human being. The other known title for the text is *Maanav-Dharam-Shaastrr.h,* meaning treatise on the righteous way of living a human life, with 2,685 verses, providing obligatory directions to a post-Vedic society divided into four occupational groups. In Sanskrit, the term "Manu" frequently refers to the archetypal human being or the first man. It is improbable that it was added to Sanskrit vocabulary from one of the Latinized languages of the migrants from the north and west of the Hindu Kush Mountains.

In Sanskrit, "manus" is a masculine noun. The fourth declension is Latin's *u*-stem declension in which almost all the nouns are masculine in gender. Ironically, the one major exception is probably the most commonly used fourth-declension noun, *manus,manūs,* feminine. This declension is unique to Latin. It is a fourth-declension feminine noun, one of the few fourth-declension nouns, which is feminine in gender. Its basic meaning is "hand." If so, then it refers to the hand, an instrument of precision, the terminal organ of the upper extremity of the modern human being. Accepting such speculation would only cause further apprehension among scholars.

The word "Manu" cannot refer to the name of the author of the text *Manu-Smriti*, a much-believed notion. If it refers to a legendary person described in mythological tales as one of the two sons of Brahma, the first man, and progenitor of humanity, then "Manu" is related to "Man, Maanushya and Maanav." Defining a being that possesses a thinking mind makes much greater sense, and the text *Manu-Smriti* is a memorandum for human beings with a thinking mind. *Manu-Smriti* could also be considered as a memorandum for beings with hands to distinguish human beings from primates with prehensile tails.

Recently, some scholars have begun to believe that "Aarya" were people who lived alongside Dravaerd all the time, and, as the word Aarya is a Sanskrit word, then there is no doubt the word "Manu" certainly refers to a human being with a thinking mind. The first "Manu" was the spiritual son of Brahma. There is also a list of fourteen Manu-kings and seven of them are still unborn. Throughout the ancient Vedic texts there are descriptions of civil laws, rules, and regulations to administer the everyday social life of the citizens. However, it is believed that there are certain social models described in the *Manu-Smriti* which predate the Vedic period and were later included in the oral Vedic compositions for dissemination among the citizens of the time. If so, then the credit for creating such an impressive original Vedic literature and antecedent mythological literature must go to Dravaerd (inappropriately translated as Dravidian) of the valley of Seven Rivers Civilization. The next step is to accept the hypothesis that the title "Aarya" was given by Dravaerd to the original peace-loving nomadic migrants, who were driven out of Turkestaan (Central Asia) by natural disasters or violent clans. However, it is very unlikely.

The objectives of developing such social models were to bring about a high standard of living through equal rights and sound administrative practices. These models were designed to initiate goal-oriented education and lifestyles by inculcating a sense of duty, high morals, and virtues in the conduct of daily life. The original Vedic social models refer to a social and occupational ranking system based on education and skill-oriented occupations, not class or "caste" divisions as commonly understood. The word "caste" is a derivative of "*castus*" in Latin, and was a much later invention by the Portuguese after they settled on the western coast of Bhaaratvarsh. It means pure or chaste. Application of similar terms in Sanskrit, such as one being "Shuddh" (pure) or "Ashuddh" (impure), was a much later adoption by Hindu society rather than an immediate post-Vedic act. How this behaviour became a regular practice is unclear. It may have been related to frequent epidemics during which that the privileged members of the society socially and physically segregated themselves and used the already existing "community matrix" of *Manu-Smriti* to lay down new social parameters. It is natural that the people in the ranks of environment maintenance by their very occupations carried a much higher load of contagions that forced their social segregation. It is possible that with this came the introduction of purification rituals and deepening of the divide and concepts such as the untouchables and numerous other practices of intense hygiene. In addition, the concept of keeping the distance of the length of one's shadow during peak public hours, morning and evening sun, in the street was likely considered a safe average distance. For an average person with a height of 5 feet and 6 inches, the shadow can be well over 6 feet long. The term "caste" was introduced among the literate population by the Portuguese, consolidated by European scholars, and put into a concrete legal mould by the divisive administrative methods of British civil servants. The number of sub-castes or the concept of "Jaatee" exceeds 5,000 in Bhaaratvarsh and is no different from the nomadic tribes and clans that have existed in the British Isles, the rest of Europe and throughout the world for centuries.

The Sanskrit word "Varn.h" (adjective) could mean colour, class, grade, and category depending on the given context. Nonetheless, in terms of Sanskrit lingua franca, it commonly refers to primary chromatic tones of red, blue, green, and other colours, and excluding black, white, and shades of grey. The original term "Varn.h vyavastha" can be loosely translated as an organization of class hierarchy. In Vedic society, there was a broad system of social hierarchy intended to classify citizens into occupational groups based on their mental capability, physical strength, financial status, education, and vocational skills rather than a rigid hereditary categorization. The classification system of rigid categorization was established much later in the post-Vedic period with the rise in migration and incessant invasions. Otherwise, according to the ancient "Varn.h vyavastha", there was full freedom of mobility to rise to a higher rank through education and improved vocational skills. In the post-Vedic period, numerous examples can be cited from the Puraanic epic tales to oppose the emergence of such social and psychological rigidity. In the last two centuries, the introduction of the concept of race and colour from Europe and misconstrued translations of Vedic literature by European scholars has further undermined and corrupted the original Vedic ideology.

To make the application of Vedic literature influential and to validate social models such as *Manu-Smriti* in daily life the credit for the creation of these texts was given to celestial figureheads rather than ordinary human beings. Therefore, much of it was linked to Brahma as the creator of the universe who dispelled darkness; his sons Manu and Bhrigu and daughter Saraswatee led the development of evolved humanity and composed the extraordinary texts for citizens to learn and vocalize in the form of prayers, as daily reminders and blissful wishes for all humanity.

However, over time with modifications and updates from oral versions to the written, much of the original texts were altered with interpolations either for better or worse. It is easy to accept that if the original Vedic and other texts were the works of Dravae*r*d Sanaatan society, then over the following centuries these texts were frequently modified to align in the name of societal progress. If so, it was transformed intentionally with the arrival of evil-spirited alien rulers at different times in history and their attitudes toward the existing population. After the complete disappearance of Ha*r*dappa, Mohenjo-Daro, and Lothai-site civilization, much before the beginning of the last millennium BCE, there must have been dramatic changes in the lifestyles of the people drifting further east with population expansion, new migrants, and frequent invasions. This introduced inconsistencies as they appear in currently available versions with variable writing styles, suggesting the involvement of multiple authors at various times in history.

Most of the changes seem to have occurred around 300 to 500 BCE with the rise in literacy and the proliferation of writing materials. It is likely that the prevalent extensive civil and administrative practices widely dispersed within the ancient Vedic texts were extracted, suitably modified, and brought together by a body of scribes or authors and compiled in the form of an easily read compendium. The title of such a compendium was very carefully chosen for wide circulation at the time, rather than making it enigmatic and for the use only of the literate members of the society. Obviously, the civil laws and social matters discussed in *Manu-Smriti* were directed at the Maanushya/Maanav, those with thinking minds and bilateral organs of manipulation, the hands, performing precision work. Although the *Manu-Smriti* was a mandate credited to the celestial figure Manu, the son of Brahma, it was, however, the work of a suitably motivated governing body.

As society became widely variegated the text was later manipulated further by the biased civil administrative bodies to form a compendium or memorandum of civil laws to superintend and regulate people's lives. It was based on social ranks, levels of affluence, complexion, appearance, education, occupation, and level of skills, abilities, inabilities, and disabilities. The whole text is filled with numerous layers of social class, outcast and tiers of occupations to minutely define the consequences and outcomes of one's activities as a citizen. It was not intended simply to monitor them, but at the same time to frame them in rigid boundaries to limit their social development, vertical hierarchy, and advancement of their literary ability. This kind of attitude enforced by the neophytes among the ruling ranks reduced the sanctity of the original works of Rishi Bhrigu, not the son of Brahma, to a new decadence. The persistence of the decadent philosophy has been experienced to this day. It has been repeatedly affirmed as racial and social bias with the rise of European culture, supposedly based on human "intelligence," which seems to many related to the shape of the skeletal frame and colour of the skin, deeply encoded in the genes and epigenetics of the melanocytes!

According to mythology, Manu is the archetype of Maanav, the human being. He was the spiritual son of Brahma (B-rah + Ahma = dispersion of light + I am); meaning the dispersed light that I am, a masculine gender, he is the source of light to erase darkness and the primal creator of the Brahmund, (Brahm + und = the egg of Brahma, meaning egg-shaped complete and unified radiant planetary system) the

Universe. Manu was the first thinking human being with organs of manipulation at the end of his upper extremities, the hands. He was "Swyam-bhu," self-replicating, with a mind of his own to be the antecedent of future humanity (Maanavata). His brother Bhrigu (from light towards darkness) carried the light source forward into the space to dispel "darkness", that is, to erase illiteracy in the future. The name of their sister-consort was Saraswatee (sarha means lake (neuter), saras means excellence (female gender), sarsah means lake, and sarasma means the reservoir of all waters), who is a divine female, maiden excellence, aqueous, a primal source of learning and euphonic sound, the one who nurtures humanity. The Manu-Kaalpaa, a man-made time cycle, has 14 periods, and currently, we are passing through the seventh period. Each period has a ruling Manu-King. When the mythological knowledge is translated from divine to the human realm it does seem to make some logical sense. In the beginning, there was darkness all around, and with the appearance of light (Brahma) space was lit up. Then came the evolution of the Maanav with self-replicating-Manu (reproduction of mankind), who had a thinking mind with organs of manipulation, and Bhrigu spread the light to erase the darkness of illiteracy and conceived equality among evolved humanity. Then, the female gender, maiden of excellence, Saraswatee, came into existence to nurture humanity and emerged as a channel of learning through sound, the medium of communication. Was there a big bang or no bang? Who saw it and heard it? Was it a silent event? What exactly was the source of the blast and the light is yet unknown; may become another tale of mythology one day.

According to the mythology, Bhrigu, the "Manas-Putra," son born of Brahma's mind, was an enlightened creative human being. The Rishi Bhrigu, one of seven famed Rishi-Muni (sages) during the civilization of the Seven Rivers, was likely responsible for the original texts, including *Manu-Smriti*. The texts were mandates prescribed by the divine figureheads as revelations of highly educated human beings for the benefit of humanity. The Rishi Bhrigu was the namesake of Bhrigu, the son of Brahma's mind. Currently, more than 50 manuscripts of *Manu-Smriti* are in existence; which one of them is a copy of the original vocalized or written text is impossible to discern. The variations among them suggest that these are works of numerous writers with interpolations, outlining prevalent civil law updates. The intentional transmutations were considered reasonable to guide or politically manipulate the illiterate common citizens by the administrators and private regulators such as Brahmans and influential street advocates. The design and objectives of such a high-powered compendium must have been intended, like modern-day articles of law and legal penal codes, to handle diverse populations by the administrative authority of the ruler.

None of the available texts can be considered authentic and original as may have been intended by the Dravae*r*d before the arrival of vicious assailants allegedly originating from Turkestaan (Central Asia) to rule over the northwestern frontier region in the post-Vedic times. There must also have occurred dramatic changes before and after the invasion of Alexander of Macedonia, in Turkestaan and across the Hindu Kush Mountain range past Sindhu River and across plains of the river Ganga.

It seems most of the alterations were intentionally made during the evolution of the rule by the so-called "Aarya," the wise, civil and noble, beginning around the fifth century BCE. The post-Vedic texts and the mythological tales written in Puraanic texts are no more than ambitious fictionalized biographical sketches. The original ancient Vedic scriptures, positive concepts of *Manu-Smriti,* and other original constitutional principles were very likely written by the Rishi Bhrigu as part of multi-volume texts, including compilations of predictive astrology under the title of *"Bhrigu-Samahita"* during the period representing the Dravaerd culture of the Seven Rivers Civilization. The name Bhrigu is synthesized from "Bhritah," meaning the one who carries, reedaM, meaning prosperous, reeitaM, meaning truth, and "Gu," meaning darkness. Thus, Bhrigu means the one who carries truth and prosperity forward to erase the darkness and is the inverse of Guru (Gu-ru, meaning who leads from darkness (Gu) to light (Ru) as a process of enlightenment). Bhrigu was an embodiment of truth and prosperity to erase darkness (illiteracy), and Samahita, meaning completely satisfactory and equally beneficial to all citizens. It can be inferred that when Rishi Bhrigu wrote the original volumes he was very clear of his goals and brought out texts espousing equal rights to enlighten his readers and relate the past to the present, so as to predict the future of the humanity. It may have happened before the extinction of the Saraswatee River and drifting of the Dravaerd and migrant communities further east of Sindhu River. The remains of the Vedic period, Hardappa, Mohenjo-Daro, and Lothai-site civilization, mostly excavated in the last century fall within the boundaries of Greater Punjab.

Of course, none of the vocal recordings of ancient Vedic primal prayers and genuine handwritten scripts are available for examination, and the reconstructed segments in existence cannot be accepted authoritatively as true copies. Attempting to fill in the blanks to complete the residual texts is another way of interpolating them; trying to present them as complete is unacceptable for analytical study. Unfortunately, despite detailed studies, these incomplete original scripts can never be read in the same way they were truly intended. Currently, their meaning and purpose are based on individual scholarly deduction and circumstantial inferences. The matters are made worse when these enigmatic incomplete texts are researched by foreign scholars and translated into non-Sanskrit languages. The original meaning is further lost in translation when recently developed vocabulary is used to describe the long-lost culture and its values, decimating the remaining authentic residue of the texts.

The copy of *Manu-Smriti* discovered by the British was Manusmriti 12.125, Calcutta Manusmriti with Kulluka Bhatta commentary. The first known English translation of the text by Sir William Jones was published in Kolkata (Calcutta) in 1794, followed by translations in French, German, Portuguese, and Russian as well. It is believed that the original text of *Manu-Smriti*, unlike current versions, did not have subdivisions. As mentioned above, the text of recent versions was extracted from ancient Vedic literature and compiled into a single volume after multiple interpolations over time. It is believed that the original *Bhrigu-Samahita* contained verses (Shaloak) on Sarvasya-Sambhuvah (globally all beings it so happens are born equal), Dharmasya-Yonih (primal source of duties and moral responsibilities), Yog-Karmasya (synthesis of work-action) meant to unite people, and many more such rules and regulations for the supreme good of the society. A divisive system based on skin complexions and the segregation of humanity into working classes was either a result of influential exogenous exigency circumstances or the creation of rogue narrow-minded not-so-civil administrators much later.

Rishi-Muni were educators and mentors, Brahman were priests to perform religious rites for all in the community, Vaishya were skilled workers and traders, and kShuderr (of insignificance) were semi- and unskilled workers employed in jobs based on the level of their education and vocational skills. A son of a charioteer trained well in warfare that holds his ground on the battlefield and a farmworker with large holdings automatically attained the title of a kShatriya (field bearer). In the text on predictive astrology by the Rishi Bhrigu, there is no mention of racial distinctions, clans, hard and fast social divisions, surnames, and family names as the mandate of the divine Creator. In the experience of the author, what is available now, whether real or fake, are hundreds and thousands of handwritten cards in an old Sanskrit dialect. If genuine they are no more than a set of mathematical analyses of planetary movements in the coming centuries as standard astrology charts. Each set has been allotted random Devnaagri letters as identifying marks without identifying a specific person by name and Varn.h.

The social classification and nomenclature of *Manu-Smriti* were altered and expanded with each new invasion of the land and arrival of a variety of migrants up to recent times. As there was no better-sounding title than "Aarya," like the earlier settlers the new assailants and many others also acquired it, despite their uncivil oppressive attitudes and restrictive behaviour towards the natives. It was the new scholarly group of migrants in each administration that interpolated and modified the *Manu-Smriti* by extracting material of self-interest from the pre-existing, already modified text from the *Bhrigu-Samahita*, to organize and administer the current society to suit the ruler of the time.

The copies of *Manu-Smriti* did not get into the hands of the Mughal scholars and administrators, and even if they did do, it seems they were not interested in the Aarya and the ancient Sanaatan society's civil legal system. They had an extensive system of civil laws in Qur'an to enforce upon the Hindus. The British formed the noun and adjective "Aryan" in English and other European languages from the Sanskrit word "Aarya/Aaryaa," confusing it with the word "Arian." The British too had the same reasons when faced with administrative challenges to rule plural social tiers of Hindu society. They accepted the material written in the Calcutta copy of *Manu-Smriti* to be true, and applied it to Hindu society, leaving out the Muslims, in the most suitable English-style legal format. After the annexation of Punjab, the Sikhs were also called Hindus, governed by Hindu laws.

Most of the British-implemented Hindu laws were abandoned when the new constitution was written with the formation of India as an independent state after 1947. Mahatma Gandhi accepted consistent parts of *Manu-Smriti* and rejected others, while Ambedkar, the father of the Indian constitution, called it a text of moral codes and justice for idiots.

20. Maraatha

This clan emerged out of rural classes of landowners and peasants in the state of Maharashtra. They raised armies against the Mughal Empire in the south-central region of the country. Among them, one of the leading personalities was Shivaji Maraatha. In the 1660s he established an independent kingdom for the Maraatha, and continued trying to dismantle the rest of the Mughal Empire in the south, preoccupying Aurangzeb and diverting most of the imperial resources. About the same time, soon after entering his adolescence, Guru Gobind Singh, fully trained in warfare, militarized his followers against the Mughal in the north for the socio-religious freedom of all social classes. Maraatha defeated the forces of Aurangzeb after long-drawn-out battles for almost a quarter of a century. Towards the end of the Mughal Empire and after the death of Aurangzeb in 1707, due to lack of a stable central rule, from the eastern and southern reaches to the Khyber Pass the Maraatha, Peshwa, Sikh, and Pathaan ruled the land. In 1803, the British defeated the Maraatha in the battle of Dilli, which gradually led to the dissolution of other smaller provincial states in the northwestern regions of Bhaaratvarsh. The British consolidated their rule further after 1857 by suppressing the uprising, often inappropriately referred to as the Indian mutiny. In fact, it was an uprising by the zealots of Bhaaratvarsh for freedom from British imperialism.

21. Masand – An official title of Persian origin, as applied to a high-ranking courtier. The title was taken into the Gurumukhi vocabulary to make the holder feel an important member of the community and take responsibility to lead new followers on the path of the Guru. The designated rank of Masand made the person a direct representative of the Sikh Guru, in a designated geographical location, within and outside the province of Punjab.

The practice of appointing a Masand was started by Guru Arjan Dev to serve an ever-increasing number of followers in far-off locations. The main objective was to hold gatherings of newly formed Sikh communities called "Sangat" locally as frequently as possible if not daily morning and evening prayers. It helped to raise funds for the development of Gurudwaras at new places to serve the locals. Once a year, over Baisaakhi celebrations, the Masand would meet the Guru to deliver the offerings of followers to assist in the Guru's activities and the growth of Sikhism. However, over time, as troubles caused by rival claimants to guru-ship became acute, there was a split among the regional Masands to support and favour the guru of their choice, causing confusion and funds ending up in the wrong hands. By the time Guru Gobind Singh took over the leading role, as the tenth Sikh Guru, the whole system of Masand had become extremely corrupt. Consequently, the Guru officially dissolved the system of Masand and asked all his followers to bring their offerings directly to Anandpur, the religious seat of the Guru.

22. Paonta – "Paon" means feet and "tikaa" means to settle. Paonta was the name given to the woodlands on the banks of river Yamuna, where Guru Gobind Singh decided to put his feet down and stayed for four to five years. The place on the banks of river Yamuna was gifted to the Guru by the Hill Chief Fateh Shah for supporting his cause, acting as a deterrent to other Hill Chiefs in the area. During these peaceful years, the Guru engaged himself in literary pursuits and hunting. His recruits had their first clash with the forces of Raja Bheem Chand and Fateh Shah, often referred to as the battle of Bhanganee. The township of Paonta now falls in the state of Himachal Pradesh, then a part of Greater Punjab. Obviously, the town has a large Sikh population and there is a Gurudwara to commemorate the time spent there by the tenth Guru.

23. Peer-e-Hind – The word Peer/Pir means "elderly person" among the Kurds of Persia and is the title for a spiritual Sufi saint in Persian. The role of a Sufi master is to instruct and guide his disciples to better their lives. A Peer would usually recommend followers to modify their daily activities based on his philosophical revelations and experience. It is a popular sect among the Muslims, but during the Mughal period, many Hindu spiritual masters who followed similar popular principles to improve the quality of life of their Hindu disciples were later included in it by scholars. Guru Nanak Dev is also classified as a Sufi master. The most famous among the Sufi masters were called Peer-e-Hind (a wise elder of the Hindostaan). To delude the Mughal forces Guru Gobind Singh announced himself as Pir-e-Hind when he left the premises of the mud-fortress at Chumkor and later, disguised as Uch-da-Peer (a Peer of the town Uch, now in Pakistan), during his escape out of Macchiwarda.

24. Raajpoot – Historically, they were associated with Hindu warrior clans in the province of Rajasthan or Raajpootanaa, the kingdom of royal blood. The word Raajpoot refers to one who is born of royal blood or the ruling class in the province. The term had been prevalent since the 16th century and the majority settled in the northern reaches of Bhaaratvarsh. Currently, there are some social groups and classes that are their descendants. Traditionally, the eldest son took over the throne from his father and younger male siblings exiled themselves willingly without conflict and spread across other prosperous parts of the country. They were well-trained in military techniques and whenever possible some of them established in other regions as rulers of small provinces. Such progeny played an active role in the Mughal forces during the rule of Akbar, and many converted to Sikhism in the 18th century and later. They joined the Khalsaa force, initially formed by common folk from all "castes" and peasants. Among Raajpoot families and many other Hindu families, the eldest son was initiated and naturalized as a Sikh to become a Khalsaa.

25. Runjeet Nagaarda – In 1684, Guru Gobind Singh installed a war drum with a diameter of nearly five feet, and called it Runjeet Nagaarda. Runjeet means one who is victorious on the battlefield and Nagaarda means a large drum. One such drum was placed at the Anandpur castle and another at the Keshgard castle. The purpose of the drums was multifold. They were primarily designed to establish prerogatives and space for his people to live in freedom in and around Anandpur. Symbolically, the beating of the drums at dawn and dusk was meant to declare sovereignty and serve as an invitation to his followers to willingly attend the morning and evening devotional prayers at the castles. It was a way to continue the tradition of Guru Nanak Dev, the first Sikh Guru, to bring together citizenry of all ranks under one roof.

26. Runjeet Singh, Maharaja – After arrival from Nanderd in Maharashtra to Punjab, Banda Singh Bahaadur took over large parts of the province and within a few years lost it back to the Mughals. Thereafter, several small and large Sikh Misls (Misl generally refers to the sovereign states of Sikh confederacy) came into being in the region during the 18th century that ruled parts of the Greater Punjab at various times after the death of Banda Singh Bahaadur up to 1849. It was Maharaja Runjeet

Singh who managed to integrate most of Punjab as a kingdom of the Sikh people with the dedicated Khalsaa spirit of his armed forces. The Maharaja administered his kingdom under many experienced commanders already leading the various Misls.

Runjeet Singh was born in Gujranwala, now in Pakistan, on November 13, 1780. As an infant, he contracted smallpox leaving pockmarks on his face. The disease also left him blind in his left eye. He was never schooled but trained actively in martial arts and combat skills. It is said that he had first real battlefield practice in the company of his father against the Afghans at the age of ten. In 1792, after the death of his father, he inherited the estate of Gujranwala and surrounding villages, to become the chief of Misl Shuker-Chakia. At the age of 15, he was married to the daughter of the chieftain of Misl Kanhaya, and thereafter his administrative affairs were directed by his widowed mother-in-law, Sada Kaur. He had a politically motivated marriage with another girl from the Misl Nakkais, putting him in an eminent position among the Sikh Misls. In July 1799, he seized the city of Lahore and was granted its governorship by the Afghan king Zamaan Shah. By 1801, he had brought together a majority of the Misls and on April 12 announced himself as the Maharaja of Punjab, and became the first autonomous Sikh ruler. He struck Nanak-shahi coins in the name of the Sikh Gurus, and began his rule as head of the united Misls, forming the Sikh Commonwealth. A year later he brought the prolific trading city and centre of Sikh religion, Umritsur (Amritsar), under his rule.

Maharaja was a liberal and secular ruler. He included Sikhs, Hindus, and Muslims in his kingdom, fulfilling the dream of Guru Gobind Singh. To train his army in the latest techniques of warfare he hired European soldiers and mercenaries to resist the aggression of the British who were eyeing the north-western frontiers to extend their interests beyond the Khyber Pass into Persia. In 1809, the British were struggling to expel the Maraatha out of the northern territory and prevent them from collaborating with Maharaja Runjeet Singh to seek refuge in Punjab. The British managed to convince Runjeet Singh and his administrators with their famed deceptive and diplomatic tactics to sign the treaty of Amritsar/Umritsur in which he agreed to expel the Maraatha already living in Punjab. He secured his territory but at the same time the treaty limited Runjeet Singh's ambition to extend his boundaries across river Satluj up to the capital Dilli. Frustrated Maharaja thereafter concentrated on taking over the remainder of the Sikh Misls and smaller Afghan territories beyond Peshawar and Kabul in the west and extending northward way beyond Kashmir including Ladaakh, bordering Tibet and China.

In the summer of 1818, Runjeet Singh pressured Shuja Shah, brother of Zamaan Shah, living in Lahore, to confiscate the diamond, Koh-I-Noor (mountain of light) for him. Once the administration of the province was under control, he turned his attention to philanthropic patronage to repair existing Gurudwaras and constructed new religious centres for all denominations in the province. However, to establish the prerogatives of the Sikh community, he completely transformed the appearance of Har Mandir Sahib and its premises. He had its dome and minarets retrofitted and covered in sheets of gold, which is why the Har Mandir Sahib is popularly known as "Golden Temple." It is the seat of the religious administration of all major Gurudwara in the country and of state politics. He also built the Gurudwara in Patna, the birthplace of Guru Gobind Singh and Hazoor Sahib at Nande*r*d where the Guru spent his final days. As his rule strengthened in Punjab he came to be known as "Shaer-e-Punjab" (Lion-of-Punjab).

Maharaja Runjeet Singh was a turbaned Khalsaa Sikh ruler, and wore an aigrette at the peak of his turban strung with pearls and tied around it. Out of respect, keeping with the Sikh philosophy, he never wanted to portray his status above the Gurus and Wahey Guru, and therefore never had the diamond Koh-I-Noor set in the aigrette of his turban, instead wearing it in original form as an armlet on his right upper arm. He married daughters of Sikh, Hindu, and Muslim families. In 1835, he married Jind Kaur, his youngest wife, and she gave birth to his youngest son, Duleep Singh, who became the last crown prince to the throne of the residual Sikh Kingdom that existed only till 1849. Maharaja Runjeet Singh fell sick at Lahore in June 1839 and died of an alcohol-related disease on the 27th day of the month. He was succeeded by his son Khardak Singh, but due to power struggles, much of the territory got split up as before within a few years. The opportunist British invaded and took over the whole territory, gradually achieving their long-awaited goal of reaching the Khyber Pass. They took the Koh-I-Noor and had it carved to set into the crown of their queen back home. To remove the young prince Duleep Singh as an obstacle they sent him to England too.

The scope for expansion of the Sikh Empire by Maharaja Runjeet Singh was limited to the original Punjab territories of the sub-Himalayan terrains of the ancient valley of the Seven Rivers. He was blocked from the banks of the river Satluj by the treaty of Amritsar (1809) and managed to reach beyond Kabul briefly with the commandership of Hari Singh "Nalwa." He did not inherit an established kingdom like the Ashoak of Mauryan Dynasty to extend his territory. This prevented him from acts of striking fear and terror among people while undertaking repeated attacks around his kingdom. Secondly, most of the region he ruled was brought together as a result of the political coalition of the various Misls. Maharaja Runjeet Singh had the opportunity to extend his kingdom past the Khyber Pass and beyond the Hindu Kush if he so desired. But the task would have meant extraordinary bloodshed between the Khalsaa Sikh and the equally strong Afghans ending in frequent stalemates and loss of life. It seems he was content to possess and bring together for the first time after many centuries the ancient territory of Greater Punjab, and probably preferred a life of peace and luxury over lust for immense empire. The eager British to some extent managed to expand westward at the first opportunity wishing to trace the path of Alexander in reverse, by employing a majority of well-trained and experienced Sikh-Khalsaa right into the last decades of the nineteenth century. However, they failed to successfully sweep away persistent resistance from the stronghold of the Afghans. Finally, by the middle of the twentieth century, British enthusiasm was quelled by Mahatma Gandhi, forcing them to vacate the Indian subcontinent without violence.

27. Sarhind – Etymologically, the word is Sar-e-Hind, the head or the frontier town of Mughal Hindostaan. According to a reference in the "Brihat Samhita" book by "Varaha Mihira" based on *Prashar Tantra*—mainly a compilation of prophecies—this geographic region was known as "Satudar Desh" said to be inhabited by Sarindhas in the fifth century BCE. It was also once the eastern frontier of the kingdom of

Brahmans of Kabul. After the passing of Mughal ruler Akbar, successive rulers were intolerant of the socio-religious practices of Sanaatan Hindus and, when Aurangzeb ascended the throne of Dilli after killing all his brothers and imprisoning his father, Vazeer Khan of Sarhind took full advantage of this, levied heavy taxes on Hindus and persecuted the non-Muslim population of the region.

28. Thanda Burj – Literally, it means "a cooling tower" or "a cold tower," and was a fortified space for a mid-day summer siesta for uniformed men near the fort of Feroz Shah Tuglaq. The Burj is situated in the town called Fatehgard Sahib in Punjab and, at present, there is a Gurudwara commemorating the passing away of the mother of Guru Gobind Singh following the martyrdom of his two youngest sons, Fateh Singh and Zoraavar Singh. This happened during December 1704, when these two children along with their grandmother were betrayed by the family cook and taken to the police station in the village Sahayrdee. Later that day they were transferred to Fatehgard Sahib for confinement in the Burj. The children survived the cold night in the bone-chilling damp air of the chamber, parched and hungry, in the warm lap of their grandmother.

The next morning they were presented to the court of the Vazeer Khan of Sarhind. Upon refusal to give up their faith, the boys were segregated from their grandmother and in isolation coerced to change their minds. Realizing their defiance, on the 26th of December, both brothers were bricked-up alive. In the evening the grandmother was informed of the tragic death of her grandchildren. Shocked by the news sometime during the night she passed away without a living soul next to her. As the news of their death spread around the town, a rich merchant by the name of Diwaan Todar Mal Jain paid for the cremation of their bodies.

In 1710, under the leadership of Banda Singh Bahaadur, the Sikhs captured the town, called it Fatehgard Sahib, and built a magnificent Gurudwara called Shaheed Ganj to commemorate the martyred Khalsaa soldiers after razing the existing fort of Feroz Shah Tuglaq. Within the premises of that Gurudwara currently, there is a conglomerate made up of Gurudwara Burj Mata Gujree, Gurudwara Jyotee Swaroop where the family was cremated, and Gurudwara Bhora Sahib housing remnants of the brick walls where the brothers were entombed alive. In remembrance of the human act of Diwaan Todar Mal Jain, there is a celebrity hall on the premises. Every year during December there is a gathering of the Sikh community to commemorate the sacrifice of the family and martyrdom of the Sikh soldiers, and a fair to celebrate the victory of Banda Singh Bahaadur.

29. Umrit – The conventional spelling in English is Amrit, which in Sanskrit means immortal. As written in Gurumukhi it would be spelled A^{n}mrit, generally meaning sacred, pure, or divine. Amrita in Greek means ambrosial, hence the accepted English translation of A^{n}mrit as usually meaning ambrosia or divine nectar is incorrect. Amrit is also the name of an ancient city in Syria on the coast of the Mediterranean Sea, south of modern-day Tartus. Two rivers, the Nahr Amrit near the main temple and Nahr-Al-Kuble near the smaller temple, cross the region. It is possible that because the Nahr Amrit flows near the temple its water is considered ambrosia and the place is called Amrit, having religious significance.

It would be a far-fetched idea to equate the water of Nahr Amrit and Amrita to the Umrit that Sahib Kaur and Guru Gobind Singh prepared in the form of sugared water in an iron bowl by stirring it with double-edged Khandah to share among the first five Khalsaa and himself. The ceremony of partaking of Umrit was a new concept at the time, and an invention of Guru Gobind Singh to cement his followers with this common factor of sharing "Umrit" from the same bowl without any social prejudice. It is neither synonymous with the Greek word Amrita (ambrosia) nor derived from the water of the Nahr Amrit in Syria. It does not refer to immortality either. For these reasons, I have chosen to spell the word differently as "Umrit" because phonetically when pronounced it sounds as said and heard in Punjabi in a way similar to words such as umbilicus and umpire.

The idea of Umrit was not conceived to make the Khalsaa think that they will become invincible or immortal (A-mrit, without death). It was not to deceive them into thinking that partaking of "Umrit" would one day raise them upon divine or a political platform by sharing the divine drink. As already has been explained, the objective of sharing Umrit, the sanctified sweetened water, from a single bowl was to break down the centuries-old barrier of social ranks and classification in the Hindu society.

This simple act of the Guru Gobind Singh was a means to encourage all citizens to willingly participate and to elevate them upon a platform of equality as Khalsaa soldiers and disciples of the Guru Nanak Dev. After partaking of the Umrit participants are called Umritdhaaree (sanctified/blessed initiated) Sikh or Khalsaa. It is a personal choice rather than a prerequisite for every Sikh to be Umritdhaaree and strictly follow the tenets of Khalsaahood laid down by Guru Gobind Singh. However, the majority of the Sikhs live by the principles of Sikhism.

The Umrit ceremony is usually staged in a Gurudwara during the morning worship. Traditionally, the Umrit is prepared in an iron bowl (symbolic of united strength) with specially made all-sugar crackers and water (symbolic of a shared source of communal energy) by stirring it with a Khandah, a double-edged sword (symbolic of saintliness and sovereignty). To anoint the new entrants, specified hymns are recited from the Guru Granth Sahib and Dasam Granth by five Umritdhaaree Sikh(s). All the aspirants at the ceremony share the "Umrit" from the same bowl for formal inclusion into the Khalsaa tradition. Non-Sikh as newly initiated Khalsaa Sikh are asked to choose a Sikh name and all the candidates are advised to abandon their existing family name to take on "Singh" for boys and "Kaur" for girls in order to become part of the Khalsaa family. The initiated are advised to follow the tenets prescribed by Guru Gobind Singh.

30. Yamuna/Jamuna – The current system of the five rivers of Greater Punjab spread across Bhaaratvarsh and Pakistan, forming the Sindhu River that discharges into the Arabian Sea. While further east the major river system in the northeastern regions of Bhaaratvarsh is formed by the Yamuna, the Ganga and Brahmaputra ultimately empty into the Bay of Bengal. This enormous water basin formed by these rivers is a magnificent creation of nature as a result of the Himalaya mountain range. The Yamuna and Ganga run almost parallel to each other to form the most fertile plateau of Northern Bhaaratvarsh. The Yamuna has its origins in the Yamunotri glacier at the height of 6,387 metres on the southwestern slopes of the Himalaya Mountains in the state of Uttarakhand. It travels 1,376 kilometres to merge with Ganga at Triveni in Allahabad to form a confluence of three rivers called Sangam, the third being Saraswatee, which is believed to have dried up a very long time ago. The Yamuna flows through the upper reaches of Greater Punjab, Delhi, and Uttar Pradesh.

In Hindu mythology, Yamuna is the daughter of Surya Dev, the Sun, sister to Dev Yama, the god of death. For almost a century, since the British began draining sewage from their residences into it, Yamuna has become one of the most polluted rivers in the country. It is a major source of water-borne diseases in Delhi and surrounding regions, famously called Delhi diarrhea.

APPENDICES

Appendix I
The Doctrine of Discovery

The "Doctrine of Discovery" was the brainchild of Pope Nicholas V, who first expressed it in 1455 CE. He urged Catholic rulers to "conquer lands and rule upon the people even in the remotest parts unknown to us" on the premise that such people were enemies of Christ. The Pope encouraged Europeans "to invade, search out, capture, vanquish, and subdue all Saracens [followers of Islam] and pagans [peace-loving civilians, non-combatant and polytheistic idol-worshippers]", rob them of their wealth, and "reduce the people to slavery." To make such an ideology a reality, on May 4, 1493 CE, at the command of King Ferdinand and Queen Isabella of Spain, Pope Alexander VI issued the papal bull *Inter Caetera* and confirmed that it was the right of the Catholics to take into their possession all newly discovered lands in the Americas.

The Papal diktat was authorized to justify the superiority and claims of Christian European explorers in Africa, Asia, the Indian-subcontinent, Australia, New Zealand, and the Americas. Upon discovery of new land, the explorer had the right to proclaim ownership in the name of a Christian European monarch, could plant a flag in its soil, report his "discovery" to the European rulers and occupy it, even if someone else was there first. This is what the East India Company did on the Indian subcontinent. The "Doctrine of Discovery" reduced the whole earth to a board game, letting loose European Christians to throw their dice and acquire the ancestral properties of ancient peoples wherever they set foot.

If the natives insisted on claiming the land as theirs, the "discoverer" could give a new name to the occupied place, and pronounce the ways of the occupants unacceptable according to European standards. The "Doctrine" justified the dehumanization of those living on the newly "discovered" lands, the removal of their wealth and export of natural resources to the explorers' homelands, and either murder or forced assimilation of the inhabitants.

The Christian Europeans considered that they were instruments of divine power and possessed cultural superiority. The "Doctrine of Discovery" was fundamentally founded on false religious beliefs and blind faith, both of which also fueled the idea of white supremacy among white European settlers, something which brought about untold atrocities and has created tragic consequences to this day for indigenous populations and non-whites in North America and Europe too.

"The Doctrine of Discovery" served as the basis for the Monroe Doctrine in the early 1800s, which declared the dominion and supremacy of the United States over the Western Hemisphere, and justified American expansion westward, propagating the belief that the U.S. was destined to control all the land from the Atlantic to the Pacific and beyond. In the 1823 Supreme Court case, *Johnson and Graham's Lessee versus McIntosh*, the "Doctrine of Discovery" was incorporated into U.S. federal law to force indigenous peoples off their homelands. In a unanimous decision, the

Court gave European nations an absolute right to lands in the New World. Thus Europeans as invaders and colonizers used the "Doctrine of Discovery" to justify their right to occupy the lands of others. They laid the foundations of towns and cities, named them after the places they had left behind in their homelands, and built a new nation, the United States of America. The American founding fathers, George Washington, Benjamin Franklin, James Madison, James Monroe, and Thomas Jefferson, were well aware of the dark side of the "Doctrine." These egotists and despots with malevolent intelligence took advantage of the ignorant natives to claim property rights and enforce political dominance as conquerors rather than act like decent immigrants and settlers. They acted with ill will towards the indigenous peoples, characterizing their own intentions as the will of God. Many others after them utilized the "Doctrine" to justify claims to property rights and political dominance over ignorant natives as God's decree. Further, Americans brought Africans over to North America and enslaved them for centuries, treated them as subhuman, causing immense physical and mental pain, and limiting their progress by design right down to this day.

The 10 elements formed as a result of the "Doctrine of Discovery" noted below were applied to establish European claims to both the North and South American continents, which were referred to as the "New World." This idea of the "New World" was an anomalous perception of European minds intended to show the rest of the world that the found land was their discovery and they had the right to own it, as if those lands were vacant for possession, and rule over the indigenous people, who had lived there for centuries. Variants of these elements have prevailed since "Crusades to Reclaim the Holy Lands in 1096–1271" and used by European explorers, particularly Spain, Portugal, England and the Catholic Church all over the world. Later these were enforced under the European legal system as the "International Law of Colonialism" intended to establish their sovereignty in foreign lands and subjugate the native inhabitants mostly as field workers, even displace them to other colonies as debentured labour. The worst-case scenario of human tragedy occurred on the continents of the Americas where nearly twelve million African people were transported under subhuman conditions and forced into slavery.

A general form of these elements is set out below:

1. Primary sovereign right to discovery of the new lands – All the lands outside the European homelands unknown to and not ruled by a European state were called the "new lands," and the primary sovereign right of possession went to the first European country to occupy the "newly discovered" land.

2. Display of evidence and validation – For a full legal affirmation the occupiers of the European state had to physically establish the entitlement by constructing garrison stations and communal encampments within an acceptable period after the first arrival to confirm claim to their title.

3. Assumed acquisition and proprietorship entitlement – The citizens of the European states were allowed under the "International Law of Colonialism" to have the exclusive right to purchase already-occupied lands of the indigenous peoples for personal use. The government of the sovereign state may frustrate an individual or counteract the wishes of a citizen of another European state to purchase the land from the indigenous occupiers.

4. Indigenous entitlement and right to real estate – The indigenous people were to automatically lose all the property rights and ownership of their ancestral lands according to the European legal system once a European discoverer announced a "newly discovered" land and had planted a European flag. The indigenous people were given the rights to remain and use the lands; however, if the natives chose to sell, then they could only sell to the government of the appropriate sovereign nation.

5. Loss of sovereignty to act in self-interest – Following the European claim to remain on the "newly discovered" land the natives also lost their inherent rule over their ancestral lands, were thwarted from opening any diplomatic dialogue, were restricted from trading outside the assumed territories, and could only trade with the occupying state government.

6. Automatic proprietorship to desirable neighbouring land – The European colonizers could acquire the adjoining desirable lands around their "newly discovered" land. It could become a zone of conflict between two or more European sovereign states, usually settled by equally dividing the unoccupied lands. For reasons of productivity and revenue if the origin of a river fell into the sovereign territory then the entire land irrigated and drained by it belonged to that particular assumed state.

7. No man's land and inappropriate utilization of the land – This open-ended element of the European legal system had a very wide long-term scope and gave immense liberty to the assumed governments to occupy and announce proprietorship of all those lands not currently occupied by other European states. Lands occupied by the indigenous peoples were not in use according to the legal system of the sovereign state, and were pronounced available as "newly discovered" even if they were owned by the natives and used productively by means of indigenous methods.

8. Religion – the mother of all elements and root cause of the troubled history of mankind – The Catholic Church was the original culprit in envisioning and constructing legal principles with the intention of civilizing and converting humanity to the "one true religion" for the "salvation of the souls of the pagans." Instead of "salvation" it brought misfortune to millions living souls and worldwide genocide. Indeed the instrument of the "Doctrine of Discovery" encouraged adventurous European voyagers to create opportunities to earn great wealth and caused non-Christians to lose sovereignty over their lands.

9. The mistaken Europeans ideals – The presumptuous Europeans thought of themselves as messengers of God who were meant to bring their kind of organization and lifestyle to the rest of humanity. They judged the rest of humanity blindfolded, believing themselves more important than others, demonstrating paternalistic rule, exercising Christian beliefs and laws in their lands, educating other peoples in their languages and making hundreds of world languages obsolete, and finally bringing success to the Christian faith in an effort to curb the spread of Islam and Judaism (see Appendix 2).

10. The military art of the conquerors – The military firepower and preparedness of the Europeans made them victorious in occupying lands previously unknown to them. To them conquering the unarmed natives of "newly discovered" lands who lacked equal firepower was an act of military "art" intended to gain claim over the people and their ancestral lands forever.

To settle a feud between Spain and Portugal, the Papal bull of 1493 divided the world between them, leaving most of the Americas to Spain and giving Portugal what is now Brazil and all the lands in Africa and Asia, as if God had given power of attorney to the Catholics to divide the earth like paternal property. The newly arrived egregious Christians from Europe exercised power over the natives and treated them in the cruelest ways. Many priests protested against Spain's dubious and illegal claim to possess native lands. They defended the Native Americans as fully developed human beings in appearance and intelligence like any European and humanity elsewhere. They wrote graphic accounts of the inhumane behaviour of the colonizers against benign Native Americans and enslaved Africans, such as evisceration of infants, physical torture of their parents, and young adults burnt alive while hung upside down. The origin of "white" ideology in Western European Christians continues to assert its "whiteness" with violence and murder. In recent years "blackness" instead of religion has become the rationale for hurting African Americans. Brutal behaviour has persisted among the European colonizers in North America in the form of gun violence by police against African and other non-white Americans. Despite the highly acclaimed American Constitution with its guarantees of equal rights and the Charter of Rights and Freedoms in Canada such atrocities continue to hurt society immeasurably. It is not surprising that non-white citizens suffer injustice more often than the citizens of European origin even in courts of law. Jews of European origin now living in America consider themselves white because "whiteness" of the skin has become the main classifier of systemic racism. It is not the anatomy of the skull and pelvis anymore, but skin pigmentation and religion which have become the visible markers for social and power hierarchy. Jews and followers of Islam along with people of other faiths, however, are often targets of religious and racial slurs in daily life. Such disgraceful behaviours are often learned by children and young adults in their family environment and continue to persist in society. How such ideologies from the past can be erased and current-day perpetrators can be brought to justice remains unclear.

During the same period in history, Catholic Christians were no better human beings than the ruling Sunni Muslims (Mughals) in Bhaaratvarsh. In 1542, Father Bartolome de Las Casas reported the genocide of nearly 15 million natives in the Caribbean and Mexico by Spaniards and a further 15 million by other Europeans over the rest of the Americas. It is believed that the number could be well over 50 million. Surprisingly, despite atrocious maltreatment for centuries, it is the failing of non-white Christians the world over not to realize the relentless behaviour of many fellow white Christians, to continue to accept Christianity as their faith, and to identify themselves using Christian first names and family names first given by the enslaving masters of their ancestors. There is no emancipation and salvation for them as long as they maintain non-genealogical European given names as the mark of their identity.

In Bhaaratvarsh, in 1498 CE when Vasco De Gama first landed on its soil, the Catholics and Jews were already living happily alongside Hindus. On subsequent voyages to impose and subject the Catholics to Portuguese values, Vasco De Gama brought inquisitors with the intention of threatening Indian (Bhaartiyae) Christians to pay allegiance to Rome or face death. The priests were forced to divorce and abandon their families. Thousands of intractable Hindus considered pagans were killed on refusal to convert to Christianity. The Jews who had come to India many centuries before Christians had been given lands by Hindu kings in the southwestern region. They had set up prosperous cities along the coast, living peacefully in the company of Hindus and Christians. Portuguese and Dutch travelers destroyed Jewish settlements and reached Sri Lanka, where Hindus and Buddhists had co-existed for over a millennium and were now treated brutally by the Dutch. They perceived the Dutch as violent, dishonourable and treacherous. Sailing east and northward the Dutch and Portuguese explorers reached Indonesia, China, and Japan. In 1904, the Dutch massacred 4,000 natives on the island of Bali. The wounds of genocide caused by the dominance of European Christians, misled by the Catholic Church, still fresh in the minds of the natives of American continents, will be very hard to erase for a very long time and cannot be ignored by those who clearly understand the implications of the "Doctrine of Discovery" on rest of the world.

The "Doctrine of Discovery" provided the Europeans with opportunity for exploration and exploitation of innocent humanity ignorant of their wily and violent behaviours. To restrict the development of indigenous peoples the principles of international law of previous times are still applicable to real estate ownership in many countries today. Attributes of "Discovery"-based international law are still widely prevalent and used even by non-Europeans. As recently as 2010 China planted its flag on the floor of the South China Sea, in 2007 Russia its flag in the Arctic Ocean, and Canada, not very far behind them, claimed authority over an island along the west coast of Greenland.

References

Pope Alexander VI, "Inter Caetera," May 4, 1493. http://www.papalencyclicals.net/Alex06/alex06inter.htm.

Robert J. Miller, *Native America, Discovered and Conquered: Thomas Jefferson, Lewis and Clark, and Manifest Destiny.* Lincoln: University of Nebraska Press, 2008.

Robert Miller, Jacinta Ruru, Larissa Behrendt, and Tracey Lindberg. *Discovering Indigenous Lands: The Doctrine of Discovery in the English Colonies.* New York: Oxford University Press, 2010.

N.F. Gier (2008). The Doctrine of Discovery and the Christian Conquest of the World. Retrieved from www.home.roadrunner.com/~nickgier/IslamPage.htm.

Robert J. Miller. The Doctrine of Discovery: The International Law of Colonialism. *The Indigenous Peoples' Journal of Law, Culture & Resistance,* 5(1), 2019.

William J. Broad, China Explores A Rich Frontier, Two Miles Deep, *New York Times,* Sept, 12, 2010, A1, available at http://www.nytimes.com/2010/09/12/science/12deepsea.html.

Robert J. Miller, Finders Keepers in the Arctic?, *Los Angeles Times,* Aug.6, 2007, A19, available at http://articles.latimes.com/2007/aug/06/news/OEMILLER6.

Canada Island Visit Angers Danes, BBC News (July 25, 2005), http://news.bbc.co.uk/2/hi/europe/4715245.stm.

Appendix II
Why, Where, and How Did It Start?

European history from the fifth to tenth centuries is filled with human cruelties and adversities. This period saw ongoing invasions by Germanic tribes, Goths and Vandals, and Saxons throughout the fifth and sixth centuries. At the beginning of the seventh century, Europe suffered ruthless strikes by Islamic forces and about the same time, the Norse and Vikings invaded the British Isles. At the turn of the tenth century, the instrument of Christianity united the diverse population of European states, making Islam their common enemy. Strengthening the spirit of the people, it transformed European monarchies into powerful forces by drawing on all available material resources. In this new model, many restless and power-hungry nobles fought with each other to take control of each other's lands and harness manpower. To control them, the Pope (French at the time) sought to divert the impulses of the aggressive French nobles outside Europe by organizing a crusade to the Holy Land to defend the Christian faith in the name of God. He organized an open-air meeting at Claremont. He pleaded to the nobility to give up fighting each other, invade the land of the infidels, and kill non-Christians.

The movement first started closer to home by attacking and killing non-Christians and heretics living in Europe. The crusade continued into the Holy Land to kill Jews and Muslims who refused to accept Christianity. It brought great material wealth to both the Pope and the ruling monarchs. This spiritual fervour and religious manipulation were adopted by later Popes and European monarchs, in the process bringing immense wealth to build magnificent churches and cathedrals across Europe. It resulted in a new face for changing Christendom, establishing a more ruthless and expansionary attitude. Thereafter the stability and rise of Catholicism were totally assured. The pattern continues to this day. Such is the power of the *"word."*

Reference
Aryk Nusbacher, Royal Military Academy, Sandhurst. In "The cultural history of the Western world." The Medieval World. Kulture International Films Ltd. New Jersey, NJ07764.

Appendix III
Author's Note

The "Doctrine of Discovery" is a "Black Paper," an evil document, revealing the dark side of European Christians, and the day it was thought of and written down was the saddest and darkest day in the history of the world. It brought down untold atrocities upon God's humanity. It was later legitimized under so-called "International law" in the interest of the few aggressors of European origin to benefit only white European Christians. Fundamentally, it was designed to enslave and dehumanize millions of other human beings in their own lands. European explorers-cum-aggressors forcefully occupied lands on other continents and destroyed the languages and cultures of the people living there for many centuries. The "Doctrine" left an indelible black mark on the whole world, making for a very sad and tragic history, and limiting the development of human beings in many ways.

The way Europeans, as Christians, acted upon the words of one man, in the name of God, has caused irreparable and grievous mental and physical injury to non-Europeans. The attitude of the European Christian leadership and "pioneering Europeans" of the time towards the rest of humanity speaks to their small-mindedness and inability to recognize variations in human physique and understand the true value of human life. They failed to realize the individual need for optimal survival in the way people thought was appropriate in their environment. It is a great shame that the killing of millions of human beings amounting to a worldwide genocide over five centuries was brought on by the European explorers blindly executing the "Doctrine" through demonstration of their ugly intellectual powers by transforming God's creation with an ill-conceived religious ideology and innovative warfare techniques.

The same "Doctrine" is continuing to play a significant role to this day in a covert fashion through control of the world economy by the same European nations, playing the same game under different rules in the lands abandoned by them, the lands that once served their economies. Those now independent nations, depleted of their enthusiasm, natural resources and facing the limitations of their development, bear the derogatory label of the "Third World." The people of these robbed nations make up three-quarters of the world population. One must ask why only those nations which were colonized and plundered by the Europeans were ultimately destined to become the "Third World" despite being home to established civilizations of long standing. And why are the Europeans and Americans continuing to fund these robbed nations? It simply cannot be for humanitarian reasons. To build their own utopia the Europeans left behind a dystopia. These debilitated nations were weakened further through financial aid, characterized as loans, designed to burden them. It has prevented their economic progress and discouraged self-development.

This note is *Zafurnamah 2020*, an instrument to give voice to the victory of now independent nations in Asia, Africa, and the Indian subcontinent over European colonizers, mostly through non-violence, with the end result being self-rule. This note expresses the anguish of people who have been gravely hurt by the "Doctrine" for the last five hundred years and continue to be in the Americas. It was a deliberate act of European states and Europeans living in North America to oppress the natives and take advantage of them in the name of God. The "Doctrine of Discovery" was just as mischievous and injurious as the false oath written by Mughal officers on the copy of the Qur'an. The Europeans are still occupying those continents and islands as their "inherited" properties, acting upon that 500-year-old "illegal" document.

It saddens the author deeply the way that such a mandate has affected the lives of millions of native people unable to fully exploit their knowledge and skills to live their dreams respectfully in their country of origin. Many highly educated professionals and skilled workers are living less than optimal lives as immigrants from the "Third World" in so-called "developed" nations out of necessity after having their future stolen.

The current environmental disaster has been brought upon this living planet by the Europeans settled in North America, Australia, New Zealand, other regions, and their native lands in Europe, with rising industrialization and consumerism throughout the 19th and 20th centuries. No doubt, recently South American nations, China, Bhaaratvarsh, and many other struggling "Third World" nations, in an attempt to improve the quality of life, have been actively contributing to the degradation of the environment, as taught and directed by the Europeans and North Americans to industrialize themselves too, to develop a mutually beneficial economy, mostly in their favour.

Unfortunately, there is only one known living planet in this universe and only one life to live, both created by the same God, if one likes to believe! Until and unless everybody living on this planet is raised to the same standard of living and able to enjoy a better quality of life, any effort to improve the environment and to save this planet will fail. All the summits and conferences will be only a farce. No amount of apologies and reconciliatory efforts by colonizers can undo the harm done to the ancestors of occupied lands or lessen the pain of their progeny. I would say, do not obstruct the progress of these broken lands and their people by undermining their self-esteem and underestimating their intellectual abilities. Nobody should ever think again that others are lesser human beings and cannot do things for themselves as Europeans have so far imagined. Their limitations have been only what they have been prevented from doing by design.

The people from the "Third World" are migrating to share what has been taken away in the first place and to make the best of their lives. They are not acting upon a religiously-motivated doctrine, but following their bliss to live a better quality of life, stolen by the colonizers. The only way to a "happy planet" is if there are no weapons, no wars, and human equality in every respect. The environment will take care of itself automatically. The Covid-19 pandemic exactly did that by locking down the whole of humanity and suddenly improved the environment! There may be one "God," but there are too many human-gods to spoil this planet!

If the leadership of any religion is acting to uphold the name of the same "Supreme Entity," as God, Allah, Yahweh, Wahey Guru, or Ishwar, in a malicious way, then it is inflaming the nature of humanity. The responsibility lies with the leadership of religious institutions, as doctrines practiced by religion are created by man to hurt others. They are not the gift of God. Such practices are a slap on the face and kick in the fundament of the "Supreme Entity." Such people are neither theists nor atheists; they are simply agnostic about *Its* "Truth,", contrary to the original beliefs.

The ability of human beings to reason and act with free will is pernicious when the choices are made at the cost of other human beings.

The *Zafurnamah* of Guru Gobind Singh highlights the failures of human relationships and it reminds that the evolution of developed societies is raised on the foundations of hurtful religious doctrines, racism and human slaughter. Since the rise of humans as intellectual beings, in organizing the world they have caused chaos and genocide time after time, demonstrating their maleficent nature.

REFERENCES

1. *Zafarnama* (Punjabi translation), by Giani Tarlochan Singh Lamba, 1998, New Delhi.
2. *Zafarnama* (Punjabi and English translations), by Naranjan Singh Noor, 2000, Publication bureau, Punjabi University, Patiala.
3. *Zafarnama* (Punjabi translation), Kapoor Singh Ghuman, Directorate Bhasha vibhag Punjab, Patiala.
4. *Zafarnama* (Punjabi translation), Giani Narayan Singh, Dr. Chatar Singh & Jeevan Singh, Amritsar.
5. *Badshah Dervesh – Guru Gobind Singh*, Dr. Brigadier Daljeetam Singh, Rojana Ajit (Punjabi), Special Edition, Monday, 21 January, 2002.
6. *Guru Gobind Singh*: Jeevan Atey Sandesh, Prof. Braham Jagdish Singh, Waris Shah Foundation, Khalsa College, Amritsar – 143002.
7. *Third Birth Centenary of Guru Gobind Singh*, Suniti Kumar Chatterjee, 1967, Punjab University, Chandigarh.
8. *Prophet of Man Guru Gobind Singh*, Sohan Singh Seetal, 1968, Lyall Book Depot, Ludhiana.
9. *Guru Gobind Singh*, Harbans Singh, 1966, Guru Gobind Singh foundation, Chandigarh.
10. *Guru Gobind Singh: The Prophet, Poet, and Philosopher (A Biography)*, 2000, Rajinder Singh Bhasin, Shilalekh, New Delhi – 110032.
11. *Dynamic of the Social Thoughts of Guru Gobind Singh*, Dharam Singh, 1998, Publication Bureau Panjabi University, Patiala.
12. *Birth of the Khalsa*, Surinder Singh Johar, 2001, Ajanta Books International.
13. *Shri Kalgidhar Chamatkar*, Bhai Vir Singh.
14. *Guru Gobind Singh Retold*, Narain Singh, 2012, All India Pingalwara Charitable Society, Amritsar.
15. *Anandpur Sahib*, Dr. Harjinder Singh Dilgeer, 2003, Sikh University Centre, 4300 Waremme, Belgium.
16. *The Story of India with Michael Wood*, Maya Vision International Ltd. Public Broadcasting Service, 2008.
17. *India Reborn: The Rise of One of the World's Emerging Superpowers*. ACBC/ZDF Production in Co-production with ZDF Enterprises, S4C and France 5, Canadian Broadcasting Corporation, 2008.
18. *Africa's Great Civilizations, with Henry Louis Gates, Jr.*, McGee Media LLC and Inkwell Films, Inc., 2017.
19. Simon Schama, *A History of Britain*, British Broadcasting Corporation in association with History Channel, 2002.
20. Alan Fildes and Joann Fletcher, *Alexander the Great: Son of the Gods*, The J. Paul Getty Museum, Getty Publications, Los Angeles, Duncan Baird Publishers, 2001, 2002.
21. Terry Shand and Geoff Kempin, *Vikings, Raiders from the North*, Eagle Rock Entertainment. An Eagle media release, 2014.
22. H. Daniel Smith, *Selections from Vedic Hymns*, McCutchan Publishing Corporation, Berkley, California, 1968.

23. Waldermar Januszczak, *What the Barbarians Did for Us. The Dark Ages: An Age of the Light*. ZCZ films, 2012, 2013.
24. David Adams, *Alexander's Lost World*, 2012 and 2013, David Adams Pty. Limited and Sky Vision, 2014.
25. Devdutt Pattanaik, *Devlok*, 2017, Penguin Books India Pvt. Ltd., Gurgaon, Haryana, India.
26. Dilip Hiro, *Babur Nama: Journal of Emperor Babur* (Translation from the Chaghatai Turkish by Annette Susannah Beveridge), 2006, Penguin, Random House India Pvt. Ltd., Gurgaon, Haryana, India.
27. Devinder Singh Duggal, *Fatehnama and Zafarnama*, 1980, Institute of Sikh Studies.

INDEX

A
Aarya, 61, 63, 109, 112, 125, 126, 134
Aryan, 126, 134, 158
Adi Granth, 38, 39, 52, 53, 55, 56, 113; see also *Guru Granth Sahib*
Ajit Singh, 20, 40, 48
Akaal Purush, 87
Akaal Takht, 38, 103
Akaali, 99, 151
Alexander, 17, 82, 92, 125, 135–137
Ardaas, 52, 138
Ashvmeydh, 76, 77, 91

B
Babr, 17, 25, 29, 30, 31, 32, 37, 59, 83, 93, 97, 103, 139–141
Babu jee, 111
Bachittrr Naatak, 45–46, 58, 80, 141–142
Baisaakhi, 18, 104, 145, 151, 159
Banda Singh Bahaadur, 10, 54, 55, 97–100, 107, 137, 160, 163
Beas River, 42, 43, 98, 128, 136
Bey-dawa, 47, 52, 152
Bhaaratvarsh, 9, 17, 18, 22, 25–27, 30–33, 37, 45, 59–63, 76, 97, 99, 103, 106–109, 111–113, 126–130, 132–133, 135–140, 143–144, 146, 148–151, 154, 159–160, 164, 172, 176
Bhaarat, 17, 127
Bhagawtee, 17, 21
Bheem Chand, 29, 40–43, 46, 142, 159
Bhanganee, 42, 142, 159
Brahman(s), 9, 18, 19, 25, 26, 28, 30–32, 37, 39, 45, 60, 61, 99, 107, 130–132, 156, 158, 163
Buddhi Chand, 48
Budhu Shah, 41, 42

C
Caste system, 28, 30, 37, 38, 44, 55, 57, 58–63, 104–108, 111, 112, 145, 151, 153–154, 160
Chumkor, 9, 20, 27, 32, 48–51, 67, 69, 72, 73, 75, 107, 112, 118, 119, 152, 160

D
Darbaars, 109
Dasam Granth, 39, 105, 138, 164
Deenae-Kangard, 51
Dravaerd, 61, 109, 127–133, 140, 146, 153, 155–157

E
Ek Lavaya, 61, 105, 143–144

F
Fatehnamah, 10, 22, 50, 67–69, 87–88

G
Gobind Rai, 17, 18, 32, 38–43, 103, 104
Golden Temple, 38, 100, 103, 152, 161; see also Har Mandir Sahib
Guru Arjan Dev, 18, 37, 40, 43, 97, 103, 112, 151, 152, 159
Guru Granth Sahib, 31, 55, 105, 140, 164; see also *Adi Granth*
Guru Taeg Bahaadur, 17, 18, 32, 38, 39, 52, 61, 97, 103, 106, 112

H
Hanumaan, 27, 105, 149–150
Har Mandir Sahib, 100, 103, 161; see also Golden Temple
Hari Singh "Nalwa," 99, 150–151, 162
Hinduism, 25–31, 37, 60, 97, 99, 104, 130, 150
Hindostaan, 25, 28, 29, 31–33, 37, 58, 61, 84, 87, 93, 98, 103, 108, 112, 139, 140, 160, 162

J
Jamuna River, see Yamuna River

K
kShatriya, 17–19, 25, 45, 59, 84, 113, 130, 132, 141, 143, 144, 158

Kaashee, 41, 42, 57, 151
Kaesh, 44, 145
Kaur, 104, 164
Kanghaa, 44, 145
Kacchaa, 44, 145
Kardaa, 44, 145
Khandah, 10, 21, 44, 57, 164
Khidrana, 46, 54, 152
Khalsaa, 9, 10, 18–21, 32, 39, 44, 45, 47–62, 67, 72, 73, 77, 78, 97–99, 104, 106, 107, 115, 120, 122, 128, 142, 143, 145, 147, 150, 152, 153, 160, 162–164
Khalsaa Panth, 59, 60, 104, 151
Khalas citizens, 58
Khalas Knighthood, 104
Khalsaa quintet, 55, 56, 67
Khyber Pass, 9, 17, 99, 108, 132, 151, 159, 161, 162
Kotkapoorah, 21, 51
Kripaan, 21, 44, 55, 57, 58, 145, 146

M
Macchiwarda/Maccheewarda, 20, 49, 50, 67, 160
Mai Bhago, 52, 122, 152
Malwa, 47, 49, 51, 54, 77
Manu, 9, 19, 60, 62, 63, 108, 112, 141, 152–158
Marathaa, 45, 53, 56, 97, 158–159, 161
Masands, 43, 159
Miri and Piri, 106, 141
Misl, 99, 150, 160–162
Muktsar, 21, 46, 52, 115, 120, 122, 152

N
Naam, 19, 61, 81
Naam Dev, 61, 105
Nanderd, 54, 55, 98, 152, 160, 161
Nihung Singh, 104, 143
Norse, 132, 137, 174

P
Paonta, 41, 42, 116, 142, 159
Patna, 17, 38, 161
Punj Piyarey, 55

R
Raajpoot, 30, 31, 38, 40, 45, 54, 56, 97, 140, 160
Ropard, 10, 20, 46, 47, 48, 117
Runjeet Singh, Maharaja, 9, 39, 99, 121, 132, 150, 151, 160–162
Runjeet Nagaarda, 40, 160

S
Sabo-dee-Talwandee, 11, 15, 52, 53, 54, 57, 121
Sanaatan, 18, 26, 28, 57, 60–62, 80, 103, 105–107, 127–131, 148, 155, 158, 163
Sanaatan Dharam, 103, 105, 107, 108, 127–130, 148
Sarhind, 20, 43, 46, 48, 50–52, 54, 55, 69, 97, 98, 122, 152, 162–163
Sarsaa/Sarsa River, 20, 47, 53
Shivaalik, 18, 38, 43
Sindhu (Sindu) River, 16, 125, 128, 135, 136, 150, 156, 157, 164
Singh (surname), 44
Sunni, 37, 97, 139, 173
Sur-Raya, 81, 92

T
Thanda Burj, 48, 118, 163

U
Uch-da-peer, 50, 160
Umrit, 10, 21, 44, 57, 68, 87, 104, 121, 163–164
Umritdhaaree, 145, 152, 164
Umritsur, 10, 121, 161

V
Vaishya, 19, 131, 132, 158
Vazeer Khan, 20, 25, 43, 48, 50, 54, 98, 122, 152, 163
Vikings, 137

Y
Yamuna, 41, 42, 98, 130, 159, 164–165